Essential Ultimate

Teaching, Coaching, Playing

Michael Baccarini
Tiina Booth

Human Kinetics

Library of Congress Cataloging-in-Publication Data

Baccarini, Michael, 1962-
   Essential ultimate : teaching, coaching, playing / Michael Baccarini, Tiina Booth.
      p. cm.
   ISBN-13: 978-0-7360-5093-7 (soft cover)
   ISBN-10: 0-7360-5093-0 (soft cover)
   1. Ultimate (Game) 2. Flying discs (Game) I. Booth, Tiina, 1954- II. Title.
   GV1097.U48B33 2008
   796.2'4--dc22

                                                    2007037498

ISBN-10: 0-7360-5093-0
ISBN-13: 978-0-7360-5093-7

The Web addresses cited in this text were current as of December 5, 2007, unless otherwise noted.

Acquisitions Editor: Gayle Kassing, PhD; **Developmental Editor:** Melissa Feld; **Assistant Editor:** Martha Gullo; **Copyeditor:** Bob Replinger; **Proofreader:** Kathy Bennett; **Indexer:** Craig Brown; **Permission Manager:** Carly Breeding; **Graphic Designer:** Bob Reuther; **Graphic Artist:** Kathleen Boudreau-Fuoss; **Cover Designer:** Keith Blomberg; **Photographer (cover):** Sarah Ritz; **Photographer (interior):** Sarah Ritz, except where otherwise noted. Photos on pages 4, 7 (bottom), 151, 153, 154, 157, 158, 159, and 160 courtesy of David R. Foster and photos on pages 6 and 7 (top) courtesy of Michael Baccarini; **Photo Office Assistant:** Jason Allen; **Art Manager:** Kelly Hendren; **Associate Art Manager:** Alan L. Wilborn; **Illustrator:** Alan L. Wilborn; **Printer:** Sheridan Books

Human Kinetics books are available at special discounts for bulk purchase. Special editions or book excerpts can also be created to specification. For details, contact the Special Sales Manager at Human Kinetics.

We thank Amherst Leisure Services in Amherst, Massachusetts, for assistance in providing the location for the photo shoot for this book.

Printed in the United States of America   10 9 8 7 6 5 4 3 2

Human Kinetics
Web site: www.HumanKinetics.com

United States: Human Kinetics, P.O. Box 5076, Champaign, IL 61825-5076
800-747-4457
e-mail: humank@hkusa.com

Canada: Human Kinetics, 475 Devonshire Road, Unit 100, Windsor, ON N8Y 2L5
800-465-7301 (in Canada only)
e-mail: info@hkcanada.com

Europe: Human Kinetics, 107 Bradford Road, Stanningley
Leeds LS28 6AT, United Kingdom
+44 (0) 113 255 5665
e-mail: hk@hkeurope.com

Australia: Human Kinetics, 57A Price Avenue, Lower Mitcham, South Australia 5062
08 8372 0999
e-mail: info@hkaustralia.com

New Zealand: Human Kinetics, Division of Sports Distributors NZ Ltd.
P.O. Box 300 226 Albany, North Shore City, Auckland
0064 9 448 1207
e-mail: info@humankinetics.co.nz

This book is dedicated to our players,
who tested our patience,
listened to our voices,
and most of all,
enriched our lives immeasurably.

Contents

part I   Skills for the Sport of Ultimate   9

3

4

5

6

Defense: Individual Skills. . . 91

7

Defense: Team Skills 109

part II   Your Ultimate Program   123

8

Ultimate Fitness 125

Preface

"Can you teach me how to throw a flick?"

We have probably heard this question thousands of times in our Ultimate careers. Almost everyone who has ever thrown a flying disc has some version of the backhand, the most common throw. However, mastery of a flick or forehand is one of the toughest and most essential skills to learn in our sport. Everyone wants to learn it, and almost everyone has difficulty at first. We usually watch the attempted forehand a few times before we say anything. It invariably turns over in the air, rolls on the ground, and stops 10 feet before the receiver. The thrower's frustration is apparent: "I'm never going to learn this throw."

We set to work. We check the grip first to make sure that the two fingers and the thumb firmly grasp the rim. Then we look at the angle of the disc, suggesting that the outer edge be tilted toward the ground, away from the body. Finally, we encourage them to snap the wrist at the point of release. This all sounds rather complicated, and it is. Rarely do players achieve this throw on the first try, or even on the 10th one.

Yet we stand by their sides, silently encouraging them to learn this new skill. Sometimes we walk away to give them time, trusting that they will work it out on their own. But we're always ready to return as soon as they call us over.

"I think I have it now. Watch." The disc sails out of their hands, wobbly and unstable, but following the correct flight path. It's not flat and it's not fast, but it finds its intended target. They turn and smile, we nod, and we move on to the next player.

Ultimate was invented in 1968, and at first the sport developed sporadically throughout the United States and the rest of the world. Throughout the early stages of development, Ultimate skills and strategies spread by word of mouth. In 1982, the first Ultimate handbook was published: *Ultimate Fundamentals of the Sport* by Irv Kalb and Tom Kennedy. It was a vital contribution to the sport at the time it was published, and other books have followed since then, including *Ultimate Techniques & Tactics* by Jim Parinella and Eric Zaslow.

Ultimate has exploded in the last 20 years. More than 40 countries have teams, and world championships are held every two years. In 2005 Ultimate was a medal sport at the World Games in Germany. Almost all major U.S. cities and colleges support some sort of Ultimate program, from informal leagues to highly competitive national contenders. The Ultimate Players Association hosts a North American series of club, college, and youth tournaments every year. Camps, clinics, and summer leagues have become staples of many Ultimate communities and are some of the primary ways in which youngsters and newcomers are introduced to the sport.

Clearly this young sport has experienced phenomenal growth and popularity without formal teaching materials or instruction. Information is still shared among players through newsletters or over the Internet. As coaches and advocates of this sport, we are constantly asked for curriculum as well as advice on how to develop an Ultimate team or program. We are often overwhelmed by the interest in our sport and our inability to meet everyone's needs.

We have more than 50 years of combined experience in playing, teaching, and coaching Ultimate. This book is a logical outgrowth of the work we have done with hundreds of student-athletes. We hope that *Essential Ultimate* clearly reflects the passion and love that we have for this sport and its players and that it invites others to enjoy all that this young, exciting sport has to offer.

Acknowledgments

Michael would like to thank all his former, current, and future Paideia Ultimate players for learning along with him and for sharing a passion for the game and its unique principles. A special note of gratitude goes to Martin Aguillera, Harper Alexander, Will Arnold, Andrew Berry, Brad Cochi, Britt Dunn, Alexis Frederick-Frost, Pauline Lauterbach, Steven Henry Miller, Moses Rifkin, Miranda Roth, Jason Simpson, Dylan Tunnell, Paul Vandenberg, and most of all, Kyle Weisbrod for their contributions and support of this project.

Great appreciation also goes out to the community of Paideia Ultimate Parents (PULP), whose support through the years has made Michael's work so fulfilling.

A tremendous thank you to the campers and counselors of Paideia Ultimate Camps, Thrower Starr, Marty Hays, and the administration and entire community that is The Paideia School.

Heartfelt thanks and much love to Mom, Louie, Laura Lea, Anna Marie, and Kimberly.

Tiina would like to thank her brother Mark, sister-in-law Austin, nephews Emmett and Dylan, her amazingly patient parents, Donald and Tiiu Booth, cousins Sue, Don, Greg, Dan, Jackie, and Pam, Emily Baecher, Jimmy Bress, Jason Chow, Woody Clift, George Cooke, Tom Cullen, Andrew Hollingworth, Sam Kanner, Aaron Kropf, Darden Pitts, Jim Pistrang, Steven Rouisse, Jeff Yu, and all of the teams she has coached in the past. The campers and counselors of National Ultimate Training Camp (NUTC) deserve a special thanks, as do all the parents of past and present Amherst Regional High School (ARHS) Ultimate players for building such a wonderful Ultimate community in Amherst. The dynamic duo of Amherst Leisure Services—Bob Brandts and Erika Cumps—should also receive their own accolades for years of Ultimate support. Kudos to David Foster for his great photos and to Paul Fisher of One Way Printing for his striking designs. Thanks also to the staff, students, and administration of ARHS, as well as to non-Ultimate friends Jan Saulsberry and Gina Fusco, who have listened to her blather about Ultimate for years. And the most heartfelt appreciation to Dr. Alan Goldberg, who taught his mental toughness system to Tiina and her teams for many years.

Michael and Tiina would both like to thank VC Ultimate, Discraft, the staff of NUTC, the past and current staff of the Ultimate Players Association—specifically Joey Gray—and Gayle Kassing, Melissa Feld, and Martha Gullo of Human Kinetics for all their professional support during the writing of this book. They would also like to thank their photographic models: Wesley Chow, Andrew Hollingworth, Sam Kanner, Darden Pitts, Maisie Richards, Lucy Salwen, Jason Simpson, George Stubbs, and Leila Tunnell. Special thanks to those Ultimate players and coaches—Dan Parrish, Ben Van Heuvelen, Ted Munter, Chase Sparling-Beckley, and Ben Wiggins—who gave us ideas about how to teach Ultimate, whether they wanted to or not.

Key to Diagrams

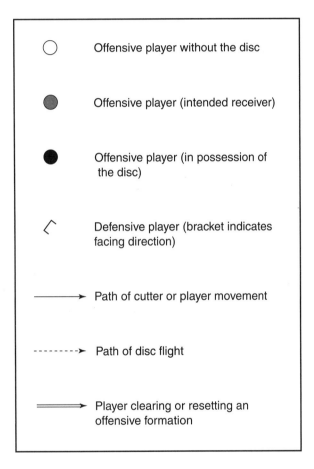

○   Offensive player without the disc

◕   Offensive player (intended receiver)

●   Offensive player (in possession of the disc)

⟨   Defensive player (bracket indicates facing direction)

⟶   Path of cutter or player movement

----➤   Path of disc flight

⟹   Player clearing or resetting an offensive formation

Note: Each key term used in this book is featured on the first page of the chapter in which it is most extensively discussed. These key terms are also defined in the glossary. Readers who encounter unfamiliar terms before they are discussed in the text may consult the glossary at the back of the book.

What Is Ultimate?

Ultimate, like all sports, is a game, and people play games because games are fun. People of all ages and ability levels enjoy the challenging and unique competitive experience of Ultimate, as well as its exercise benefits. Aside from a flying disc, all that is needed to get a game going are a few friends and an open playing area. As with any athletic pursuit, those who want to participate at higher levels must make a greater commitment in time, money, and equipment, although these costs are not as high as they are with most sports. Playing a game with a flying disc includes several unique aspects. In Ultimate, a disc can be manipulated to fly in a variety of ways, as compared with a ball. It can be made to curve right or left, climb up like a plane taking off from a low release point, drop abruptly, or hover gently to its intended target. This quality promotes the distinctive movement and flow of the game and its participants. The sport is simple, with relatively few rules, allowing participants to learn it quickly. Running, throwing, and catching are the primary skills required to play. And because each player on the field acts as a referee, personal responsibility and integrity are demanded of all involved. This exceptional and compelling aspect of the sport, along with its physical challenges, makes Ultimate an appropriate activity for physical education curricula and recreational environments.

History of the Sport

Ultimate is a fast-paced transition field sport that originated in the late 1960s on the campus of Amherst College in Amherst, Massachusetts. In the summer of 1968, Jared Kass, a student at the college, was a summer camp counselor at nearby Northfield Mount Hermon School. Kass introduced the game of Ultimate to kids attending the camp. One of the camp attendees was Joel Silver, now a Hollywood producer, then a high school student from Columbia High School in Maplewood, New Jersey. Joel took the game back home and taught it to classmates at Columbia High. Together these kids developed and refined the game, composed the basic rules, and founded CHS Varsity Ultimate, the first Ultimate team.

Soon other high schools in the Newark, New Jersey, and New York City area began playing. Later, after graduating from high school, these kids introduced the game to a broader audience, and teams formed at the various colleges and universi-

ties they attended. Princeton and Rutgers universities played the inaugural intercollegiate Ultimate game. Coincidentally, the game took place on the same pitch as the first American football game did, played by the same two schools before the turn of the century. The rest, as they say, is history.

Nearly 40 years later the popularity of Ultimate has grown tremendously. It is one of the fastest growing sports in the world, and hundreds of thousands of people play it in more than 40 countries. Over 300 colleges and universities have programs. Hundreds of high schools and middle schools have teams. Ultimate is being taught to students in physical education and recreational settings, such as the Cub Scouts, the Boys & Girls Clubs of America, and similar organizations all over the world.

The Ultimate Players Association (UPA), founded in 1979, is the governing body of the sport in the United States. The association has more than 25,000 members and is itself a member of the World Flying Disc Federation (WFDF), the organization that oversees the sport on a global basis.

Human Kinetics and the authors of this book recognized the great interest in the sport of Ultimate. With little written about this relatively new game, a sizable need remains unmet. Our goal in writing *Essential Ultimate* is to help meet the demands of the rapidly increasing number of people who are playing, coaching, or teaching the sport. Provided here is knowledge that the authors have acquired and continue to gather from our more than 50 years of disc sports experience as players, coaches, and schoolteachers. From individual skills to team concepts and strategies, from physical to mental preparation, from running an effective and efficient practice to starting a program, this book offers the reader the fundamental building blocks to achieving success in this exciting team sport.

Basics of the Game

Ultimate, like many great sports, is a game of keep-away. It is played on a field roughly the size of an American football field, 40 yards (36.6 meters) wide by 120 yards (109.7 meters) long, including end zones 25 yards (22.9 meters) deep. Seven players from each team start a point standing on the front line of the end zone that they are defending. Play begins as one squad throws off to the other, similar to the way that a kickoff initiates play in football. Figure 1.1 illustrates the layout and dimensions of an Ultimate field.

The object is simple. Each team plays keep-away from the other team by completing successive passes and progressing down the field, with a team member catching the final pass in the opponent's end zone. Sound easy? It would be, except that the opposing team is using various strategies to force an interception, a blocked or errant pass, or a drop. What makes this tricky, and what makes Ultimate unique, is that the object of play is not a ball but a high-tech plastic flying disc (figure 1.2)!

A concept called Spirit of the Game™ (SOTG) is another aspect of the game that makes it exceptional. Part of the game's official rules, SOTG is based on the belief that respect and honor between competitors make it possible for control of the game to be in the players' hands. Each athlete is obliged to trust every other player on the field to act as an official throughout play. Together, those 14 players are responsible for making their own calls. What results is more thorough coverage of the field than any set of referees could provide, perhaps making Ultimate the closest there is to being the perfectly officiated sport. Respect, trust, and a sense of honor pervade the sport, influencing more than just what takes place during competition.

Easy to Play

Some games have more mass appeal than others. Those that provide the most fun are usually the most popular with kids of all ages (including adult-age kids!). As a health and physical education teacher, one of this book's authors has noted that team games that provide sufficient but readily learnable physical challenges, serve as competitive outlets, and offer ample social interaction are usually favorites. Ultimate involves all that and more. Although developing the acute skill and peak physical condition needed to play at elite-club level requires considerable time and effort, a person can enjoy the sport of Ultimate at any measure of ability.

First, throwing and catching a flying disc is fun, for both beginners and elite-level players. Releasing the disc and watching it float on its intended path toward the target taps into a child-like desire to watch things fly and, even better, to possess some control over their flight. No one seems to tire of throwing a disc, and throwing is the foundational skill of the sport. And because

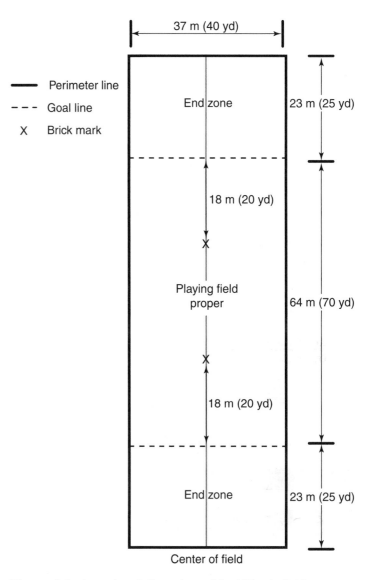

Figure 1.1 Layout and dimensions of the Ultimate field.

Figure 1.2 An official 175-gram playing disc.

Postgame circles are a common sight in Ultimate, particularly in international competition, like this gathering that followed the bronze medal match between Australia and Colombia at the 2006 World Junior Ultimate Championships.

fewer athletes (seven per team) are on the pitch during play than in field sports such as soccer or football, Ultimate ensures that more players are consistently involved in the action. This engagement allows each athlete to improve quickly and have fun while doing so.

Additionally, when a game is fun to play, participation increases, not only for those already involved but also for newly introduced players. People, particularly children, love to teach each other new games. The more, the merrier, and the simplicity of Ultimate is evident to all who learn it. The Ten Simple Rules (see sidebar on page 5) cover the basic instructions for play and the most common infractions of the sport. Although a complete set of rules exists, knowing only these 10 rules is enough to get started.

Finally, anyone who can throw and catch the disc can play Ultimate. As with any sport, higher levels of play demand greater skill, physical conditioning, and athleticism, but participation is relative and learning the basics is easy. Many cities are developing youth and adult recreational leagues and conducting tournaments, so opportunities to play and learn the sport in organized settings are constantly increasing. Most colleges and universities have Ultimate clubs, and many high schools and middle schools now have teams or are developing programs. As a result, chances

are good that an opportunity is available in your community or that you can help create a club at school. Contact the Ultimate Players Association for a list of contacts in your area or for additional information about how to organize a league or club in your community or school. Also see chapter 10, Starting a Program, which offers a wide variety of ideas and approaches to help you.

Inexpensive Equipment

Of course, most organized athletic endeavors involve some costs. Uniforms, appropriate footwear and protective equipment, practice and game space, travel, coaches' salaries, and compensation for officials are expenses that can add up. A school's athletic department, parents, and the competitors involved usually bear these expenses. But one of the great advantages to playing Ultimate is the relatively low cost of participation. In fact, little is needed to play the sport—a flying disc and eight cones representing the landmarks of the playing field will get a match going.

Currently, the official disc of the Ultimate Players Association is the Discraft 175-gram Ultrastar. The UPA established the standard dimensions of

Ultimate in 10 Simple Rules

1. **Field**—A regulation field is 40 yards (36.6 meters) wide by 120 yards (109.7 meters) long, including a 70-yard (64.0-meter) playing field proper and end zones 25 yards (22.9 meters) deep.

2. **Initiate play**—Each point begins with both teams lining up on the front of their respective end-zone line. The defense throws ("pulls") the disc to the offense. A regulation game is played with seven players per team.

3. **Scoring**—Each time the offense completes a pass in the defense's end zone, the offense scores a point. Play is initiated by a pull after each score.

4. **Movement of the disc**—The disc may be advanced in any direction by completing a pass to a teammate. Players may not run with the disc. The person with the disc ("thrower") has 10 seconds to throw the disc. The defender guarding the thrower ("marker") counts that stall count out loud.

5. **Change of possession**—When a pass is not completed (e.g., sails out of bounds or is dropped, blocked, or intercepted), the defense immediately takes possession of the disc and becomes the offense.

6. **Substitutions**—Players not in the game may replace players in the game only after a score or, in the case of injury, when replacing that injured player during an injury time-out.

7. **Noncontact**—No physical contact is allowed between players. A foul occurs when contact is made. Picks and screens are also prohibited.

8. **Fouls**—When a player initiates contact with another player, a foul occurs. When a foul disrupts possession, the play resumes as if possession was kept. If the player committing the foul disagrees with the foul call, the play is redone.

9. **Self-refereeing**—Players are responsible for their own foul, line, and possession calls. Players resolve their own disputes.

10. **Spirit of the Game**—Ultimate stresses sportsmanship and fair play. Competitive play is encouraged, but never at the expense of respect between players, adherence to the rules, and the basic joy of play.

Ultimate Players Association, Steve Courlang, Neal Dambra, 1991.

the Ultrastar, which has been the official disc since 1996. The disc is available at various retail outlets and can be purchased in bulk from Discraft, Inc. (follow links to merchandise on the UPA's Web site). Discraft offers both stock designs and custom-designed discs—for example, with team or tournament logos. See their contact information in the appendix.

To conduct a productive practice, a team will want more than one disc and eight plastic cones. Having several flying discs will provide more touches for the players and ensure a more rapid development of their skill. Having extra cones to supplement those showing the field layout will be useful for directing the flow of technical skill and conditioning drills. Players should bring to practice both a dark jersey or shirt and a white one so that they can form easily distinguishable teams for scrimmages or competitive drilling. Some teams invest a few dollars in mesh practice pinnies to differentiate teams.

Ultimate is a fast-action transition sport, demanding frequent cutting, acceleration, and deceleration. Cleats are an essential piece of equipment to ensure proper footing and effective traction. Most players prefer the various soccer-style stud patterns available, whereas others choose the broader base provided by a football turf shoe. Either way, footwear is usually the most expensive equipment that an Ultimate player must buy.

Uniforms can involve as much or as little cost as the team desires. High-performance fabrics that wick moisture away from the body are beneficial but not essential. As long as opposing squads are clearly identifiable from one another, the chosen material is not important. Of course, numerous options are available to outfit a team in lightweight performance sportswear that helps regulate body temperature. Several companies produce uniform choices appropriate for the sport, and in recent

These players from Australia's and the United States' national teams possess the skill, physical conditioning, and athleticism required to face off at the 2004 World Championships in Turku, Finland, but a person can enjoy the sport of Ultimate at any measure of ability.

years, several marketers have targeted the Ultimate community. Vicious Circle Ultimate is one such company whose product lines focus on the unique requirements of the sport. For more equipment and educational resources, refer to the appendix.

As mentioned earlier, each competitor on the field acts as a referee, eliminating the need to pay officials to monitor an Ultimate game. Fees for officials can be significant in other interscholastic athletic events but are nonexistent in Ultimate. This aspect is one of the most beneficial attributes of the sport, both in cost outlay and in player control of a competition.

Emphasis on Personal Responsibility

Ultimate does not use referees, although there has been some experimentation with an inactive observer system that still leaves players in charge

of calls. Each player on the field, as described in the official rules, is an acting official *of* those rules. This personal responsibility is an attractive feature of the sport and integral to its success. Each participant is committed to and responsible for ensuring fair play and safety. This underlying principle demands that the correct call be made. Whether that call benefits a player's team or the opposing team is irrelevant; fairness is the objective. Ironically, by omitting outside officials and keeping control in the players' hands, a more accurately officiated game can result. If the athletes involved in any infraction know what actually occurred—and they are more likely to have this knowledge than an outside (and at times out-of-position) official is—and honesty prevails, fairness will more often result. Although admittedly a challenge in the heat of competition, this system has the potential to be a purer system of officiating and it encourages respect among opponents, especially when both sides honor Spirit of the Game.

Furthermore, Ultimate's expectation of respect for opponents, the sport, and the community of

Opposing team members show mutual respect following a championship final between fierce rivals The Paideia School in Atlanta, Georgia, and Amherst Regional High School, Amherst, Massachusetts.

players and organizers as a whole values individual integrity in competition. This system provides frequent opportunities to "practice" fairness and respect, and it provides a framework to continue developing personal and team (group) integrity. Given the demand for forthright conduct, it is not difficult to see how Ultimate emphasizes sound citizenship. Young or old, novice or elite, this is fitting exercise for all participants in sport.

Ultimate Meets Physical Education Standards

Any active lifestyle will result in physical gains that have far-reaching benefits. In physical education settings, teachers seek activities that improve the fitness levels of their students as well as promoting motor, cognitive, and affective development. Ultimate offers many such opportunities. It elevates fitness while improving motor skills. Like basketball and soccer, Ultimate involves continuous running. Players are more effective when they have conditioned appropriately and sufficiently and are able to sprint repeatedly during games, resting only between points. Players move at various speeds and levels. Of course, for younger children, such as those of middle elementary ages, the game is fun and challenging without as much running.

The sport requires constant movement of a transitional nature. The experience of play is enhanced if a player possesses endurance, speed, agility, the ability to decelerate and accelerate rapidly, and the ability to make quick changes of direction. Besides developing the multiplanar, nonmanipulative skills

Players from Canada and the USA demonstrate endurance, speed, and agility in the 2006 World Junior Ultimate Championsip Final.

(e.g., cutting, jumping, changing speeds and directions) common to other court and field sports, Ultimate promotes the acquisition of manipulative skills (hand–eye coordination) because participants must throw and catch the flying disc. Manipulative skills increase because people enjoy developing control of the disc. Catching the disc is also an interesting challenge because participants must learn to track its flight before they can catch it.

Developing an understanding of individual and team movement, strategy, and the fundamentals of the game is also essential for successful Ultimate play. Participants are challenged to conceptualize, process, plan, and perform complex movements throughout the course of play. These cognitive challenges are demanding in Ultimate, as with any team field or court sport, but the flying disc can have an especially dynamic effect on individual and team performance.

Because Ultimate is a team sport, students have many opportunities to work on important social (affective) skills. The unique self-regulatory nature of Ultimate allows constant practice in the skills of negotiating and resolving conflict, developing respect for teammates and opponents, and recognizing that competition, at its finest, can and should be fun for all. Why else play?

Summary

Given the many challenges and benefits of playing Ultimate, it is clear why the sport is rapidly gaining popularity worldwide. The sport is inexpensive and easy to learn, has a structure that allows for complete player control, and fosters honor and respect among teammates and opponents alike. The system works, and this rule of conduct—of honoring the game—is demanded of competitors at all levels of play, making Ultimate a rare sport experience.

part I

Skills for the Sport of Ultimate

Principles of Throwing

A seasoned Ultimate coach who sees a group of people throwing the disc around can determine within seconds whether they play Ultimate. All she has to do is watch the type of throws, the flight of the disc, and the movement of the thrower and receiver. Ultimate throws are distinctly different from other disc throws. The underarm throw that works for Uncle Ed on the beach is worthless on the Ultimate field.

This chapter begins with the basic throwing concepts necessary for almost every throw. These concepts are mental approach, snap, and follow-through. We then show how to master the three essential throws in Ultimate: the backhand, the forehand, and the hammer. We break down each throw into distinct parts so that the throws are easy to learn and teach. Those who are having difficulty with a specific throw can refer to the troubleshooting chart to address common throwing problems. When a throw is not working, often only a minor adjustment is necessary.

Parts of a Disc

Before you attempt to make a disc fly, you must be able to identify the parts of a disc. Put a disc in your hand as you go through the following descriptions.

The disc comprises the following parts (see figure 2.1, *a-b*):

▶ Top—the domed part of the disc

▶ Bottom—the underside of the disc

▶ Flight rings—the grooves on the top of the disc

▶ Shoulder—the curved part of the disc outside the flight rings

▶ Inside edge—when throwing, the edge closest to the body

▶ Outside edge—when throwing, the edge farthest from the body

▶ Leading edge—the part of the disc closest to its destination

▶ Trailing edge—the part of the disc farthest from its destination

Make sure to consult this diagram as you continue through this chapter. We will use these terms to explain how to execute the different throws.

Basic Throwing Concepts

All throws that an Ultimate player will ever want or need have the following in common: mental approach, snap, and follow-through. To learn a new throw, the novice must prepare mentally, develop snap, and execute the correct follow-through. These concepts are essentially the same for each throw, and the new player must understand the theories behind them before trying to put them into action.

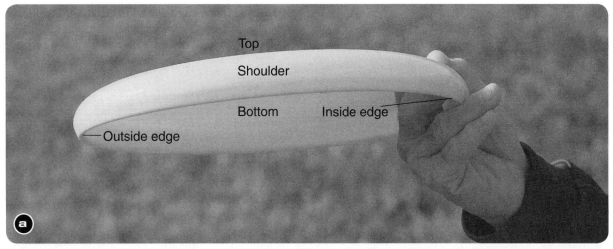

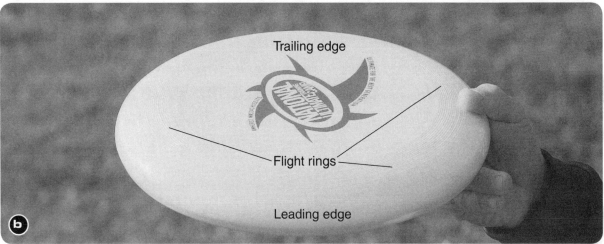

Figure 2.1 Parts of the disc.

Mental Approach

A disc is not a ball. A disc is not a ball. Repeat. A disc is not a ball. Throw out all the old beliefs about what makes an object fly, because a disc and a ball share few flight characteristics. Young children with little ball-playing experience often learn how to throw a disc more quickly and easily than their ball-throwing counterparts do. They do not have any habits to unlearn. Here are some suggestions that will help you prepare mentally for what you want to do physically.

▶ **Be prepared to fail.** Throwing a disc poorly can be frustrating, despite the popular myth that anyone can throw one. When a throw turns over immediately in midair and rolls across the ground, or flies errantly over a partner's head, you may want to give up. But don't throw in the towel, because you will forget all your mistakes once you make the disc fly beautifully.

▶ **Choose a patient person who is a better thrower than you are to practice with.** Do not be afraid of looking silly. Watch your partner carefully and try to identify the steps of his throwing process. Mimic what you can and move around the field, throwing in all directions. Watch how your partner adjusts his throws and movement. Ask questions but don't put too much pressure on yourself to learn a new throw immediately. Relax. Finally, if you cannot find someone who wants to throw, you can always . . .

▶ **Throw by yourself!** Don't be embarrassed about spending time alone in a big field with a stack of discs. Many serious Ultimate players have probably done this a few times. You need internal dedication to see external results, and throwing by yourself gives you the time and focus to achieve this. Throw long and short. Pick out a target and see how many throws it takes to reach it. Throw the discs into a strong wind and try to run them down.

And don't wait for a warm, sunny day to work on throws. Ultimate players compete in a variety of conditions. The sooner you make the wind and rain your friends, the better off you'll be.

Snap

Snap is what makes a disc fly. A throw with little snap will wobble and die. Snap, an elusive quality, is the result of many hours of practice and experience. Snap is what gives spin to the disc. The more spin a disc has, the farther it will fly. The rotations, or Zs, stabilize the disc and cause it to fly farther. Some Ultimate throwers produce an audible finger snap when they execute the pull—the throw that begins a point, much like a

kickoff in football. Imagine that you are snapping a wet towel at someone. (We do not suggest that you actually do this.) The noise that you hear as the end of the towel makes contact is snap.

How do you achieve snap when you are throwing? Regardless of the throw, you want to snap your wrist at the end of your arm swing. You swing your arm smoothly and rapidly, and then, at the last moment before release, you snap your wrist forward in the direction of your target. Your arm continues moving forward, and the swinging motion translates into rotational motion (see figure 2.2). This action imparts spin to the disc, which leaves your hand flying. The more you practice throwing, the more snap you will learn to put on each throw.

Follow-Through

You can have the right mental approach and develop lots of snap, but if you don't have the correct follow-through, the disc will not fly where you want it to go. Think about a basketball player getting ready for a free throw. She is most likely mimicking her shot before releasing it, including making an arcing motion toward the basket. She is reminding herself that she needs to follow through after releasing the ball. Ultimate throws are similar. Each throw requires a specific type of follow-through to get the disc to its intended destination. Novice players should practice their follow-throughs without a disc to develop a smooth, clean

Essential Throwing Tip

When teaching a group of players to throw, a coach should begin by having someone model the correct stance and throwing mechanics. Doing this demonstration in slow motion often helps. Then, *without discs,* players should mimic what they have just seen. This approach enables them to focus on what they are supposed to do without being distracted by a disc that flies poorly. After a few minutes, players try the stance and motion *with discs.* Chances are that the initial flights will work, and players will have a good idea of how to self-correct.

Figure 2.2 Practicing snap and follow-through with a backhand.

motion. Releasing too early or too late means that the throwing partner will either be diving or leaping during a simple game of catch, quickly leading to frustration for both partners.

These are the basic throwing concepts for every throw. Now it is time to learn the first throw that all players use when they begin to play Ultimate—the backhand!

The Backhand

Television commercials that show people throwing a disc usually have them using a backhand. It is the most common throw and the one that most novices rely on. But throwing a backhand well, particularly with defensive coverage, can be difficult in a competitive game of Ultimate. Mastering each facet of the throw—grip, stance, and movement—will make a player a real offensive presence on the field.

Grip

The correct grip for the backhand can be seen in figure 2.3, *a* and *b*. Pretend that you are shaking hands with someone and grab the disc. The thumb should rest on the outer flight rings, and the four fingers should be clenched along the rim. The thumb should not point toward the center of the disc, and the fingers should not be splayed away from the rim. The disc should lie comfortably in the V formed by the thumb and forefinger. At first this grip may seem uncomfortable and unnatural, but eventually it will feel as though you are putting on a favorite, well-worn glove.

Stance and Movement

Stand perpendicular to the receiver, with the right shoulder closest to the target (see figure 2.4, *a-c*). Bring the disc back, past your left side, rotating your hips and trunk, while transferring your weight to the back foot. Keep the disc flat and parallel with the ground. Continue to look at the receiver; don't look at the ground or at the disc. Terminate this backswing and begin to move the disc forward, increasing the speed throughout the swing. Rotate the hips and trunk back in the direction of the target. You should be transferring weight from the back leg toward the front leg, in tandem with the disc. Just before you release the disc, speed up the arm and spin the disc with a quick wrist snap. Release it and point the right hand at your target. Hold the hand there for a second, as the disc is flying. The left foot should have stayed stationary, and the right foot can point in the direction of the receiver. Remember that, for a right-handed thrower, the left foot will eventually become the foot on which you pivot from side to side, so you cannot move it at all during the throw without risk of being called for a travel (see figure 2.5, *a-b*).

How did it fly? Did it fall away to the left? If so, you released it too early or with the outside edge

Figure 2.3 Correct grip for the backhand: *(a)* inside view; *(b)* outside view.

Figure 2.4 Throwing the backhand, from the beginning to the end of the backswing.

Figure 2.5 Always keep your pivot foot on the ground when throwing. Otherwise you will be called for a travel.

dropped too low. Did it turn over, hit the ground, and roll? If it did, you released it too late or with the outside edge raised too much. Was it wobbly? If so, the disc needs more spin, and your release needs to be smoother. Did it make its way to your partner, perhaps spinning slowly and erratically but still staying in the air? If it did, you are well on your way to mastering the first throw in Ultimate!

Variations

After learning how to throw a nice, flat backhand, players are ready to learn two variations of this throw: the outside-in backhand and the inside-out backhand.

▶ **Outside-in backhand.** The technique is simple: Throw a regular flat backhand but raise the outside edge just a bit when releasing the disc. You should also extend the throwing arm slightly away from the body, more than you do with the regular backhand. But do not raise your arm upward toward your left shoulder. Release the disc at chest height, not at shoulder height. Now break the wrist slightly so that it looks as if the disc is turning over. This technique will make the disc fly in a left-to-right, slightly arced path to the receiver. The receiver should not have to move toward the disc; it should still fly directly to him (see figure 2.6). Ultimate players often use this throw to throw around a defender, particularly in a zone.

▶ **Inside-out backhand.** Drop the outside edge of the disc. Prepare to throw a regular backhand but swing the throwing arm closer to the body than you do with a regular backhand, almost like a pendulum. Your wrist should hold steady. The disc should fly for most of its flight with the outside edge angled downward, on a gentle right-to-left course. Again, of course, make sure to follow through (see figure 2.7). This release is certainly not as common as the outside-in backhand release because the player must throw across the body and a marker could be in the way. This throw is not the easy choice into the passing lane; that's what a forehand is for. But learning both the outside-in

Essential Throwing Tip

When putting a curve on any throw, you do not have to raise or lower the edge much at all. A minor variation in your release will result in a major variation in flight path.

Figure 2.6 Outside-in backhand.

Figure 2.7 Inside-out backhand.

and inside-out will help later with longer throws into the wind.

Common Problems With the Backhand

Although the backhand appears to be an easy throw and, of course, is the throw of choice for most non-Ultimate players, it is a difficult throw to make under defensive pressure. Table 2.1 shows some common mistakes and ways to solve them.

The Forehand

A thrower will be closely guarded by an opponent, known as the marker (or mark). She will need a backhand *and* a forehand to throw into the right-hand and left-hand passing lanes. A player who knows only one of these throws is vulnerable, in the same way that a basketball player who can dribble in only one direction with one hand is vulnerable. A veteran Ultimate defender can immediately tell whether the thrower has only one throw and will defend accordingly. A thrower needs to be a threat from both sides of the body and be able to throw efficiently into both passing lanes.

Throwing a forehand is thrilling. A backhand is utilitarian. A forehand, for whatever reason, is much more fun to throw. Players who master the forehand sometimes abandon the backhand. But a player who relies on one throw, even an impressive forehand, is still a liability. So, as players learn to master this popular throw, they must not forget the trusty backhand!

Grip

The grip for the forehand can be tricky. The forehand is also called the flick or two-finger, because you first put your index and middle finger together, along the inside rim of the disc. The thumb pinches the shoulder, and the ring finger and pinky are either folded into the palm or slightly outstretched, depending on which feels more comfortable and secure. The thumb should grip the edge but, unlike its position in the backhand, it should not be parallel to the ground (see figure 2.8).

Stance and Movement

When throwing a forehand, face the receiver. Hold the disc slightly back and away from the body, with the elbow near the side. Keep the left foot stationary and move the right foot sideways and slightly forward. Put weight on the right leg and bend the right knee slightly.

Bring the arm back a bit and then begin to move it forward at waist height. Continue to look at the receiver. Make sure that you do not bring the outside edge up. Lead with the elbow and follow with the forearm. The wrist should then break under, with a motion similar to that you use when skipping a stone. Release the disc with snap and point your hand toward the receiver. The palm should be facing the sky. A recognizable forehand should then be making its way to the receiver (see figure 2.9, *a-b*)! The arm swing and release is the most difficult part of this throw. Again, do not try to throw the disc as you would throw a baseball overhand. This throw is much more like a sidearm toss of a ball or a forehand in tennis.

Table 2.1 **Backhand Troubleshooting Tips**

Common mistakes	Solutions
Disc flies over the receiver's head.	Lower the leading edge just a bit.
Disc hits the ground in front of the receiver.	Raise the leading edge just a bit.
Disc wobbles.	Hold the disc tighter, snap it more, and release smoothly.
Disc will not fly flat.	Imagine a glass of water on top of the disc that you don't want to spill. Maintain a flat release throughout the entire swing of your arm.
Disc does not have a lot of power.	Make sure that you are *not* facing the receiver. Maintain a stance perpendicular to the receiver. You may be transferring your weight to your front leg too early. Your weight should not shift forward until the very end of your release.
Disc always flies to either side of its intended target.	Adjust the timing and vary your angles of release. Experiment with raising or lowering the outside edge. Maintain follow-through.

Figure 2.8 Forehand grip.

Figure 2.9 Throwing a forehand.

Variations

The forehand has the same two variations as a backhand does: the outside-in and the inside-out. A player needs to be able to throw these different types of forehands in the same way that a tennis player needs to be able to hit both sides of the court with a forehand return.

▶ **Outside-in forehand.** When throwing an outside-in forehand, simply lift the outside edge a bit. If the disc starts turning over, or rolling, put the outside edge down again. By moving the elbow farther from the body for this throw, eventually you should be able to extend the arm considerably. Raising the arm somewhat toward the shoulder will cause the disc to fly in a slight right-to-left arc (see

Figure 2.10 This exercise helps the thrower keep the release low when throwing a forehand.

figure 2.11, *a-b*). Again, putting too much curve on this throw will turn it into a blade, an extreme version of the outside-in that is difficult for beginners to catch. Players use the outside-in throw for throwing down the line around a defender, often in a zone, or for a long throw to open space, where a sprinting cutter will run to the disc.

▶ **Inside-out forehand.** The inside-out forehand is a prized weapon in a thrower's arsenal. A player who has an effective inside-out forehand, often simply called an IO, has clearly elevated her offensive game. You throw an IO to the left side of the body, with the right arm crossing over in front. The leading edge of the disc should be slightly raised, and the outside edge is lowered somewhat. The weight should be on the left foot this time, with the right leg initially back or slightly to the side. You then step forward with the right foot. The arm swings close to the front of the body, and the left shoulder rotates back as the right shoulder comes forward until the chest aims squarely at the target. You snap and release the disc, and the hand points toward the receiver (see figure 2.12, *a-b*). The IO is essential in breaking the mark (see page 51), which is the main reason that it is so valued. Players usually throw the IO to a cutter (receiver) coming up the left side of the field, which, in a traditional one-on-one defense that has chosen to force the offense toward the forehand passing lane, is usually devoid of defenders.

Common Problems With the Forehand

The forehand is the most difficult throw to learn in Ultimate, as well as the most satisfying. Table 2.2 shows some common problems and ways to solve them.

The Hammer

The hammer is unlike the backhand and forehand in that it flies upside down. It is the third member of the triumvirate of Ultimate throws. The disc may never have been intended to fly upside down, but early Ultimate players became enamored with the many trajectories that a disc could follow. Having the disc fly flatly to a receiver in either passing lane wasn't enough. Someone turned the disc upside down and kept tweaking the throw until it became more predictable and catchable. The careful Ultimate player relies mostly on the backhand

Figure 2.11 Outside-in forehand.

Figure 2.12 Inside-out forehand.

Table 2.2 Forehand Troubleshooting Tips

Common mistakes	Solutions
Disc flies over the receiver's head.	Lower the leading edge just a bit.
Disc hits the ground in front of the receiver.	Raise the leading edge just a bit.
Disc hits the ground and rolls.	Stop throwing the disc like a ball. Make sure that your palm faces the sky when releasing the disc.
Disc wobbles.	Hold the disc tighter, snap it more, and maintain follow-through.
Disc always flies to either side of its intended target.	Adjust timing and vary your angles of release. Experiment with raising or lowering the outside edge. Maintain follow-through.

and forehand, with a variety of release points and a range of angles, and uses the hammer discreetly. Yet the hammer is sometimes the perfect throw for breaking the mark or picking apart a zone defense. A well-placed hammer is almost impossible to block and exciting to watch and catch.

Grip

The grip for the hammer is the same as the grip for a forehand. The only difference is that the grip should be tighter than the grip for the forehand. Many Ultimate players have experienced the embarrassment of winding up to throw a hammer but holding it too loosely. The result is a falling disc that bumps down the back of the thrower and an empty hand in front of the thrower's face. So make sure to grip the disc as tightly as you can, while still being able to release it smoothly.

Stance and Movement

The hammer is similar in motion to a serve, or an overhead, in tennis. Face your throwing partner. Start with the disc at the side, as if you are going to throw a forehand. Tighten your grip and move the disc above your head, with your right arm slightly bent. Do not bend your neck; keep looking at your receiver. The disc should be above your head, held upside-down and at about a 45-degree angle to the ground (see figure 2.13, a-b).

The right leg should be out to the side and back. You must maintain the left leg as a pivot, and the left foot cannot move from its position. As you wind up, most of the weight should be on the right leg. As the arm moves forward, the weight transfers to the pivot leg.

The most unusual aspect of this throw is that you should not aim at the receiver. Instead, pick a spot to your left of your partner, well above his right shoulder, and aim the hammer at that point.

The hammer will not sail past your partner but instead will fly in a left-to-right arc down to him.

You also must release the disc well above your head. You will feel as if you are throwing upward, rather than forward. You may want to imagine that between you and your partner is a tree that you must throw over, not through. You will need some forward momentum, of course, but the disc will be flying up and then coming down to your partner. It should not fly in a flat line. Your follow-through should be well above your head. The disc should fall toward, not away from, the receiver and be easy to catch.

The value of the hammer is that it is a quick throw. It often takes defenders by surprise and can therefore start a quick succession of passes before the defense is able to recover. In addition to the inside-out forehand, players often use the hammer to throw to a cutter coming up the left side of the field. Do not overuse the hammer, because it can be difficult to throw and catch. Use it rarely and wisely. If your teammates are frequently dropping your hammers in games, you should put it away until you can perfect it and your teammates can become more successful at reeling it in.

Common Problems With the Hammer

Forget most of the troubleshooting tips that you learned for the backhand and forehand. The hammer does not fly like they do, and problems with the hammer call for different solutions (see table 2.3).

Switching Grips

After beginning players learn the basics of throwing backhands, forehands, and hammers, they must

Figure 2.13 The hammer.

Table 2.3 **Hammer Troubleshooting Tips**

Common mistakes	Solution
Disc flies over the receiver's head.	Aim lower. Release later and reduce the strength of your snap. Make sure that you are not releasing the disc too horizontally.
Disc hits the ground in front of the receiver.	Aim higher. Snap the disc more. Make sure that you are not releasing the disc too vertically.
Disc helixes back and forth.	Release should be more vertical. Aim upward, not forward.
Disc falls away from the receiver.	Aim more to the left of the receiver.
Disc does not fly very far.	You need to practice to develop a long hammer. Increase your snap, making sure that you are still aiming at the correct spot. Slowly have your partner move backward as you throw and be sure to maintain good form as you try to achieve distance.

become skilled at switching grips. According to the rules of the game, a player has only 10 seconds to throw, and if the disc accidentally falls from the thrower's hand without being touched by a defender, a turnover results. Being able to switch grips swiftly and smoothly allows the thrower to release the disc more efficiently. The thrower must be able to do this while pivoting from one side to another and faking his releases (see page 48), timing these actions perfectly so that the defender on the mark has little idea of where and when the thrower intends to release the disc.

Hand Movement

A proficient thrower has to be able to put the disc anywhere on the field, assuming that a receiver is moving into that area. Like a baseball pitcher, an Ultimate player does not want to telegraph what the next throw will be. The element of surprise is important. If a mark has an idea of where the disc is going, the defense can adjust accordingly. The easiest way for a player to avoid tipping her hand is first to stand with the disc in both hands as she surveys the field, looking for the next pass. The defender will not be able to determine anything from the grip, and the offense will gain another advantage.

To practice the skill of switching grips, start with a backhand grip and hold it at the left side of the body. Pretend to throw the disc but hang onto it. Make sure that the fake is realistic. One of the joys of having a realistic fake is fooling the opponent. A convincing fake can result in an "Up!" call from the opponent's sideline. If you can fool the sideline, you can most likely fool your mark, as well as other defenders on the field. Move the disc quickly to the other side of the body, as if now preparing to throw a forehand. As you switch from one side to the other, you also should be switching your grip. You may want to use your nonthrowing hand to help maneuver the disc. Your backhand grip should be morphing into a forehand grip. You are moving from having four fingers under the disc to having two fingers under the disc. Slide the disc along your hand, putting the correct two fingers under the rim and either curling the last two under the rim or keeping them slightly outstretched, depending on your personal preference and comfort. The thumb moves slightly, from along the shoulder to slightly across the shoulder, pointing toward the middle. This movement will feel uncomfortable at first, and the disc may flip out of your hand and hit the ground a few times. But continue to practice wherever you can—on the way to school, while you are waiting for practice to start, or even at home. All this practice will pay off when you step onto the Ultimate field.

Timing

Switching the grip while simultaneously pivoting and faking potential throws is a complex skill. A new player will often frantically try to do all this at the same time, thereby letting everyone know that he is a novice and has no idea where or when he is going to release the disc.

Stand in front of a full-length mirror. Don't even put a disc in your hand yet. Pretend that you are holding a disc and pivot on your left leg. (For more about this skill, see page 48).

Perform the pivot so that it looks realistic. Always face the mirror and make sure that you extend outward with your right leg.

When you feel comfortable pivoting and faking, pick up a disc with both hands. Now incorporate switching grips with pivoting and faking. Try to complete the grip switch to the correct throw just as you are extending your right leg. Then fake the throw (see figure 2.14, a-b). Do not fake a forehand if your grip is still in the backhand mode. This is a dead giveaway that you lack experience.

Practice the entire pattern of movements slowly. Don't speed it up until you feel comfortable and look believable. Eventually you will be operating at game speed, which is quick and deliberate, but not frantic.

When warming up before a game or practice, incorporate these movements into your routine. Standing still while throwing with a partner does not prepare you for competition. Move around, use all the throws, and pivot and fake away from

Figure 2.14 Switching the grip from backhand to forehand while pivoting.

an imaginary mark. The more skills you can simulate in warm-ups, the better you will perform in a game.

When players have a basic concept of how to throw the three main throws, as well as how to switch grips, they are ready to practice these throws in a drill. We like to use Speedflow for this purpose, because it is a low-pressure drill that players at all levels can perform.

Speedflow: A Drill for All Throws and Throwers

PURPOSE

To improve the skills of catching and throwing in a challenging situation.

EQUIPMENT

One disc for every two players

SETUP

Two lines of players face each other at a distance of 10 to 15 yards, depending on their skill level. Each person should be facing a partner, and each set of partners has one disc. If the number of players is uneven, three players can do the drill in a triangle formation with one disc. The pairs or groups of three should be separated by at least 7 yards, to minimize collisions while players chase down errant throws (see figure 2.14).

PROCEDURE

Pairs warm up for a few minutes by throwing any kind of throw to each other. They should try to catch every throw, even those outside their comfort range. If they have to chase down a throw, they should return quickly to their place in line before throwing the disc back to their partner. If they do this drill properly, players should be very active. After warming up, players stop throwing, hold on to their discs, and listen for instructions.

To start the drill, the coach calls out a throw that they should try first, such as "Backhand." The players then attempt to throw a simple flat backhand to the player opposite. The receiving player focuses on the catch and then returns the disc with a backhand. The short distance between players makes it simple for them to adjust their throws to be more accurate. Players must not move closer to each other, and they must not attempt throws that they can't control from too great a distance. At some point, the lines may look a little ragged, but this is fine. Each pair is working on individual throwing skills.

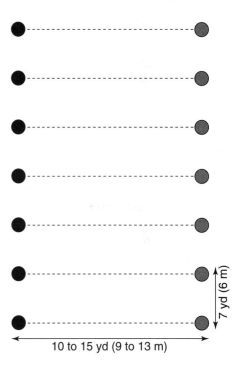

Figure 2.14 Speedflow drill.

Players continue throwing back and forth, trying to catch and release again as quickly as possible. The coach then calls out a different throw, such as "Forehand." The drill continues as the players work on the weaker aspects of their forehands. The coach or team captains can walk around the outside of the drill, offering appropriate suggestions. The coach then switches the call to "Hammer." As the drill continues, the calls change frequently, forcing the players to switch grips and concentrate on throwing and catching a new throw. The drill ends after players reach a predetermined number of completions (perhaps 50 throws) or time limit (three minutes is usually an optimum time).

(continued)

THROWING VARIATIONS

▶ Players can throw more complicated throws, such as inside-out forehands or outside-in backhands.

▶ Players change sides on the command "Switch!" This plan works particularly well on windy days because players must adapt their throws to the wind.

▶ Players can race to achieve a certain number of completions, within a time limit or not. This approach adds a competitive, slightly more pressured edge to the drill while requiring players to maintain their focus on form and accuracy.

OTHER VARIATIONS

As the participants become familiar with the drill, non-throw-related commands can be incorporated.

▶ Players can perform various exercises like push-ups, sit-ups, or jumping jacks immediately after the call, where they stand.

▶ On the call "Sprint," players immediately take off at a full sprint in opposite directions. After reaching a certain point or on a signal, players plant hard, come back to their previous position, and resume throwing.

▶ Players catch with only one hand or with the off hand.

▶ Players must incorporate a fake or a quick pivot before each throw.

Speedflow is an excellent way to have players work on mechanics and fundamentals. The purpose of the variations is to challenge and distract the players and still require them to complete their throws and catches, as they would in a game situation. As the skills of the players improve, adding new challenges will help them move up to the next level of competency.

Throwing in the Wind

"How do you throw that thing in the wind?" The answer to this frequently asked question from non-Ultimate players is "With lots and lots of practice!" Great throwers are successful because they have spent hundreds of hours outside, throwing on their own or with a partner. Throwing indoors is essentially useless, unless no other option is available, and players who want to improve their throws should greet windy conditions with enthusiasm. To make the wind your friend, you should understand some basic concepts about how the wind works and how it can affect the flight of the disc.

Determine the Wind Direction

Although the suggestion to determine the direction of the wind seems obvious, novice players and teams often figure it out too late. You can always begin by using the tried-and-true method of throwing some grass in the air and noting which way it falls. Then move on to throwing with a partner in various parts of the field. This exercise will give you information about how you will need to alter your throws to make the disc fly correctly.

Start Throwing Close Together

When beginning to throw, start close to your partner, just as you would at the beginning of basketball practice by starting with layups and short-range shots before going to the three-point line. As you and your partner gather knowledge about how the wind is affecting the disc, gradually move farther apart.

Throwers who have the luxury of the wind at their back may yearn to move farther apart because the wind is pushing and assisting their throws. But the thrower facing the wind won't have it as easy. Additionally, one of the most difficult throws in Ultimate is the short downwind variety. The goal is to keep the disc up and have it approach the receiver at a comfortable speed. You also must focus on how hard you will need to snap the disc.

Increase Snap

When thrown into the wind, the disc has to overcome tough flight conditions, just as a plane does when flying into a headwind. The more spin you impart to the disc, the more stable its flight will be. For a backhand, the wrist must curl back toward the forearm more than usual, and toward the end of the forward arm swing, the wrist must snap more powerfully to provide the abundant spin necessary to combat the effect of the wind. For a forehand, snap also needs to be harder. Done correctly, it should be felt along the inside of the forearm.

As for the hammer, put it away. Why would you use a risky throw such as a hammer on a windy day?

Change Stance

Changing your stance can help you counteract the forces of the wind. Adjust your stance in the following ways for the three basic wind directions.

▶ **Upwind.** When facing into the wind, you must lower your body to have the disc fly correctly. Drop your hips rather than bending over from the waist. Then release the disc from a low position of power with the leading edge tilted slightly up. To help develop this power while getting comfortable with the lower release point, do the following. Face the receiver and lunge forward with your right leg at a 45-degree angle to the left of the target. Place your trailing knee (left) on the ground. From this position, reach out in front of the right knee and throw the disc, but with tremendous spin. As you gain proficiency, try to lunge farther and release lower and lower. Eventually you will lift your left knee from the ground too.

▶ **Downwind.** A strong wind at the thrower's back will push the disc into the ground, so you should be more upright when throwing in these conditions. You also must aim higher, probably above the receiver's shoulders or head. Keep in mind that such a tailwind necessitates a higher release (about waist level or slightly higher) because the disc wants to lose altitude, and rapidly, as it flies. You should reduce some of the velocity and a little of the spin to avoid overpowering your downwind receiver.

▶ **Crosswind.** No hard-and-fast rule dictates a change in stance in a crosswind. Your stance will vary depending on the direction and velocity of the wind. Sometimes you will want to get lower, and sometimes you will need to stand up straight. In dealing with a crosswind, the angle of release is much more important.

Vary the Angle of Release

A slight variation in the angle of the disc can make a significant difference in its flight. If you are constantly having problems controlling the disc in the wind, practice varying the angle of release until you have once again gained control. Do not continue to throw randomly and hope it all just works out.

▶ **Upwind.** When throwing into a headwind, try tilting the leading edge of the disc up, about .5 inch (1.25 centimeters) more than if it were lying flat on a table. This modification will allow the disc to climb as it approaches the receiver. Drop the outside edge a bit as well; otherwise, the added wind resistance will cause the disc to turn over in the direction of the spin as it flies, driving it off target and into the ground. Be certain to give the disc plenty of spin and forward velocity. Don't overdo the upward tilt or your receiver will be chasing the disc all over.

▶ **Downwind.** If you are throwing with the wind at your back, tilt the leading edge of the disc up again, about 1 to 2 inches (2.5 to 5 centimeters). Remember, you will be aiming higher than you usually do on a still day. Tipping the leading edge up will counteract the effect of the tailwind and delay it pushing the disc into the ground. The danger of throwing downwind is that the throws tend to gain so much velocity that they are very difficult to catch. By tilting the leading edge of the disc upward, you are putting the brakes on the disc, or adding something called touch. Touch is when a thrower changes the angle of the disc to slow down its flight a bit and make it much easier to catch.

▶ **Crosswind.** A wind coming across the field can wreak havoc with your throws, particularly pulls. If the wind is coming from left to right and you are throwing a backhand, keep the outside edge of the disc angled downward enough to overcome the crosswind, allowing the disc to hold its intended line of flight (and do the opposite for the forehand). You do not want to show too much of the underside of the disc to the wind, because the wind will quickly toss the disc away and to the right, often into the middle of a game on the adjoining field.

If the wind is right to left, do the opposite. Flatten out your backhand and do not allow the wind to have any effect on the underside of the disc. You want the disc to be able to slice through the air, nullifying the force of the wind.

In windy conditions, throwing comes down to understanding the amount of spin and the adjustments in stance and angles that are necessary to overcome the effects of the wind on the disc. Although we have given you the basics to understanding the wind, you must learn much of this on your own. Experiment in the wind. Discover how you can use it or overcome it to get the disc to fly where you want it to go. But if there is one thing to master, it is spin, spin, spin!

Summary

Throwing in Ultimate is as essential as dribbling is in basketball. Players must have these skills to advance the object of play, and they must practice them over and over. An Ultimate player can throw with a partner or alone and should not be afraid of poor weather. Improvement is the natural outcome of hard work. Even a player who has developed a high level of expertise has more to learn.

Throwing a disc is probably the main reason that most people get hooked on Ultimate. Remember to have fun when you throw. When you feel confident in your throwing, find someone new who wants to learn to throw and will benefit from your teaching. After all, that's how we all started, and that's how the sport will continue to grow and evolve!

Principles of Catching

What good is a well-placed throw if the intended receiver drops it? As with throwing, catching a disc is much different than catching a ball, and this fact is evident to receivers new to the sport. They unwittingly expect to be able to track a disc the same way that they do a ball, and they believe that a disc and a ball will behave in a similar manner. But the two are different animals. Like a ball, a disc can be thrown hard or with a soft touch, over long or short distances. Unlike a ball, however, a disc can be made to fly in myriad arcs, can stay aloft longer by hovering like a spaceship, or can be made to drop like a rock to its intended target. Add to this the unpredictability of flight in windy conditions and what can happen when an inexperienced player launches a throw. All these factors contribute to the necessity of learning the nuances of a disc's flight and the principles of catching one. Although experience can teach a player how a disc flies, this chapter accelerates the learning process by presenting the basic techniques and approaches to successfully catching a disc in Ultimate action.

Basic Catching Concepts

Like throwing a disc, catching a disc is a unique skill that you must practice if you are to develop proficiency. Ultimate demands that you be able to secure a disc while running at top speed and then make a smooth transition from receiver to thrower, all while a defender is vehemently breathing down your neck. A strong mental attitude will allow you to be aware of defensive pressure without letting it affect focus. To catch the disc, clamp on the rim to stop it from spinning. After you have secured the disc, the transition to thrower begins. Besides offering mental focusing exercises, this chapter shows various catching techniques and several drills to help you become proficient with them.

Mental Focus

To be a reliable receiver, you must be able to remain focused and gain a level of comfort with the considerable pressure applied from defenders. You must find the right mixture of intensity and relaxation in game situations. Drops often result from lack of focus or anxiety under pressure. To gain comfort catching at full speed, practice doing so—at full speed—accelerating through the disc as it approaches. Repetition is crucial to developing not only soft, sure hands but also the focused and relaxed confidence needed to secure the disc under pressure.

Simulating mentally challenging situations that commonly occur, as well as others that would rarely take place on the Ultimate field, aids in developing a strong focus, comfort, and confidence in your ability as a receiver. Before discussing specific types of catches, we offer several drills that help with focus and relaxation in catching (see the sidebar on page 31).

Stop the Spin

Novice players seem to think that the disc is going to come gently to rest in their arms. They believe that they can catch it as they would a football or envelop it as a goalkeeper would a soccer ball. But then the disc abruptly darts out once the spinning plastic object meets the skin. Other beginners reach effectively for the disc with outstretched hands, intending to grasp its rim, only to misjudge the direction and effect of the spin and watch it ricochet away. A key to securing the disc is to clamp down firmly to stop its spin. This task is not so easy if the disc is thrown with some velocity, if the receiver's hands are sweaty, or if the receiver can reach it with only one hand.

The suggestions listed in the sidebar on page 31 will help receivers learn how to recognize and react to velocity and direction of spin, where to grab the disc, and which technique to use to secure the plastic most effectively. Add the exercises following this paragraph to your list to further challenge athletes' hand–eye coordination, visual perception, and grip

Selected Catching Focus Drills

▶ Partners stand 10 to 20 yards (meters) apart and throw soft, medium, and hard passes to different and awkward locations to make the receiver work on reacting and securing the disc when throws are not ideal.

▶ A teammate stands behind or alongside the receiver, gently nudging and bumping him to challenge his balance and focus, distracting him as the disc draws near.

▶ A third teammate, holding a lightweight and opaque object like a large cardboard panel or large towel, stands between the two partners. This teammate stands nearer to one of the athletes and holds the object up as the disc approaches. She then drops or pulls the object out of the way before the disc strikes it. The receiver must react to the speed, spin, and level of the disc and attempt to catch it. Distraction is the key here. Try other means of distraction.

▶ Fatigue challenges focus, so try Yo-Yo's, an exercise in which one partner remains stationary while the other cuts away and back in, in an upside-down V pattern. Partners continue throwing to one another in this fashion for a set period of time or a total number of throws. Then they switch roles and begin another set. As the receiver improves, the partner can challenge her with purposely bad throws.

▶ Players should practice telling themselves mental affirmations when receiving the disc, saying, "Go get it," "Sweet! Here it comes. I can't wait to get to this," and so on. Come up with your own internal cues to prompt focus and a relaxed confidence.

---

strength. In each of these suggested drills, stand 10 to 20 yards (meters) apart from one another.

▶ Throw a stack of discs to an athlete who is wearing soft synthetic or cloth gloves. The disc meets less friction that way, and the athlete must learn to clamp down hard to stop the spin.

▶ Coat a disc with spray silicone or furniture polish to make it more slippery and harder to get hold of. Then use any challenging drill intended to develop catching skills, such as those listed in the sidebar. (Afterward, wash the disc with mild soap and water to remove any residue.)

▶ The receiver closes his eyes (or turns his back to the thrower). As the thrower releases the disc and calls, "Up," the receiver opens his eyes (or turns around) and must read the type of throw and subsequent spin to catch the disc.

▶ One partner sits or lies down. Once the thrower releases the disc, the receiver springs to his feet in time to successfully make the catch.

▶ In any catching drill, ask athletes to clap two (or three) times before catching, catch with one hand only, catch only with the nondominant hand, and so on.

Whatever techniques are employed to learn how to stop the spinning disc, raising cognitive demand (reading, tracking flight, and identifying direction of spin) is helpful in developing sensory awareness and the ability to recognize subtle differences in disc flight dynamics. Varying manipulative challenges (handling of the disc) is also critical to developing overall disc skill.

Secure It Before Throwing It

In the excitement of competition, a receiver's concentration often gets ahead of the current task—catching the disc. The player should focus on completing the reception first, and then make the transition to the role of thrower. The ability to move rapidly from receiver to thrower is, of course, an important skill in Ultimate, but players cannot afford to be hasty or careless. As legendary UCLA basketball coach John Wooden would exhort, "Be quick, but don't hurry."

Here are some additional techniques to help in the development of this critical skill. To improve players' focus, add these variations to other catching drills.

▶ Players in practice drills must pause after each catch and say, "Zero" before they throw the disc. After a drop, they say, "One," and so on. The goal is to keep the number as low as possible or try to beat the last lowest score following a predetermined length of time.

▶ Distractions—physical, visual, and audible—will agitate players and challenge their concentration as they attempt to receive the disc and transition to the role of thrower.

▶ Players must read something on top of the disc before they throw.

▶ While drilling, athletes must make the transition to the role of thrower following a reception with the appropriate fake, *without* releasing the disc.

▶ After any break in concentration, players must complete a fitness task to reinforce focus.

Players can secure a flying disc in many ways, but some are more effective than others, particularly in certain situations. The following sections discuss and then demonstrate a variety of catching techniques, and offer exercises designed to improve specific techniques.

Clap Catch

The basic receiving technique is referred to as the clap catch. Figure 3.1, *a* and *b*, shows how one hand claps down on top of the disc while the other does so from underneath, effectively sandwiching the disc between the hands. This tactic is most effective when the disc is arriving at a middle level, that is, between the navel and the chest. The shoulders must be squared (perpendicular to the flight path) as the disc approaches. This positioning, like that of a baseball infielder or catcher getting her body in front of the ball, allows the trunk to serve as a backstop if the disc slips through the hands or is bobbled, providing a second opportunity to secure the disc. Another reason to use this method is that the body acts like a shield, boxing out trailing defenders and making a block more difficult to achieve.

Many players find the clap catch effective at different levels—above the chest by jumping up as the disc approaches, or below the waistline by lowering the body and sliding to meet the disc (see figure 3.2, *a-b*). And when conditions are windy or wet, the clap catch is a more sure-handed method because it keeps the disc in front of the body.

Although both reliable and effective, this technique has its limitations. As figure 3.3 shows, clap catching too high puts the hands and forearms in

Figure 3.1 Clap catch: *(a)* preparing for the clap catch; *(b)* executing clap catch at chest level.

Figure 3.2 *(a)* High-level clap catch; *(b)* low-level clap catch.

Figure 3.3 Making a clean reception using the clap catch overhead is difficult.

Figure 3.4 The clap catch is unreliable when catching discs away from and to the side of the body.

an awkward position for a clean reception. The forearm of the top hand is at an angle perpendicular to the plane of the disc, making it likely that the disc will strike the forearm before the hands secure it. Far too often positioning the arms this way results in a drop. The clap catch is also unre-

liable when catching discs away from and to the side of the body (see figure 3.4). First, with each stride the shoulders rotate forward and backward in opposition to leg action, causing alternating arm length. This circumstance affects the timing and precision of the clap of the top hand of the outstretched arm onto the bottom one, especially at top speed. Instead, the hands are often misaligned when clamping down on the plastic and the disc flips out of the hands. Another reason to avoid using the clap catch to the side is that the player should use the arms in the action of running until the last possible moment before reaching out for the catch. When the disc arrives out and to the side of the body with any velocity, clamping on it at just the right moment and with just the right pressure is difficult. The receiver is often tardy with the hands, and the disc squirts through.

As stated earlier, players should use the clap catch primarily when the disc is approaching at midlevel and squarely into the torso of the body. Receivers can increase the range of this technique by elevating the trunk with a jump or lowering it with a baseball-type slide toward the incoming disc. The key is to adjust the trunk level, not the forearms. The forearms must remain parallel to each other and to the flight plane of the disc. If the disc is to the side, too high, or too low to accomplish this, players should choose the two-handed rim catch or catching one handed.

Two-Handed Rim Catch

In some situations a cutter must use his reach advantage, and the two-handed rim catch (TRC) accomplishes this. Besides offering greater reach, this catch makes the transition from receiver to thrower quicker because the hands are immediately grasping the rim when making the reception.

TRC Out Front

As figure 3.5 demonstrates, the two-handed rim catch (some call it the crab claw) increases reach and extends the point of reception. This method provides the thrower a safer, wider target area and reduces the likelihood that a defender will get a block because she has more distance to cover to reach the disc. A call that offensive teammates should communicate loudly to the cutter when a defender is fast approaching is "Go to!" (the disc). This call alerts the cutter that he must assertively accelerate *through* the oncoming disc and perhaps even extend his arms with a two-handed rim catch to foil the defender's hope of getting a block or interception. Notice in the photo that the disc is arriving at a middle

level. The cutter can therefore lean forward and accelerate through the arriving disc with a fingers-up, thumbs-down orientation to make the catch. The cutter should keep the hands close together so that the disc will not slip between them and angle the palms slightly toward one another so that they meet the rim simultaneously.

TRC High Level

If the throw is approaching at a higher level, the cutter should keep the thumbs down while leaning into, and reaching for, the disc. The TRC allows the cutter to continue cutting at top speed, extending the arms for the catch at the necessary moment. Again, this method pushes the point of reception farther out in front of the body, even while catching high-level passes or high-arriving hammers. Note the reach advantage gained by the cutter in figure 3.6. This technique screens out the defender while allowing a secure two-handed catch at top speed.

TRC Low Level

As the disc arrives at a lower point, somewhere near the navel and all points below, the hands must rotate down into a thumbs-up position. This principle is analogous to the way in which an infielder uses one technique to field a ground ball (thumbs up) and another to make a play on a pop fly (thumbs down). The TRC for a low pass allows

Figure 3.5 The two-handed rim catch increases reach and extends the point of reception.

Figure 3.6 *(a)* TRC high-level catch alone; *(b)* TRC high-level catch with a defender.

the cutter to run through the disc, not having to slow down as much as he would when using a sliding clap catch (see figure 3.7). The concept behind the arm position used when making a clap catch at high levels also holds true for a clap catch at a low level. The disc often strikes the forearm and will ricochet away before being secured by the receiver's hands.

The following technique progression helps determine a player's range with both the high and low TRC orientations and where the switch from one to the other should take place.

1. Hold a disc in both hands in front of the body as though you just caught it, at head level and using a thumbs-down grip, with fingers on top of the disc (see figure 3.8a).

2. Slowly lower the disc, keeping it flat (parallel to the ground) throughout.

3. Note the point at which maintaining a flat orientation with the disc becomes difficult and you feel a strain in the muscles on the top of the hands, wrists, and forearms (figure 3.8b). This position indicates where to switch to a thumbs-up hold (figure 3.8c).

4. Repeat the progression starting low with a thumbs-up grip. Again, keep the disc flat as you slowly raise it. As before, note the point where it becomes difficult to keep the disc flat. (You will notice your elbows extending and your shoulders creeping up toward your ears as you try to keep the disc parallel to the ground. You want to avoid this tension.)

5. Perform this exercise in front of a mirror to add a visual association.

Figure 3.7 Low two-handed catch in action.

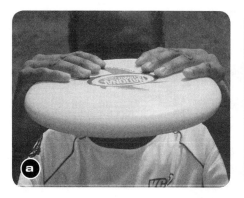

Figure 3.8 High and low two-handed rim catch: *(a)* high grip with thumbs down; *(b)* when to switch to *(c)* a thumbs-up hold.

Although players vary somewhat in their range of comfort in catching thumbs down and thumbs up, in general, when the disc arrives anywhere below chest level, go thumbs up. Depending on throw level, using the appropriate TRC approach allows you to readily lean forward from the ankle, optimizing both acceleration and reach.

Having completed the preceding progression, try the Go to Pair drill, which puts the two-handed rim technique into practice.

While the clap catch is as reliable as they come, particularly in windy or wet conditions, competency with the two-handed rim catch will raise your playing level.

Go to Pair Drill

▶ Partners throw back and forth standing 12 to 15 yards (meters) apart, keeping their arms at their sides.

▶ As the disc approaches, the receiver steps forward toward it with one leg (alternating right and left on successive repetitions) and, depending on the level of the arriving disc, catches it with the appropriate two-handed technique.

▶ After a couple minutes, partners step forward and decrease the distance between them (to increase difficulty and improve quickness).

▶ Finish with each partner taking two or more game-simulated steps toward the disc each time it approaches and attempting a TRC. (Drilling with a group of three players forming a triangle will make this last step smoother, allowing more time to return to the starting position.)

▶ Try moving closer together to raise reactive demands.

Players use their imaginations to enhance or expand on this exercise. Progress to any Go To drill and focus on using the proper hand position and technique for making a two-handed catch.

Catching One Handed

As stated earlier, players should catch with both hands whenever possible. Often, however, the cutter can reach the disc with only one hand, such as when a throw sails high overhead, is too low to reach with two hands without slowing down, or is thrown far out in front of, or behind, the body. Furthermore, although the cutter may be able to get both hands on the disc, doing so may be mechanically awkward or impractical (e.g., clap catching to the side of the body). For these reasons players should practice one-handed catching.

Some new players not well acquainted with the consequences of dropping the disc during an important game prefer to catch one handed. When watching new players in action it is easy to identify those stubborn athletes who insist on using one-handers, just because they can, when two would have provided more certainty. In a hard-fought game of keep-away, in which even one unforced drop can be the difference between success and failure on the scoreboard, it is essential to do everything possible to approach a 100 percent completion percentage. If a two-handed catch is less practical, or a quick reach with one hand will help beat the defender, then by all means, go get it. The following section describes the best method for securing the disc one handed.

Grab That Rim!

Stopping the spin of the disc one handed can be tough, particularly in wet conditions—which is why two are preferred—but the way to do it is to grasp the rim firmly in the webbing of the thumb and index finger and across the palm. Getting the correct hand in the desired position to stop the spin can be quite a challenge. Inexperienced players often fail to recognize the direction of spin of a particular throw. The predictable and typical reaction, as the plastic spins abruptly out of the cutter's hand, is a look of astonishment and wonder: "How did I miss that? It was in my hand!"

Recognize and Prepare for the Spin

The spin of the disc is clockwise when the throw is a right-handed backhand or left-handed forehand. Likewise, the spin is counterclockwise if the throw is a right-handed forehand or left-handed backhand. Recognizing the rotation is important

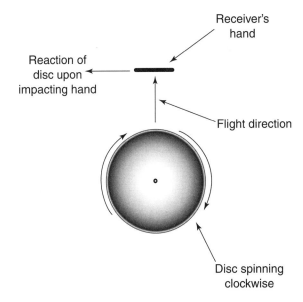

Figure 3.9 Reaction of spinning disc when it hits the cutter's hand. The disc will carom in the opposite direction on impact when spinning counterclockwise.

for catching, as well as reading purposes, because spin affects flight dynamics too. When the plastic meets skin it ricochets in the direction of the spin, which can add to the difficulty of the catch. Figure 3.9 illustrates how the disc will react at the point where it strikes the hand, and how to overcome this effect.

When going toward an incoming disc, apply the same principles to catching one handed that you would use when catching two handed—generally, use thumbs down above the chest and thumbs up for lower receptions. Both hands should cover any throw toward the middle of the body. But when throws are high, low, wide, or behind you, a single-handed catch may be necessary.

Hand Orientation and Location on Rim

The hand closest to the disc is generally the best one to use. But because the disc reacts according to the direction of spin, to stop it successfully, you must not only use proper hand orientation but also meet the disc at the correct position on the rim. As an example, if a clockwise-spinning disc is arriving to the right of a cutter at or below chest level, a thumbs-up orientation with the right hand is best. As figure 3.10*a* demonstrates, the disc will spin toward the thumb and forefinger on contact. With one-handed grabs, this is desirable. If the disc is arriving out to the right but higher than chest level, a thumbs-up orientation becomes awkward and difficult to maintain. Here, the cutter must switch to a thumbs-down orientation. If a clockwise-spinning throw is arriving high and farther away from the right side of the body, however, making this catch with the right hand can be a challenge. Figure 3.10*b* displays how to reach across the body with the left hand, thumb down, so that the disc is properly blocked and will spin into the thumb and forefinger. A cutter must be able to reach the leading edge of the disc if it is spinning away from her body, whereas reaching only the inside edge of a disc is sufficient if it is spinning into her body. Apply these principles to both sides.

These approaches are helpful in developing one-handed catching skill:

▶ Practice one-handed grabs using the same progression that you did for TRCs.

▶ During Speedflow drills or when warming up, devote some time to catching with only one hand, with both the dominant and non-dominant hand.

▶ For more of a challenge, throw outside-in and inside-out curving throws and hammers with a partner to help determine which technique and hand position work best for you.

▶ Alternate soft, hard, and purposely errant throws, and put extra spin on some.

Jumping for the Disc

Ultimate is played at multiple levels, from low to the ground to high in the air. Therefore, you must maximize your vertical reach. If the throw is low enough to secure with two hands, catch it that way. If the disc is too high or a defender is rapidly approaching, quickly snagging the disc one handed will provide an advantage. The keys to success in catching higher throws are reading the flight of the disc, gaining favorable position on the defender, and timing the takeoff to reach the disc at the highest point of your leap.

Reading Disc Flight and Timing the Catch

For simplicity of discussion, we will assume conditions of little or no wind. When cutting for a disc that is hovering high overhead, you benefit by being able to recognize the direction of its spin. From the perspective of a downfield cutter facing the thrower, a hanging, clockwise-spinning disc will eventually fall back to the right (or left, if the cutter is instead chasing the disc downfield). Reverse this for a counterclockwise spin. Expecting this result, you can more quickly reach the point where the disc will be falling so that you can leap and catch it first.

Figure 3.10 *(a)* The disc will spin toward the thumb and forefinger on contact; *(b)* reach across the body with the left hand, thumb down, so that the disc is properly blocked and will spin into the thumb and forefinger.

Essential Catching Tip

When facing the throw, a high-hanging disc spinning clockwise should eventually fall right, whereas a counterclockwise-spinning disc should fall left.

Leaping and Jumping Technique

A takeoff from two feet is referred to as a jump, whereas a takeoff from one foot, with a landing on the opposite foot, is a leap. At times, when standing under a high-hanging disc, a standard jump, like that of a basketball player when rebounding, will get you high enough to secure the disc, particularly when going up for the disc with both hands (as you would for a rebound). If you are alone in the end zone, for instance, or you have effectively boxed out—gained position that seals out the opponent from where the disc is arriving—a strong two-foot takeoff may do the trick. But to attain greater elevation and reach, you must leap, taking off from one leg and going up with one hand. The same applies when you and an opponent are swiftly chasing a high throw, stride for stride, out in open space.

If you are alone in open space, going up for the high catch is easier. But when the throw is hanging, hovering in the air above you and allowing a defender (or two) time to arrive and make a play on the disc, you must be familiar with how the disc will behave and gain favorable position to jump or leap and get it at the earliest possible moment. You should be able to leap off either leg as well as catch with either hand. When a defender is applying pressure, taking off from the favored leg or catching with the dominant hand is not always feasible, so you should work hard to develop this ability from either side. Practice time should be devoted to these skills.

The following drills help develop reading skills and timing of leaps.

Dog

This drill is a lot of fun for new players, because they get to run fast and hard for the disc. Athletes start near the thrower, who launches long passes to individual cutters. The cutters then return on one side of the field with the disc, drop it at the feet of the thrower, and return to the starting position for another opportunity. Athletes can start from the other side of the field after every turn or following a couple of tries, or can even begin sprinting after throws from opposite sides.

It's Up

As pure as they come, this drill has two players take off from a cone near a thrower. The thrower purposely throws long, hanging passes (sometimes unflatteringly called jump balls) for the two players to read. They jockey for position as they run and battle for the disc. After the players catch the disc, or not, they return with the disc to wait for their turn to try again. As in Dog, players can switch sides after each turn, leaving from the other side of the thrower to get a different view of the same throw. Throwers should be predictable at first, using the same release, and then proceed to vary their releases, throwing hanging, bending, or plain long throws for the players to chase down.

Old-Fashioned 500

Several athletes are downfield again, awaiting high, hanging throws. Before the throw, announce the possible points scored if a throw is caught or make it a standard 100 for every catch. After a player reaches a score of 500, he either becomes the new thrower or he is declared the winner and all scores are reset to 0. This drill works on stationary

(continued)

reading skills and timing when facing the thrower, gaining position, and then jumping or leaping for a catch.

When the disc is thrown high to an in cut—in which the cutter is coming back toward the thrower from a downfield position—the cutter must carefully time the leap to meet the disc, slowing down as little as possible. Sometimes the cutter can leap and secure the disc with both hands. But if the disc is too high to use this technique, the leaping cutter should go with one hand. The challenge, again, is timing the leap correctly without losing speed. In this situation, inexperienced players often take to the air too late, and the disc slips through their outstretched but tardy hands.

Essential Catching Tip

If the disc is arriving high on a hard in cut, especially if the throw is approaching with some velocity, the cutter should prepare sooner and leap earlier for the reception.

Skipping for height, along with a variety of other exercises explained in chapter 8, does wonders for working on the footwork and mechanics of leaping for high catches. On every repetition, players should reach up as high as possible with the forward-swinging arm. As always, to gain the most benefit, players must have the legs and core thoroughly warmed up before jumping, leaping, and skipping for maximum height.

Layout Catch

All situations discussed so far have centered on relatively catchable throws, those reachable throws that are low, high above, or wide to either side of the body. The grab that sets Ultimate apart from most other sports is the layout, or diving, catch. Athletes dive in countless other sport settings, but the frequency with which it occurs in Ultimate is unique. In fact, many elite players claim that they became serious competitors on the Ultimate field only after they began to lay out for the disc. The willingness to dive extends the reach significantly, enabling the cutter (or defender) to make spectacular plays on the disc. There is a right way to dive and there are many wrong ways to dive. Done incorrectly, diving will result in failure to make the play and may cause injury. The following step-by-step progression will help players gain proficiency in one of the most distinguishing skills in the sport of Ultimate.

A note of caution: Although diving is an important skill in Ultimate play, *never* require players to perform this skill before they have practiced sufficiently and are prepared to do so with proper form and technique. *Diving can lead to injury.* Emphasize to players that they should try diving only when they feel ready to do so.

Commitment

Diving demands a decision from the athlete. A player must commit to hitting the ground. The more comfortable the player is with that prospect, the easier and more instinctive the commitment to and execution of the skill become. To help players gain comfort and overcome initial fear, lead them in this simple exercise.

1. Roll around on the ground. Simply roll back and forth, noting how the ground feels and how the grass smells, perhaps even whether it itches. Be aware of the senses as much as possible. Try closing the eyes, too.

2. After a few moments progress to all fours. Fall forward from the knees, with the arms outstretched and palms facing forward, so that the heels of the hands slide across the ground first, followed by the forearms, inside of the elbows, chest, belly, and finally the upper legs. See figure 3.11a.

3. Next, rise higher, to the knees, and do the same as you did in step 2. As your comfort level increases, attempt to cover more ground with each effort, as if jumping forward from the knees. See figure 3.11b.

4. Apply the same progression and positioning while falling forward from the feet. At first, try bending at the ankle, knee, and hip—crouching down, like a swimmer on the blocks at the start of a race, to get a lower starting position. But keep in mind that staying flat—landing on the heels of the hands, inside

Figure 3.11 Steps to learning how to dive: *(a)* from all fours; *(b)* from your knees; *(c)* from the feet but crouching down to get to a lower starting position; and *(d)* diving from a jog or short run.

of the elbows, chest, and belly—is the key to safe and successful diving. See figure 3.11*c*.

5. Finally, try jogging into a dive using the preceding principles. Wet ground will make this easier because less friction will occur on landing. Another key to remember is that as you move faster, you overcome some of the friction and disperse more of the ground impact. See figure 3.11*d*.

An effective technique is to practice diving into a pool or into shallow water at the beach. If a team has access to a crash mat, like those used for the high jump or pole vault, players can practice diving form without fear of injury. (But be aware that these mats can cause surface friction burns, so wear a long-sleeved shirt and long pants while

practicing laying out.) Other soft, yielding surfaces to make use of are powdery sand at the beach and snow (probably not found at the same soft, powdery beach). Finally, a child's Slip 'n' Slide kit is helpful and plenty of fun, but don't get too carried away!

Some athletes have had experience diving in other sports, and others simply have a knack for it and are not afraid of this aspect of the game. Still other players are understandably reluctant. After all, diving headlong after a plastic disc is counterintuitive; but like throwing, it is a learnable skill.

Body Position

You can achieve good diving form, first, by leaning forward from the ankle and committing to the fall. Imagine leaning forward into a strong wind, as if it were strong enough to hold you up in this leaning position. This is precisely the position that you should employ when preparing for a smooth layout. Do not bend your upper body forward at the hips. This action will slow you down. Maintaining a hips-tall, back-straight orientation while leaning forward from the ankle creates a positive shin angle and increases acceleration. This is because the ground reaction force is now focused on propelling the body forward (see figure 3.12). Ultimate players make seemingly impossible catches by laying out, due as much to the increase in acceleration in the last few steps before launching as to the increased reach by the body being stretched out horizontally. By using the proper body position, leaning into a fall while staying tall (long), the form will be flat and the landing will be smoother.

Landing

After leaving your feet, you must keep the body extended, not allowing either knee to come underneath the body. Doing so may cause a bruise, or contusion, to the knee. As much as is within your control, land correctly—that is, flat (see figure 3.13). When laying out properly, players look relaxed, and the subsequent landing is smooth and seemingly effortless. Given the opportunity, focus on players with good form and study their preparation and execution when diving. Visually going backward from the landing is a helpful exercise, providing a different perspective on the progression of movements. Following a landing, go back through the sequence in your mind. Did you land flat, on your side, or on one shoulder? Did you bring a knee underneath for protection? Just before takeoff, did you have the sensation that you could not turn back, that you were leaning so far forward that the only option was to "get horizontal"? Mentally revise and rehearse every step, so that the process becomes familiar. The more familiar the sequence is, the more natural or normal laying out will become.

Look for these telltale signs:

- Are grass or mud stains on the lower chest and belly, where they should be, or are these signs of impact on the back of a shoulder or side of a hip?

- If slight scrapes are present, are they on the heel of the palms, inside of the elbows, or on the top and front of the hipbones, as desired?

- After a practice or tournament in which you laid out, are you sore? If so, where? Until you build up specific strength, postevent soreness should be present in the muscles of the upper back and back of the neck (normal). Soreness in the shoulders, in the rib cage, sides of the hips, or knees is a sign of incorrect form and landings. Your form needs work.

Figure 3.12 Layout catch body position at point just before takeoff.

Figure 3.13 Landing flat.

Visualization

As mentioned earlier, mental rehearsal and review are extremely useful tools. This exercise gives the athlete the advantage of having been in the situation before. Players who use visualization actually practice and experience success before they achieve it on the field. The benefits are obvious, and here is how to apply it.

▶ Picture yourself in action, in the third person, as though watching yourself on television.

▶ Next, visualize the action in the first person, as though the play is happening to you directly. This approach is more realistic and even more effective in preparing you to be *in* the action.

Employing one of these approaches, rehearse all steps in the sequence of laying out (or any game situation or skill).

Visualization can improve execution and enhance performance significantly, but only if you take it seriously and practice it regularly. Persistence leads to mastery, so don't sell this exercise short. Visualization is particularly effective in overcoming the apprehension that often accompanies laying out.

Common Catching Errors

Drops are usually due to lack of experience in reading the spin or flight of the disc or a lapse in focus, and with newer players, often both. To overcome unforced drops, be aware of the common mistakes (see table 3.1).

Table 3.1 Catching Troubleshooting Tips

Common mistakes	Solutions
As you cut in, a defender bolts by you for the block.	Make the defender's job tougher by accelerating to (through) the approaching disc. Do not slow down!
You are wide open, about to receive a pass and then throw (unmarked) to a teammate who is alone in the end zone, but you drop an easy catch.	Do not think about throwing until the catch is complete. Secure it before throwing it. See it all the way in.
In your attempt to clap catch a pass above your head, the disc caroms off your forearm.	Adopt instead a thumbs-down two-handed rim catch, reaching up and forward for the disc.
As you cut straight in, a right-handed forehand (spinning counterclockwise) is arriving at a middle level. Reaching to make a thumbs-up rim catch, the disc spins to the left, out of your right hand.	Go with the clap catch or two-handed rim catch, or use the left hand so the disc will spin toward the thumb and index finger.

Summary

Catching a flying disc in Ultimate is a challenge, but it becomes much easier when you realize that a disc behaves much differently from other objects of play and then take appropriate measures to adapt to this fact. Practice the exercises offered in this chapter while paying attention to these principles: Learn to recognize the spin, how it affects disc flight as well as how it reacts upon impact with the skin; choose the most effective catching technique to stop the spin; be certain to secure the disc before transitioning to throw; and whenever possible, use two hands. After all, the game *is* all about possession.

Offense:
Individual Skills

Key Terms

backfield

bailing

breaking the mark

break side

clearing

clogging

downfield

force side

pivot foot

straight-up force

weak side

Ultimate offense at its most basic is merely throwing and catching. You pick out a receiver, or a group of receivers, throw the disc in their general area, and someone figures out a way to hang on to it.

Ultimate offense at its finest is a thing of beauty. Everyone is following some sort of pattern, varying his speed and sprinting his hardest at times. The disc is flying true and crisp. Strong defenders challenge many catches, often in the air. Turnovers are rare, and the opposing team converts almost every one to a goal.

This chapter will show how individual players can contribute to a team's overall offensive plan. Players will learn how to cut effectively into open space and cleanly complete a throw against an effective mark.

Our basic philosophy about offense is exceedingly simple: Do not turn over the disc. Everyone has a simple and direct throw that she can make to a cutter. A spectacular screaming hammer that boinks off the fingertips of a diving receiver is still a turnover. A slicing blade up the sideline that a smart defender intercepts is a turnover. The fancy high-release, break-mark backhand over the cup that is blocked by the savvy wing is, again, still a turnover. The spectacular throw is often not the best choice.

The theatrics of stylish throwing can be compelling but, without internal discipline and poise, can make for terrible offense. As your team's offense improves, keeping turnovers to a minimum correlates directly with winning more games and playing better Ultimate.

Throwing

In the previous chapters you learned the basics of throwing and catching. Although you may have developed some confidence in your skills at this point, all bets are off when you join a real game. The goal of the other team is to make it difficult for your team to throw and catch. They are committed to forcing a turnover. So, to develop additional strengths in game situations, imagine that a point has just started and you are putting the disc in play.

Choosing a Receiver

You have just received the pull, and the disc is in your hands. You face downfield, and your job is to put the disc into play and start your team's offensive drive. The last thing you want to do is serve up the first pass to a rabid defender.

Your team's offensive plan may already dictate exactly where this first throw is supposed to go, particularly if you are initiating a pull play (see page 71) or are trapped on the sideline. But you still need to scan the field. Make sure that you have a panoramic view. Look backfield and downfield, left and right.

You now have a receiver picked out. She is sprinting at top speed toward an open space where you can easily put the disc. No one from either team is in her way. Make sure that your receiver has enough separation from her defender. Some receivers need only a step on the defender; others need yards of daylight.

All these calculations happen in the first seconds of your possession. Skipping any of these steps can result in a turnover and a score by the opponent because you are so close to the other team's end zone. A turnover on the first throw can lower your team's morale and pump up the other team. Why would you ever want to do that?

Essential Offensive Tip

The first choice of the player who receives the pull should be to center the disc. The first pass, therefore, should go toward the middle third of the field. The throw should not go toward the sideline because the defense can then create a trap at the beginning of the offensive drive. Initial cutters should know this, so that they do their best to become open in the middle third of the field.

Throw-and-Go Drill

PURPOSE

To teach throwers how to complete a pass to open space. To teach receivers how to "go to" the disc, to accelerate through the disc at full speed while making the catch. To encourage the thrower to become a receiver as quickly as possible.

EQUIPMENT

10 discs—8 for throwing and 2 to indicate the beginning of the two lines

SETUP

Players make two lines, single file, facing each other about 15 yards apart, depending on their throwing abilities. If the lines seem too close or too far apart, players adjust as necessary. This drill works best with at least 14 players, with 7 on each side. The first player in line A does not have a disc, but the next 4 players do. Each of the first 4 players in line B has a disc. See figure 4.1.

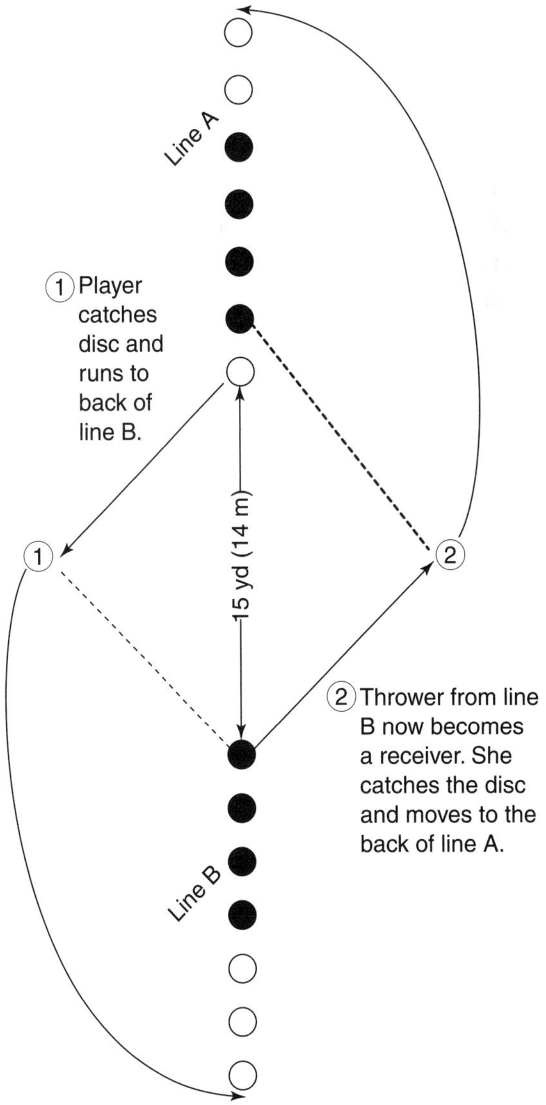

PROCEDURE

The first player in line A runs hard at a 45-degree angle toward line B. He is running to receive a flat backhand thrown into space. He accelerates to the disc, makes the catch, and runs to the end of line B, without breaking stride. He then hands the disc to the next person in line B who needs a disc. If he drops the disc or if it is out of his reach, he quickly retrieves it and continues to line B.

As soon as the first player in line B has thrown, she takes off immediately at a 45-degree angle toward line A and does the same thing. The thrower must not look at her own throw but instead must immediately make the transition to becoming a cutter for the next throw.

The drill continues in this way, with each player having at least 10 chances to throw and catch a backhand. The drill should move along quickly, with teammates encouraging both the thrower and cutter loudly and constantly.

Figure 4.1 Throw-and-Go drill.

1 Player catches disc and runs to back of line B.

2 Thrower from line B now becomes a receiver. She catches the disc and moves to the back of line A.

(continued)

The drill ends when the players have completed a required number of throws or after a set time elapses.

THROWING VARIATIONS

▶ After a while, tell players to throw the forehand. Cutters must cut to the other side of the thrower.

▶ Throwers can add a pivot or a pump fake to the opposite side before making the proper throw.

▶ Advanced throwers can practice the inside-out forehand or hammer when cuts are to the backhand side and inside-out and high-release backhands when cuts are to the forehand side.

OTHER VARIATIONS

▶ Receivers catch with only one hand or with the nondominant hand.

▶ Move the line around to allow players to experience different wind conditions.

▶ Receivers add a juke (change of direction) before they decisively cut to the disc.

▶ Add a marker to both lines to increase the difficulty of the throws, making the drill even more realistic.

REMINDERS

Novices often throw the disc directly to the receiver, instead of to the open space in front of the receiver. This tendency often results in throws that are behind the cutter, which defeats the purpose of the drill. Cutters should not have to torque the body backward to make the catch. The thrower must force the cutter to move at top speed by putting the disc well out into open space. All cutters should be running hard, laying out, or missing the disc in front of them. They should never have to stop their sprint to make a catch.

Pivoting and Faking

As in basketball, a player in possession of the object of play must always keep one foot in the same place when he wants to make a pass. In Ultimate, the pivot foot is the one opposite the throwing hand. (If you are right-handed, your pivot foot is your left and vice versa.) You can rotate on that foot, but if you move it, or even lift it, you will commit a travel, which is a violation and stops play.

Assume that you are right-handed and are being marked straight up. Also known as a flat mark, your defender is squatting directly in front of you, on her toes, and is going to try to block either your backhand or your forehand. (Chapter 6 will discuss the straight-up mark and other forcing in detail.) The defender wants to make it difficult for you to throw to either passing lane. To get off either throw, you will have to "move" her out of the way without touching her.

Pivoting wildly will only make you dizzy, and you will not fool your defender. You want to develop a deliberate, quick pivot that is believable. You also may want to pivot just before you are ready to throw to prevent the defense from having time to reset. You probably will pivot only once or twice in a possession, and sometimes you may not pivot at all. As you begin to pivot, make sure that you continue to face downfield so that you can see any teammates who are developing their cuts. Only if committing to throw to a reset cutter in the backfield should you turn your back to the downfield action.

You have decided that you are going to throw an easy backhand to a cutter who has beaten his defender and will shortly be all by himself in the open passing lane. You want to hit him quickly to gain maximum yardage, but your mark is overplaying the backhand side, which means that you are unable to make a clean, easy throw. The defender is forming a human blockade between you and your intended receiver. See figure 4.2, *a* through *c*.

Break eye contact with your intended receiver, pivot toward the forehand side, and snap the disc without releasing it. You have to sell this fake. The more you practice throwing, the more realistic your fake will be. Again, if you fake frenetically, your mark will know that you have no idea when you are going to throw, and you may hear "Not a thrower!" from the opposing team's sideline. If your fake is believable, the defender will have to move over to your forehand side to cover it.

Your defender has now bitten on your fake and has overcommitted to the forehand side. Suddenly you have lots of room to throw. This window of opportunity will be open only for a split second, so you must act immediately. Quickly pivot back to the backhand side, still facing downfield, and put most of your weight on your outstretched right leg. Your receiver is still there because he knows the importance of completing a cut. You snap off a quick flat throw and immediately take off, away from the disc and the open passing lane, because you have done your job.

These are the basics of pivoting and faking against a straight-up mark. As the force changes from straight-up to backhand or forehand, or to a middle force, your pivoting and faking will change too. You may want to use a shoulder or head fake to move your defender. You can also fake high, which may get your defender to raise her hand, and then release low, or vice versa. We also suggest that you watch players who are adept at pivoting and faking. Watch how they move their marks around. Try to

Figure 4.2 Faking and pivoting in order to release an unobstructed backhand.

incorporate their technique into your game. All these methods can work, as long as your defender believes what you are doing.

You also must practice changing your grip back and forth between a forehand and backhand, as discussed in chapter 2. You must be able to execute a quick, smooth transition from one to the other. A smart defender will recognize immediately if you do not change your grip, even if the fake is otherwise believable. See figure 4.3, *a* through *c*.

Figure 4.3 Faking a forehand, then pivoting to a backhand fake.

Pivoting and faking well is an art. You must practice both skills together and practice them often. You don't even need a disc to practice pivoting and faking. While you're standing in line, hanging out in your kitchen, or standing in front of a mirror, work on the rhythm of these movements. Remember, start deliberately and gradually increase the speed of these movements to game speed. Eventually the movements will become second nature.

Throwing to Space

Athletes who play soccer or hockey often develop into good Ultimate players because they understand the concept of putting an object into open space where the next receiver can gain control over it. Whether a team is using a ball, puck, or disc, its offense will be effective if everyone understands the concept of a leading pass, or throwing to space, and can execute it.

A player first learning to throw understandably wants a stationary target. As he gains mastery of his throwing skills, he should be able to hit someone who is moving. The Throw-and-Go drill helps players work on these skills in practice and prepares them for competition.

When warming up for a practice or game, do not play catch with someone who is standing in one place. You want your warm-ups to mimic a game situation, so choose someone who understands the importance of incorporating moving, cutting, and pivoting into the warm-up routine.

Here are some simple suggestions for making your warm-up routine true preparation for a game or practice, not just an opportunity to chat. The receiver should first run at a 45-degree angle toward the thrower. A mistake that novice receivers commonly make is running across the passing lanes like a duck at a shooting gallery. This poor habit can ruin your team's offense in an actual game.

You then throw the disc to the area where the receiver has not yet arrived. The receiver should not have to slow down, or lunge backward, but should meet the disc midstride while accelerating, as in the Throw-and-Go drill. The receiver now becomes the thrower, and you are the receiver. You have already started to set up your cut before your partner makes the initial catch. Go as soon as you throw! You should run away from the new thrower, plant hard, change direction, and then accelerate toward the disc. This routine should run smoothly, in preparation for beautiful offense during a game. If you do this simple drill correctly, you should have warmed up your legs, broken a sweat, and fine-tuned your throws.

In game situations you usually want to be throwing to space. An exception might be when you are hitting a straight-in cut, when your receiver is running directly toward you. You still will want to make sure that the disc goes to the side of the receiver where the defender is not. You should always have your receiver picked out, and sufficient space should be available in front of her to put the disc (see figure 4.4). The amount of space required depends on how fast your receiver is and how fast you assume her defender to be. Your judgment on this kind of call will improve with experience. If you do not see enough separation, do not throw the disc.

In addition, you must be aware of poaches. A poach is a defender who goes off his person for a second or two to make a block. If you are zeroed in on your receiver, believe that she is clearly open, but do not see the rest of the field, you run the danger of throwing into a poach. A block by a poach brings jubilation to the defense and despondency to the offense. See the field, see the receiver, and see the poach.

Figure 4.4 Throwing a backhand to space.

Breaking the Mark

Breaking the mark means that the thrower is still able to throw to the area of the field that the marker is trying to obstruct. This is probably the single most useful skill that you can acquire as a thrower. You must have competent throwing, faking, and pivoting skills before you can excel at breaking, but you should start to develop this skill as soon as possible.

Breaking the mark means that you throw exactly where the defense doesn't want you to throw. You attempt to break the mark only when you are being forced to throw to one passing lane or the other. You can use a variety of throws. If you are able to break, your team will have a much easier time scoring.

Assume that you are being forced to flick, perhaps trapped on a sideline. This means that your mark is standing near your left side. She is encouraging you to throw a flick to the force side and obstructing you from throwing a backhand to the side that she is covering, also called the break

side. You see a cutter sprinting to your backhand throw, the break side, and you want to hit her with your backhand. The first thing that you do is face your defender. This is one of the few times when a thrower will not be facing directly downfield; you will be turning toward a sideline instead.

Facing your mark has now turned it into a straight-up force, and you already know what to do in this situation. You fake a realistic quick flick downfield and move the defender one way. You then pivot quickly to your backhand, lunging low and reaching wide, and throw a low backhand around her right side that will meet your receiver midstride on the break side.

Of course, timing is important to completing a good break-mark throw. You have a smaller margin of error than you do when throwing to the force side, because you are throwing to a smaller area. You must make sure that the disc arrives in front of the receiver and that the defense does not have a chance at the disc. Another advantage of throwing to the break side with a low backhand is that

> ## Essential Breaking the Mark Tip
>
> Once you have faced your defender, do not turn back downfield. Your receiver expects you to make the break throw, and pivoting away will only confuse everyone on your team.

Figure 4.5 Breaking the mark.

the defender will often poach and try to block the inside-out flick passing lane. She will lag off her person to obstruct the lane, you can get off the backhand break, and your receiver can easily continue the offensive flow to the far sideline without a mark being set up.

Your other throw of choice for breaking a force forehand is the inside-out flick. In this case, you do not have to face your defender. You watch the cut develop again on the break side, move the defender around by a fake and pivot, if necessary, and step forward past the mark or lunge wide to throw by the mark on her left side (see figure 4.5, a-b).

Time your throw to gain maximum yardage. You want to throw this flick as soon as you can and not wait until the receiver is close to you. Throwing a long inside-out flick takes quite a bit of practice, but when you and your teammates feel confident with it, your offensive plan will have another serious weapon.

Finally, you have the option of the high-release backhand to break the mark. Continue to face downfield. The cutter goes break, and you fake

a low backhand and quickly pop a high release over the right shoulder of your defender. The disc starts flying quite high, with enough spin to keep it aloft. It will move toward the ground rather quickly, but not before your cutter makes an easy grab.

We are not great fans of this break throw for a number of reasons. Novice throwers often release it at the wrong tilt or without enough Zs, or rotations, which makes it wobble in the air, thus making it easier to block. This throw is difficult in the wind, and if a thrower has not developed the two break throws described earlier, it becomes the default throw. In other words, a thrower who develops only the high-release backhand cannot adjust when conditions call for it. Finally, the player who relies on the high-release backhand for most of his breaks is a limited thrower. Strong handlers have a full arsenal of throws and know when and where to throw them. Becoming enamored of only one throw to do a variety of jobs leads to fewer effective options and more turnovers.

Break the Mark Drill

EQUIPMENT

Six discs for 12 players

SETUP

A thrower is trapped on a sideline by a mark forcing her flick. A line of five players, each with a disc, is off the field, next to the thrower, ready to take her place. Another line is in the middle of the field, stacked in a single line, about 30 yards (meters) away from the thrower (see figure 4.6).

PROCEDURE

The thrower has a disc in her hand and sees a cutter running up the break side. She begins to fake and pivot, moving her defender around. (Note: The defender can be marking at 50 percent intensity or less to start this drill. As the skills of the throwers increase, so can the intensity of the defender.) The thrower then chooses to throw either an inside-out forehand early to the cutter or some type of backhand (a low backhand or a high-release backhand) around the defender. After catching the disc, the receiver clears quickly to

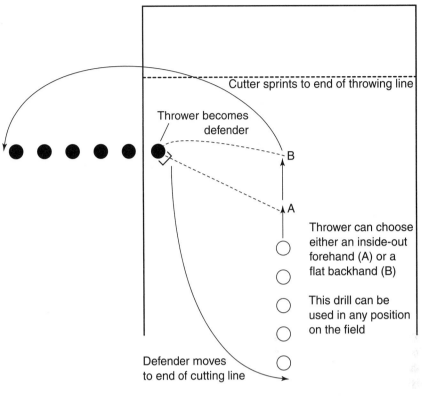

Figure 4.6 Break the mark drill.

the back of the thrower line, the defender marking the thrower moves to the end of the cutting line, and the thrower becomes the new mark for the new thrower. Each thrower should attempt 10 of each kind of throw. Throwers should vary their throws throughout the drill and not rely on one more than the other to break the mark.

VARIATIONS

The cutter can add a juke before cutting to the break side. This action will encourage both the thrower and the cutter to work on their timing.

As players become adept at this drill, they can cut for the swing and continue to make throws after the first throw occurs. This variation will improve team timing and help players see how this drill leads to an overall offensive plan.

Cutting

Throwing is an important part of Ultimate, but some teams become too focused on making good throws and spend too little energy developing the skills necessary to secure those throws. No team wants to be one of those whose main thrower often yells, "No one is open!" because a turnover is usually the result. Remember, the goal of the individual offensive player is to reduce turnovers,

and learning appropriate cutting techniques is an essential part of the overall plan.

Cutting Techniques

Cutting effectively means that you identify yourself as an open receiver at the right time and in the right place. So how do you get open on your defender? You can be an outstanding thrower, but if you can't get open, you will not be part of your team's offense. In fact, if you are not cutting effectively, you will probably stymie your team's offense. Most novice players merely try to outrun their defenders, and this tactic may work for a while. But what do you do when you are being covered by someone who is clearly faster than you are? If you can't beat your defender to the disc in an all-out sprint, you can still get open. Regardless of what type of offense you are playing, you need to remember three things when starting, making, and completing a strong cut.

1. Get low. Sprinters do not stand upright at the starting line when they are getting ready to run the 100. They settle into the blocks and get low. The same is true for Ultimate players who want to sprint to the best of their ability. If you get your legs under you and drop your butt, you will be able to launch yourself almost immediately into a full-on sprint. Although you still may not be able to outrun your opponent in a dead sprint, you will be in position for the next step.

2. Chop your feet. You are now running low at close to maximum speed, but you want to change direction to find some open space, and, perhaps, the disc. You do not want to slow down, stand upright, and then go in another direction. If you do, your defender will be in your back pocket.

What you want to do is slow down slightly, stay low, and chop your feet, in preparation for moving in a direction that will surprise your opponent. Put your weight on the balls of your feet and move

them as quickly as possible, as if you are stamping out a small fire. As you are doing this, mentally prepare for the direction in which you are going to move. You may be chopping your feet directly in front of your defender and then plan to burst past him, to either the right or the left. You may be going short or long, and then change direction completely to get your defender to overcommit as you run past him.

3. Explode! In the last stage you explode in the direction that you want to go. You are low, you have chopped your feet, and you are sprinting as hard as you can to open space. If you have done this correctly, you will have left your defender in the dust. No one on the other team knows for sure which way you are going to cut, so no one can be completely sure how and where to cover you. See figure 4.7.

Essential Cutting Tip

If you are constantly slipping on an Ultimate field, you are making a mistake. The problem is most likely neither the conditions nor your cleats, but your poor form. If you practice staying low and chopping your feet and do not explode until your feet are under you, you will be much less likely to slip.

Figure 4.7 Getting open by running toward your defender and then sprinting away.

Basic Cutting Drill

EQUIPMENT

About six players. You don't need a disc.

SETUP

Five or six players are in a line, facing a defender. The defender should be only about 15 feet (4.6 meters) away.

PROCEDURE

The first person in line gets low, runs toward the defender, and chops her feet four or five times. At the beginning of this drill, the runner should actually count, "1, 2, 3, 4, 5" as fast as she is moving her feet. The runner then explodes in either direction past the defender and runs a few steps. The runner should accelerate noticeably as she blows by the defender. The runner then becomes the defender, and the defender goes to the back of the line.

Having a coach watch this drill helps. The coach should encourage players to move through each of the three stages by saying, "Get low. Chop your feet. Now explode!" Many players do not realize how low they need to go and how quickly they should chop their feet. Some may even fall over at first.

The arrival at the defender should be at about 75 percent speed, and the explosion should be at 100 percent speed. Players should make a clear distinction in speed between these two stages. Each player should run through this drill about 10 times.

Every cut may not have these distinct stages, and eventually, as you gain experience, these stages may blur together. You may not have to chop your feet so much, or you may be able to fool your defender with a body fake or change in acceleration. Watch any veteran player and you will see a variety of ways to beat a faster defender. But knowing and performing the techniques of cutting are useless if you don't know when to cut.

Timing Your Cuts

So now you have an idea of how to make an effective cut, but what happens when you are in a game? You can't have five or six people chopping their feet and exploding all over the place. But you want to become part of the offensive action. It's time to show what you have learned about cutting.

You really want that disc. You don't want to arrive too early or too late. You don't want to cut off a teammate. And you surely don't want someone diving past you and making a heroic D block. How do you know when to make your move?

In general, beginning players cut too much. Actually, what they often do is hover around the disc, calling out the thrower's name and clogging the passing lanes. This activity is not cutting.

If you don't know when to cut, then don't. Stay out of the play and watch what is going on around you. Is your team working it up the sideline? Are they hitting the dump (getting the disc off the sideline) and continuing the disc to the opposite side of the field? Try to anticipate where the disc will be in two or three throws.

Essential Timing Tip

Become a student of the game from the sideline. Watch what works and what doesn't work. Choose someone who is an excellent cutter and watch what he does when he is *not* cutting for the disc. Chances are that he is not standing around but is moving in a calculated manner, planning his cut to the disc before the defender has a clue. You can learn a lot about timing and other aspects of the game from off the field.

Then look at the field and figure out how you can be part of this flow.

You have now selected a space where you can easily and realistically catch the disc. You know where you want to go, and you know where you don't want your defender to go. You are reasonably sure that you can claim this space over any teammate. First, choose an area to cut toward that is *away* from where you want to go. Sprint to that space at about 75 percent of your speed, and after you chop your feet and plant hard, explode past your defender at 100 percent. You should be open, be an easy target, and be part of the offensive action!

Clearing

You make the catch and complete the next pass. Your job here is done. Or is it? Where do you go now? Clearing means getting out of the way of the offensive flow, and it is just as important as catching and throwing the disc. You can go to a number of places, depending on what your team is doing. If you are cutting out of your team's vertical stack offense and have not received the disc, you will most likely clear out wide, on the outer edges of the passing lanes. However, if you just completed a pass downfield, you will want to clear to the inactive or weak side—that is, away from the current position of the disc. Immediately after a completed pass there is a moment when the offense will attempt to continue flow in that same direction. This provides you a brief window of opportunity to clear in the opposite direction, away from your completed throw. If your pass was for a short gain, perhaps you will become the reset option for the person to whom you just threw.

Why are so many options available? It all depends on your team. Each of these destinations

Essential Clearing Tip

The one place where no one should clear is near the person who has just received the disc, particularly in the currently active lanes. Often a thrower will have just received the disc and be looking for a way to continue the offense. The rest of her team, and their defenders, will thunder past her like a herd of buffalo, thereby cutting off any of her potential throws. This commotion essentially prevents her from throwing to anyone who may be making a good downfield cut.

for clearing can work, as long as it is part of your team's offensive plan. You should know exactly where to go based on what your team has decided. Staying out of the way is an essential part of your overall strategy and, like all aspects of your offense, your team needs to discuss it before stepping on the field.

Bailing

Suppose that in the middle of your next cut you suddenly see someone in your peripheral vision. It could be a teammate or a poaching defender. Obviously, something has gone wrong, and you should not complete your cut. This action is called bailing.

Do not slow down, because you will only clog the lane and prevent the thrower from being able to throw to anyone behind you. Plant hard and go in the other direction, away from the disc and any other cutters, possibly bringing your defender with you. You may want to yell, "No," or "I'm out," to the thrower and other teammates, to signal that you are going to bail.

After you have changed direction, you are still a viable receiver. Chances are that your defender has remained in a passing lane to poach for a second or two. Yell, "Poach!" which translates to "My person is poaching and I am wide open right this second!" Immediately sprint to the easiest place for the thrower to hit you. When your teammates hear "Poach!" they should clear out of your way immediately.

If you don't get hit then and your defender starts covering you again, you are still a viable receiver. You just have to wait for your next chance.

Sometimes you will have to bail because the thrower can't make a certain throw or because he has a tough mark. The rules for bailing remain the same: Sprint away from the disc and the passing lanes and watch how the offense is developing.

Bailing is honorable and not a sign of weakness. Although not finishing a cut and not catching a disc may sound like the antithesis of Ultimate, removing yourself from the offensive flow allows your teammates to complete a pass. All seven players do not have to touch the disc during every possession. In fact, a smart team knows how and when to use its personnel most effectively. Staying away from the disc and creating space is as much a part of the sport as throwing and catching are.

See table 4.1 for individual troubleshooting tips on offense.

Table 4.1   Individual Troubleshooting Tips on Offense

Situation	Result	Solution
THROWING		
Looking off open receivers early in the stall count.	Count goes up; defense clamps down; receivers panic and clog.	Hit first viable cut. Look dump after "5."
Throwing disc behind the receiver.	Easy D for defender; potential collision.	Throw the disc to space; let receiver run to it; practice your throws more!
Main handler picking up disc regardless of her field position.	Shows no trust in other players; ruins any chance of a fast break; identifies main handler as someone defense should shut down.	Closest capable player puts disc in play, usually with a very easy throw.
Receiving disc from trapped teammate and returning disc back toward the trap.	Defense has easy time to reset; little offensive advantage has been gained.	Look immediately to continue the disc to the open side of the field; break the mark if defender sets up quickly.
Picking up disc after making a layout block.	Disc is thrown away because of the adrenaline rush.	Run away from the disc and out of the play; you are already a hero!
Pivoting frantically and panicking.	Thrower sees neither field nor cutters; mark holds force; count goes up.	Slow down, breathe, keep facing downfield; pivot toward your receiver and throw an easy pass.
Calling for a specific receiver by name; pointing to where you want to throw the disc.	Defense now knows where the disc is going; shows no trust in other teammates; telegraphed throws are easier to block.	Open your eyes and see all the options on the field; stop throwing to your friends!
CUTTING		
Not accelerating as you are catching the disc.	Layout D.	Make sure there is enough separation between you and your defender; sprint 100% as you are finishing your cut.
Not finishing the cut.	Miscommunication with thrower; disc is thrown at the receiver's back; offense bogs down.	Finish cut or clear immediately; have eye contact with thrower.
Making a cut that is loopy or straight toward the sideline.	Defense can cover these cuts with little effort; blocks are easy to come by.	Cut hard either toward or away from the disc.
Colliding with one of your own players while cutting.	Clogging, injuries, picks.	Cut with purpose; know offensive plan; check where other potential receivers are; anticipate developing cuts; get out of the way!
Clearing too close to the thrower.	Passing lanes are clogged; count goes up; thrower has few options.	Know the best place for clearing depending on your offensive plan; in general, you want to clear away from the disc and route of the next logical pass.
Getting a block and picking up the disc, even though all potential receivers are behind you.	Count goes up; covered receivers are slow to arrive; offense slows down.	Get out of the way and out of the play; your job is done!
Wanting and expecting the disc every other throw.	Passing lanes are clogged; little yardage gain; shows lack of trust in teammates; no one improves.	Let others become part of the offense; Ultimate is a team sport!

Summary

• •

Ultimate, like any team sport, relies on the expertise of individuals who come together to form a team of experts. Your responsibility as an individual offensive player is to develop all the skills necessary to contribute to the success of your team. Individual players can always improve their throwing and cutting skills, and if everyone on the team commits to doing this, offense will become effective and effortless.

5

Offense: Team Skills

Key Terms

continuation

counter-cut

dead space

deep

deep fill

fast break

fill

flow

give-and-go

handler

horizontal stack (H-stack)

huck

iso cut

L-stack

middle

pick

popper

pull play

red zone

reset (also called dump)

reverse (also called swing)

seventh person

short fill

side-handler

slice cut

spread (also called split stack)

stack

strong side

wing (offensive)

A team whose players develop the individual skills of the sport will not necessarily have success on the field if the team does not have a structured approach to offense. Outrunning or outthrowing the defenders in a chaotic fashion is simply not enough. A team that has a plan to help prevent such chaos will gain more from the efforts of its players. Every competitive Ultimate team employs one or more formations among its offensive sets. Teams can use several strategic variations, and imaginative planning can create yet another. We will discuss a few commonly used strategies. Although many options of attack have been designed, the straight, vertical stack has stood the test of time and remains the most prevalent formation used in Ultimate.

A thorough description of the stack offense follows, along with an exploration of several flow patterns commonly seen with it. In addition, we will discuss concepts universal to team field sports, such as positions, spacing, and situational protocols. Other types of offensive designs will be introduced, such as the spread formation and the horizontal stack, more common at elite levels of play. Next, we will discuss end-zone offensive practices and strategies that teams can use in that all-important area on the field where offenses have less space in which to work and normally face a stifling defense. And how does a team handle the immediate switch from defense to offense after forcing a turnover? Teams must spend time to develop a plan for transition offense. Finally, all this discussion centers on tactics that are effective against individual defensive pressure. We will then examine how to conduct an efficient offensive attack when facing a zone coverage style of defense.

Stack Offense

. . . .

A stack is a single vertical line of cutters downfield from the thrower and placed in the center of the pitch (see figure 5.1). This is a familiar sight in Ultimate. The formation keeps both the forehand and backhand passing lanes open for one receiver at a time to perform a cut. While one player is setting up his cut, his teammates are staying in, or clearing

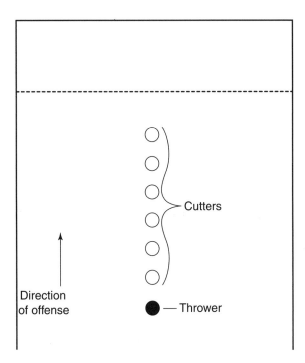

Figure 5.1 The vertical stack.

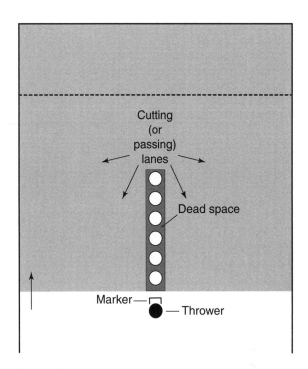

Figure 5.2 Passing lane and the dead space.

to the stack, looking for the next opportunity to cut. Players must keep lanes uncluttered in Ultimate, free of those *not* moving. Disciplined adherence to this offense can be quite effective. The stack is lined up downfield of the thrower. The area where the offensive players are stacked is referred to as the dead space—the area in which the offense is setting up cuts. The area the offense is using to receive the disk is called the passing lane, and should be kept clear except for active cutters preparing to receive the disc(see figure 5.2). Flow—fluid offensive movement—is more readily achieved using a stack because recycling it is easy. When a player is not open or the thrower "looks her off" by turning to another cutter, she simply clears out of the passing lane and moves back toward the dead space. She should clear as swiftly as possible. A rapid, effective clear by a cutter not only creates the space needed for teammates to offer cuts, it can provide another cut for good throwers.

Ideally, a stack is a dynamic arrangement that keeps adjusting and moving so that those about to cut briefly occupy the dead space and lanes are open for those cutting. Using a stack, weak teams get one cut at a time, with little deception and modest flow. Strong squads get multiple cuts with deceptive fakes and ample flow, even against good defense. Teams should strive to achieve this—an offense with smooth-flowing motion.

Spacing Between Players

The first cutter in the stack should be no closer than 5 or 10 yards (meters) from the thrower, with a space of 3 to 5 yards (meters) separating cutters in the stack. Adequate space between each player will help reduce clutter and prevent picks from occurring. A pick occurs when an offensive player moves in such a way as to cause a defensive player guarding a cutter to be obstructed by any other player (offensive or defensive). Contact need not take place for a pick to be called. If the defender has to slow down or alter his path to avoid a collision when attempting to maintain coverage, a pick has occurred. For this reason, offensive players must maintain sufficient spacing.

The stack of cutters can move farther from or closer to the thrower, or to one side of the field or the other. In fact, locating the stack left or right of center creates more space in which to isolate cutters in favorable one-on-one matchups, which can be difficult to defend. This overloading on one side is effective in creating more cutting space. Teams often use it when calling sequences, such as the four-person play discussed later in this chapter. And by reducing the space between cutters, the stack becomes shorter, or shallower. This formation will keep the long game open, and the threat of hucks—akin to bombs in football—opens up the

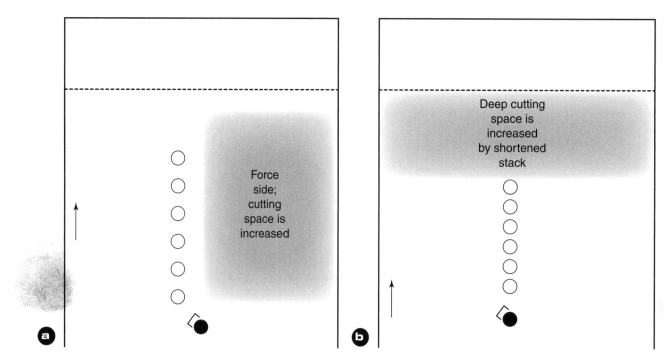

Figure 5.3 *(a)* Offset stack; *(b)* shallow stack.

field for underneath (or in) cuts. Figure 5.3, *a* and *b,* shows these variations.

Positions and Cutting Patterns

A basic concept of the vertical stack strategy is to assign the following positions to the seven players on the field: handlers (three), middles (two), and deeps (two) (see figure 5.4). These three positions have overlapping responsibilities.

HANDLERS

Handlers are like point guards in basketball, distributing the disc to cutters in a variety of ways and usually touching it more often than players at other positions do. An effective handler is precise and poised with the disc, is able to break the mark readily, and comfortably leads the cutters into space as they run. Handlers are typically a team's finest throwers and sharpest cutters, able to get open quickly with short bursts of movement. Teammates do not want their handlers taking big risks and turning the disc over repeatedly. Handlers should focus on maintaining possession while taking calculated risks (i.e., hitting the first open receiver or safely breaking the mark). Handlers should have good field vision, make solid decisions, and show consistent precision.

MIDDLES

Middles are traditionally the continuation cutters, possessing good disc skills and the ability to cut in, toward the front of the offense, as well as away for

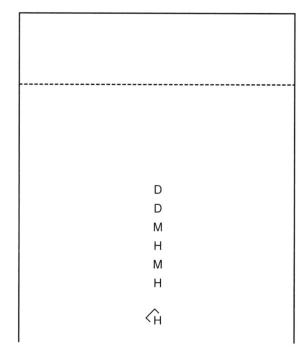

Figure 5.4 Offensive positions in a vertical stack formation.

longer throws downfield. Like a two guard or a small forward in basketball, they are able to create on their own or receive the disc from one of the handlers. They remain primed and at the ready for break-mark receptions. An effective middle sees and uses the entire field and throws well off movement, making the transition fluidly from receiver to thrower.

DEEPS

Deep cutters are often their team's tallest or fastest athletes. Depending on where a team places its deeps, they may be cutting in from the rear of the stack or away from the front. Some teams with accurate long throwers place their deep cutters near the handlers, toward the front of the stack so that, off movement of the disc, they can set up long streaking cuts that often cover the length of the field. Exciting plays often result!

Variety of Placement (Keeping Opponents Guessing)

Of course, regardless of position, teams move their players to different places in the stack to make it harder for a defense to anticipate the offensive plan. Note the various position placements and sequences suggested in figure 5.5. Whereas one team (see figure 5.4) puts its deeps at the back awaiting a middle to receive a pass from a handler before cutting, another team (figure 5.5) begins its offensive flow

by bringing a handler in off the back of the stack for the first cut, followed by a deep who cuts away long from the middle of the stack.

ADDITION OF THE RESET CUTTER

Many teams place a handler, referred to as the reset position, out of the stack, either diagonally behind the thrower, when positioned on the force side, or level with her on the break-mark side (behind the marker; see figure 5.6). This placement reduces the number of downfield cutters, which creates more space for others and allows an easier and quicker reset if no downfield cutters are able to get open. A reset is a useful tool to initiate and maintain movement and retain possession, particularly if a team lacks depth in disc skill.

RECYCLING THE STACK

Recycling the stack is an essential team skill that results in players cutting from the obstructed dead space and clearing out of the lane and back into the stack—in effect, recycling their offensive flow. By clearing quickly, observant and active players alternately create and seize opportunities for themselves and their teammates. Recycling requires communication, selfless discipline, and practice. Otherwise, players will cut each other off, creating traffic in the passing lanes, and the team will struggle to move the disc downfield. One common way to help reset the flow is to clear weak side, or away from the current

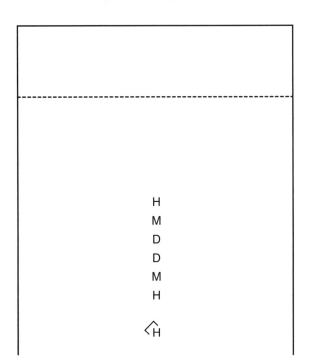

Figure 5.5 Varying the placement of the offensive positions in a vertical stack formation.

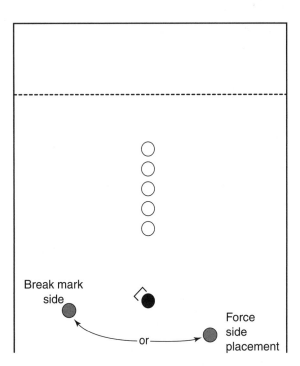

Figure 5.6 Positioning of the reset cutter(s).

path or position of the disc. The side of the field that the disc is on or its direction of movement is called the strong side. If offering a cut to a thrower who received a pass on the forehand side, the player should clear to the weak side (toward the backhand) if not thrown to. Some teams always clear on the same side as their cut, turning sharply around and back downfield, then returning quickly to the stack. Regardless of the protocol that your team chooses, you should have a plan to which all are committed. The assignment of positions makes it more evident where individual players clear to, when not cutting, to recycle the stack. The stack offense offers numerous possibilities. Be creative with your team's placement of players and work hard at the valuable team skill of recycling the offensive set.

To help your offense develop good flow and timing on cuts for stack offenses like this one, make liberal use of the Three-Line Flow drill. This drill is realistic, fast, and fluid, and a team favorite that will do wonders for your offense. Set a goal at practice, challenging the team to score a certain number of goals in succession without a turnover or to score as many as possible in a set length of time (e.g., 5 or 10 minutes).

Three-Line Flow Drill

PURPOSE

To develop flow and good timing on cuts and clearing in a vertical stack offense.

EQUIPMENT

One disc and three cones

SETUP

Set up three cones along the centerfield line 15 to 20 yards (14 to 18 meters) apart, such that 30 to 40 yards separates the two end cones, as shown. Cutters are placed at each cone, with one or two fewer cutters at the center cone.

PROCEDURE

A player begins with the disc in the forehand (or backhand) lane and throws to cutter #1 cutting out of the middle cone. Before that reception is made, cutter #2 jukes away and cuts in toward the new thrower for the reception. If this pass is not caught beyond the end cone another cut comes from that line until the plane has been broken (see #3). Once this plane has been broken, the drill immediately reverses direction in this same passing lane, heading back down the field. Cutter #4 (as shown in figure 5.7) cuts downfield for the player whose reception broke the plane (scored the goal). Cutter #5 is now out of the middle line (as shown). Before the reception is made the next player has initiated his cut (see #6) out of the end line. And, as discussed earlier, if this pass does not break the imaginary plane marked by the last cone, another cutter (see #7) will come from the end cone. Finally, having broken the plane, the drill continues in the opposite direction. Players should clear to the line to which they threw.

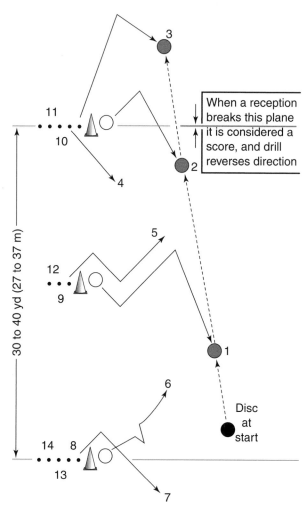

> When a reception breaks this plane it is considered a score, and drill reverses direction

Figure 5.7 Three-Line Flow drill.

EMPHASIS

▶ Throwers should place the disc out in space in front of the cutters.

▶ All players should throw the correct throw. For right-handed players this means a forehand while cutting in the forehand lane and backhand while cutting in the backhand lane.

▶ Players should strive to set cuts up before their teammate has made the reception and is looking for them in the lane.

▶ After releasing a throw, players must clear rapidly wide and out of the cutting lane, away from the direction of their throw.

VARIATIONS

▶ Run drill on opposite side of the field.

▶ Using end line cutters, reset and reverse the field every time there are "scores" at one or both ends of the field.

RESET AND REVERSE

The reset reverse is a way to improve field position by coupling two types of passes. As discussed earlier in this chapter, the reset option provides a high-percentage short pass to a thrower who may have few choices, particularly if trapped on a sideline. After a dump pass is completed to the reset (dump) cutter in the backfield and toward the center of the pitch, the player pivots immediately to throw to a teammate cutting in a diagonal direction

(see figure 5.8). This is the reverse cut (sometimes referred to as the swing), which moves the disc farther across and hopefully downfield from its former trapped and stagnant position.

As implied by its name, the reset reverse is more of an offensive protocol than it is a specific play. Although teams can set up and run plays from the reset reverse sequence, its primary function is to provide a situational structure—one that helps reset the disc, the stall count, and the offense,

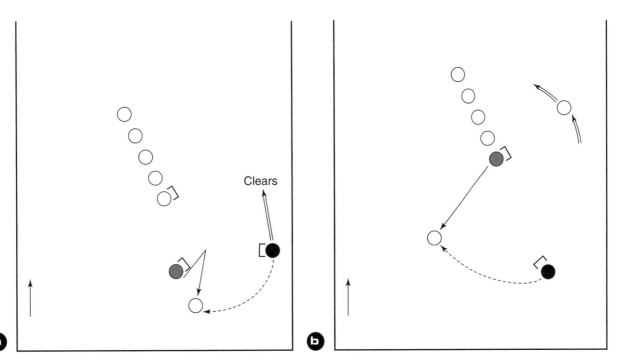

Figure 5.8 *(a)* Backfield reset (note trapped thrower clears *away* from current flow); *(b)* reverse.

while reversing the field and opening up new passing lanes.

Indeed, any time a stack play breaks down or the disc gets stuck on the sideline, near the end zone in particular, the reset reverse option is effective in putting the disc (and teammates) in motion. It is useful both to obtain a fresh stall count and to get the disc moving again. The defense will have a tough time stopping a team from completing a backfield reset, and even more difficulty in stopping the next pass, the reverse, because the defense is overcommitting to their force side.

Suppose that your offense has reversed the field on the smooth flow of two timely cuts. You, the swing cutter (the player providing a continuation cut, reversing the field), find that you have the luxury of a couple of stall counts with which to scan the break side (where the defense is not) before your defender arrives to mark you. As you turn to look for the continuation, the last cutter in the stack is already cutting in toward you, and a cutter from the middle of the stack is streaking deep downfield, away from you. You have the choice of either putting the disc to the underneath cutter, who can turn to throw to the deep cut, or to throw to the teammate breaking long (see figure 5.9).

Teams frequently find that they are trapped against a sideline, particularly if that is the defense's intention. The ability to break the mark to get out of the trap is important, whether by an inside-the-mark or around-the-mark throw, or even an over-the-mark throw, such as the hammer. All are difficult and higher risk choices. Using the backfield reset to get a fresh count and escape the trap also breaks the mark, but only if the reset cutter then hits the field-reversing cutter to switch the field. Reset, reverse, and when flow has slowed, repeat! Your teammates' work will not be in vain, and the defense will be forced to adjust or change their plan altogether.

Most competitive teams use the reset reverse, and they should. Committing to this offensive strategy can reopen options on the force side. When a defense begins to tire of having to cover the entire field, they begin to shift their marks to prevent the easy reset. Defenders often begin covering the force side much closer to their person, concerned with giving up too much to the break side. This circumstance can serve to stretch open-side (or force-side) options and, because of the shifting mark, enhance the opportunity for break-mark throws. A defense will have difficulty stopping both sides of the field if the offense can effectively hit the reset reverse, in addition to breaking the mark. In fact, there *is* no open side of the field for teams that use this approach. It's *all* open—*wide* open. To get a clear idea of how this strategy unfolds, use the helpful reset reverse drill.

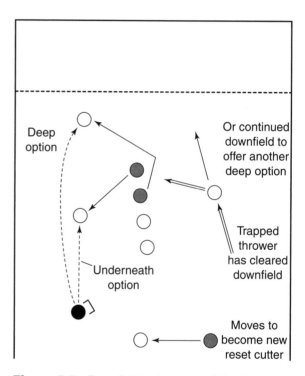

Figure 5.9 Downfield options open following a reset and reverse.

Reset Reverse Drill

PURPOSE

This is a helpful drill to teach players how to reset the disc from the sideline and then reverse the field following the reset.

EQUIPMENT

▶ Minimum of 5 discs

▶ 2 cones

SETUP

▶ Line of throwers/markers with the discs just off the field.

▶ Thrower with marker 3 yards (meters) away from sideline on the field.

▶ Reset cutter 10 yards (meters) away and level with the thrower (see figure 5.10a).

▶ Line of reverse cutters just past the centerfield line 10 to 15 yards (meters) downfield of the thrower.

▶ Cone 5 yards (meters) downfield of the thrower and one placed at beginning of the line of reverse cutters.

▶ Give the thrower and the first four players in the thrower/marker line a disc.

PROCEDURE

Marker starts the stall count at 1. At a stall count of 4 the thrower looks at the reset cutter to initiate the reset. Reset cutter makes a backfield cut. Thrower throws to the reset cutter in the backfield. As throw is released, first player in the reverse cutter line cuts diagonally across the field (as shown in figure 5.10a). Reset cutter pivots and quickly throws the pass to the reverse cutter.

Immediately upon receiving the disc, the reverse cutter pivots and throws a fake downfield. As soon as the original thrower releases the disc he clears downfield past the cone without watching his throw. The reverse cutter runs the disc back into the thrower/marker line (behind the drill, as shown in figure 5.10b), reset cutter clears hard to the reverse cutter line, thrower becomes the new reset cutter, marker becomes the new thrower, and the next player in the thrower/marker line hands his disc to the thrower and becomes the new marker.

EMPHASIS

▶ Throwers should place the disc out in front of the cutters.

▶ Reset cutter must turn in the correct direction when receiving the reset and hit the reverse cutter on the first look. Hesitation will allow the marker to cut off the reverse.

▶ Timing of the reverse cut is key—it must give the reset an immediate option on his pivot.

▶ Once making their throws, both the thrower and reset should clear wide as quickly as possible.

VARIATIONS

▶ Move drill to other side of the field.

▶ Switch the direction of the force.

▶ Add a reset defender.

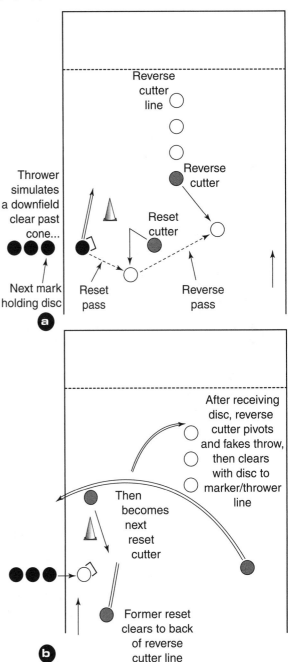

Figure 5.10 Reset reverse drill.

(continued)

▶ Allow reset cutter the option to make an upfield reset (into the trapped side).

▶ Introduce the slice cut (when the reset can not complete the reverse throw, she fakes the reverse throw, which prompts the reverse cutter to plant and cut perpendicular to the sideline, sweeping back across the field into the force side).

FOUR-PERSON PLAY

This play is simply a sequence in which four players are assigned a position in the cutting order before receiving the pull. The team stacks 3 to 5 yards (meters) from the center of the pitch, toward the side of the field on which the pull lands (the side is called by #2 while the disc is in the air). The player catching the pull (#1) throws a crossfield, centering pass to #2, who is set up opposite the stack, ideally gaining some yardage as well. This

second player throws to #3, who had already slid out a couple of yards (meters) from his teammates into the expanded cutting lane. The #3 cutter is juking, changing direction and speed in an attempt to shake his defender, so that he can receive the disc from #2. While #3 is about to make the catch, #4 is streaking toward the end zone for the finish. The team has scored in three throws, or even two if #3 instead breaks free deep. Keep such options open. Figure 5.11 illustrates this sequence of play.

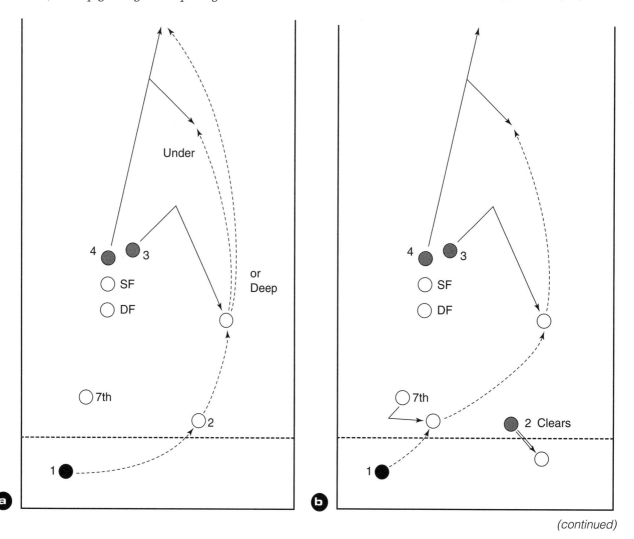

(continued)

Figure 5.11 (a) Four-person play as called; (b) breakdown when #2 is not open; (c) breakdown when #3 is not open for #2. (SF = short fill; DF = deep fill)

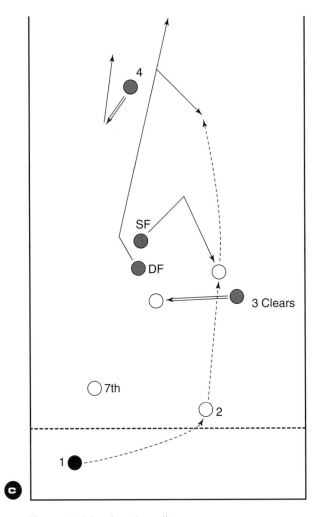

Figure 5.11 *(continued)*

The four-person play is another simple, effective arrangement that helps create space and minimize clutter. The three other positions in this play are the short and deep fills and the seventh person. This latter position is placed at the front of the offense on the stack side to provide another option if, because of a hustling defender, #1 cannot get it to #2 or if the play should break down at any point. If the seventh person receives the disc from #1 rather than the intended #2, then the play runs as called—hitting #3, who looks to #4. If the defense has denied #3 from getting the disc, then the short and deep fills become the new sequence for #2 (or the seventh person).

In addition to moving the stack from side to side, you can bring the stack closer to the thrower by reducing the space between individual cutters. Be careful not to pick a teammate's defender when you are stacked closer together. A structured sequence will help. By shortening the stack, deep options open up considerably. Increased traffic up front may be the tradeoff, but knowing who is cutting can help prevent that. Simulation is a practice drill that helps you achieve the desired movement and flow of any play or offensive scheme. It gives your team the opportunity to work out kinks and to respond positively when spontaneity is demanded of the offense. You run this exercise without a defense.

Simulation

To simulate the four-person play, offensive players line up on their receiving end zone line. The coach, a captain, or a player not on the field tosses a disc to various places on the field and shouts, "Go!" By simulating a pull, you have just started a point. All players sprint to their respective positions, with #1 picking up the disc. The offense runs the play as called (#1 to #2 to #3 to #4). On the next repetition, have #1 pump fake, not throw, to #2 and then run the first breakdown (#1 to seventh to #3 to #4). Then run the second breakdown (#1 to #2 to short fill to deep fill, and finally to #4). Have fun with the challenges when running a simulation. Ask players to close their eyes or lay down on the ground. Have #1 stand where he intends to start the offense, deep in a corner or in the end zone near a sideline, counting down from five as though the pull and the defense are on their way downfield. Counting down like this simulates the time it takes to get a real pull-play offense set up and in motion. Players have to hustle to position.

SIDELINE (TRAPPED) OFFENSE

Defenses love trapping the offense near the sideline. This strategy, discussed further in chapter 7, is successful because the offense then has a much narrower force-side passing lane in which to operate. The marker shifts to a position that is closer to parallel to the sideline, making the backfield reset and the break-side passes more difficult while only marginally contesting the force-side pass. But because the sideline has become an extra defender, the downfield defenders are overplaying in this skinny lane, trusting the mark not to permit an easy reset or any break-mark throw. An offense must work hard to learn how to deal with this common scenario. This team skill takes time to develop.

First, pull your stack farther away from the strong side, the side of the disc's current location on the field. This adjustment creates a larger force-side space for cutters and throwers (see figure 5.12). You must resist the common temptation, if your team becomes anxious, to move closer to the strong side. By doing so, you will strangle your offensive flow by narrowing the width of the lane that the opponents must defend. Naturally, this makes their job easier. Instead, position the stack *at least* to the centerfield line, or even beyond, favoring the weak side. The increased force-side space provides cutters more room to cut and gain separation, thus presenting better options to the thrower.

Second, line up one or two players level with the thrower, but about 10 and 15 yards (meters) away, respectively (see figure 5.13). This formation is referred to as the L-stack. These cutters are available to go quickly either up the line on the force side or for a backfield reset. The formation shortens the center stack, reduces the number of players downfield by four (two offensive and two defensive players), and creates options that are easier to complete and more rapidly available. An L-stack keeps the defense honest—they still must cover the force side because you have a formation that presents more options there. Note here that you must strive to set up these short reset cuts so that the reception occurs farther from the sideline than the previous thrower's position. Otherwise, despite the reset and fresh stall count, the trap will still be on, the defense will still be jacked up, and the disc will still be near the line, which is serving as an extra defender.

An effective way to use the L-stack formation is to identify the closer reset as number 1 and the farther reset as number 2. By calling out any odd number, you are identifying the nearer teammate as the primary reset cutter. Depending on her defender's position, she may choose to dart downfield into the force-side lane or juke for a backfield reset. Whichever she chooses, the other reset cutter does the opposite (counter-cuts), giving the thrower two options coming in rapid succession.

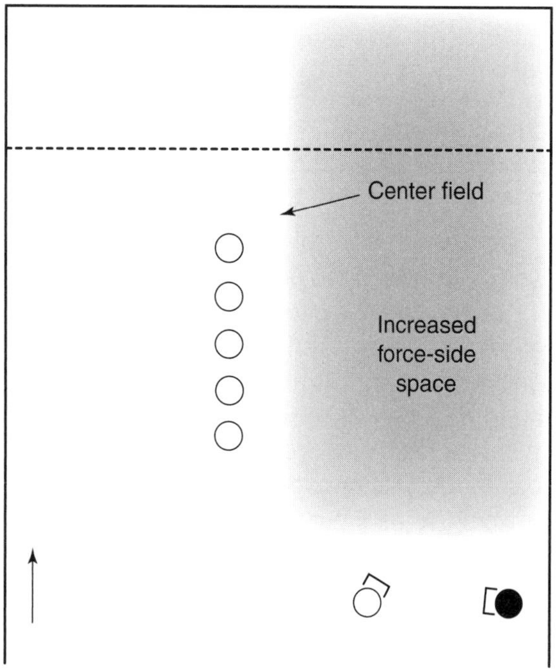

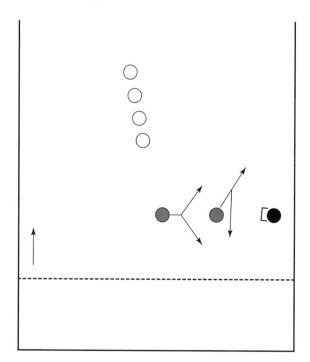

Figure 5.12 Wide stacking when trapped on or near a sideline.

Figure 5.13 L-stack spacing and cutting options for both reset cutters.

If the pass goes to a reset in the backfield, do you know what follows? Absolutely. Hit the field-reversing pass! If your teammate hits that reversal, the trap is broken, and now you are flowing again, with options on both sides of the field and a diminished defensive presence. The receiver offering the reverse (swing) cut should come from second position in the stack to gain more yardage upfield while providing an easier passing angle for the thrower. This also leaves the first cutter in the stack available for a quick step-up (counter-) cut option if the reverse cut has been defended or is not available for some reason.

Your team may have throwers who can deftly get the disc off the sideline by breaking the mark, besides using the reset reverse. This ability makes your team much more effective when presented with limited space in a trap. These players make a marker and defender's job more difficult, and your team's confidence will rise. However, beware: A defense will target less experienced or skilled players to trap, creating opportunities to defend them zealously.

If a defender is poaching, playing considerably off of the offensive player he is guarding in order to help defend the trapped force side, the receiver he is covering can cut in on the break side for a wide open, field-reversing swing or short pass. The defender will not be able to recover immediately, so the poached teammate may be quite open. Be certain to rehearse this situation so that all players know how to react to it. Poachers must pay the price! Make them pay dearly by finding a way to get the disc to that uncovered teammate. You want to keep the defenders honest and paying close attention to the offensive player for whom they are responsible.

One more tactic when facing a trap on the sideline is to set up the stack in a diagonal fashion, as shown in figure 5.14. The advantages are similar to the two earlier suggestions—creating more space on the force side and keeping short reset options available relieves the pressure of the trap. A diagonal configuration provides more room for a lateral or a shallow-positioned reset cutter and, because the defensive pressure has been reduced, increases the space in which to operate downfield on the force side. Your team can have a deeper receiver cut in toward the thrower, a reset cut diagonally upfield toward the line, or a moderately positioned cutter streak deep.

When the reset cuts upfield into the force side, an immediate counter-cut response should come from the front of the stack to offer a quick new

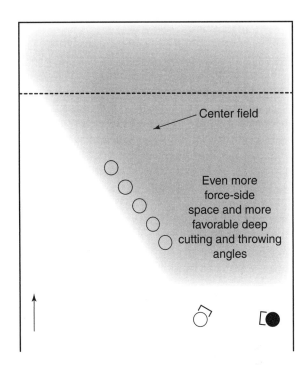

Figure 5.14 Diagonal stacking when trapped on or near a sideline.

backfield reset option, or at least a positioning of the next reset cutter. We cannot state the next point strongly enough: If the reset pass goes to anyone in the backfield, the next pass *must* continue across to reverse the field. Ultimate is a game of space even more than speed. The best teams make the most of both.

Another strategy to help your team prevail in a trap is to place your stack wide, over toward the weak side, and isolate a cutter in a larger open-side lane. This action supplies that teammate with a one-on-one matchup for several counts. If completed successfully, another isolated cut will follow, or a strong cut heading deep from the back of the stack in rhythm with the isolated cutter. A steady diet of this strategy alone will be ineffective, as poachers will feast on hanging force-side passes. But using this approach in tandem with other suggested options will be helpful. Prepare your teammates to handle the pressure of sideline situations. Good defenses make a living there. So do good offenses. Practice breaking the mark and using the reset and reverse strategy. You will be glad you did.

Specific Pull Plays

A pull play is a full-field plan that an offense runs when receiving the disc at the start of a point. Top club teams may have several pull plays in their playbooks that they run out of a stack, but they will rarely use all of them in a game. In designing your team's full-field offense keep in mind that simplicity is crucial to success. Use your imagination and create new approaches in attacking a defense. Remember, though, that your opponent could come downfield and play a zone defense that will foil your best pull play. Keep it simple and work toward total team commitment to whatever your offensive plan may be. Virtually any reasonable offense will work if everyone agrees to run it.

Your team can choose any configuration or sequence of cutters. By assigning the receivers numbers, as in the four-person play described on page 68, you can design specific cuts so that each player will be prepared for the play called. Basic pull plays that many teams use include Deep Strike, Hot, Money, and Give-and-Go Strike.

DEEP STRIKE

Deep Strike is a basic yet effective play that also runs well as a practice drill (see below) to help develop timing of longer cuts and the accuracy of longer throws. In Deep Strike, a handler cuts in from either last or next to last in the stack. While the disc is still in the air (not yet caught), a deep cutter takes off downfield for a long gain. An option for this play is for the last receiver in the stack to cut to the force side. One or two counts later, the next-to-last receiver cuts to the opposite side, the break side. The thrower then has a choice on either side of his mark and a little time before the second cut to see if the first is viable. To whichever side the disc is thrown, the deep, set up at #2 or #3 in the stack, strikes downfield for a big gain. His shallow placement in the stack allows the long cut and throw ample time to develop.

Deep Strike Drill

PURPOSE

This is an effective drill to work on your offensive flow, particularly timing, setting up, and throwing to deep cuts.

EQUIPMENT

- ▶ 4 discs
- ▶ 3 cones

SETUP

- ▶ Line of throwers at the brick mark.
- ▶ Line of cutters 15 yards (meters) downfield of the thrower line and 3 yards on the forehand side of the centerline.
- ▶ Line of cutters 25 yards (23 meters) downfield of the thrower line and 3 yards (meters) on the forehand side of the centerline.
- ▶ Cones marking the front of each of these lines.
- ▶ Discs with first four throwers in the thrower line.

PROCEDURE

First cutter in the far line (line C) makes a cut into the backhand lane and first player in thrower line (line A) throws the disc to this cutter. Just as the thrower releases the disc the first player in the near line of cutters (line B) cuts to the forehand side and then out and around line C deep into the backhand (flow side) lane (see figure 5.15). When cutter from line C receives the disc he throws it downfield to the player cutting deep from line B.

Once the deep throw goes up, the cutter from line B adjusts to attack the disc at the first point that he can catch it. This may require that he cut back toward the disc. Once the cutter from line B receives the disc, he throws it back to the cutter from line C, who

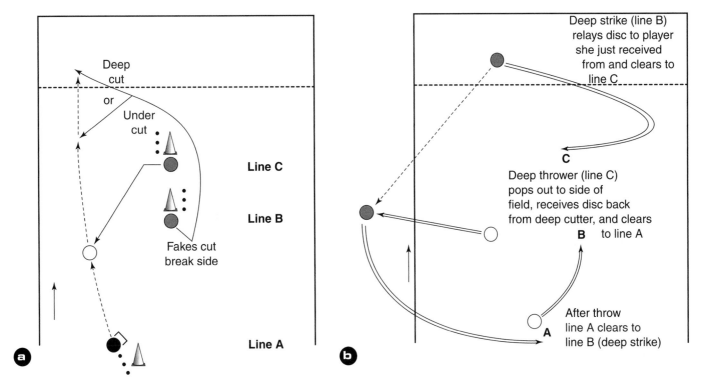

Figure 5.15 Deep Strike drill.

threw it to him and who has now cleared off of the field to receive the relay. The cutter from line C runs the disc back to line A, the cutter from line B clears hard to line C, and the cutter from line A clears to line B.

EMPHASIS

▶ Throwers should place the disc out in front of the cutters.

▶ Deep cutter should provide a good angle for the deep thrower to throw the disc and should go to the disc aggressively once it's in the air.

▶ Deep cut should be timed so that the deep thrower can turn and throw the disc without hesitation.

▶ After throwing, all players clear fast and wide, out of the way of the next group.

VARIATIONS

▶ Run drill on forehand side of the field.

▶ Run drill both upwind and downwind and have players make necessary adjustments.

▶ Deep thrower fakes long throw and deep cutter cuts under on the cue of this fake.

HOT

Most teams have some version of this long throw, or huck play. The last two receivers cut in aggressively off the back of the stack, the deepest one first, followed immediately by the next receiver cutting to the opposite side (figure 5.16). Whereas one of them would receive the disc in Deep Strike, here they are merely decoys. As the third cutter from the rear of the stack sees both of these cutters passing by, he turns and strikes straight downfield, angling toward the huck that has been put up by the handler. Just in case this "hot" cutter is not

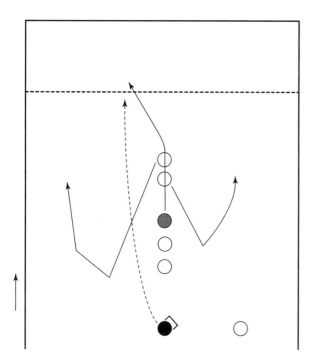

Figure 5.16 Hot play.

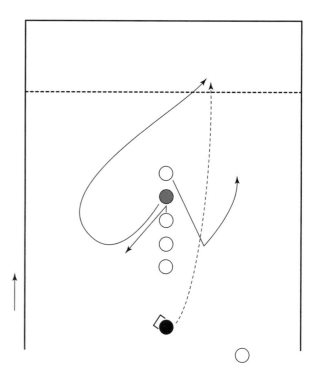

Figure 5.17 Money play.

going to score, the two who originally cut in from the back have since turned sharply downfield to help finish the play.

MONEY

This pull play, a variation on Hot, is particularly effective after the offense has run Hot a time or two (see figure 5.17). After the last two receivers have cut in from the rear, the break-side cutter reverses direction and streaks downfield for the big throw. That deep cutter in Hot (third from the rear) fakes a juke deep and instead counter-cuts break side toward where the now long cutter was originally headed. And, if the thrower decides to hit the new underneath break-side cutter, that player can also launch it "for the money." As with Hot, the force-side cutter loops sharply out and downfield to help finish the play. If the Money cut doesn't score, a teammate will be arriving soon to offer an option.

GIVE-AND-GO STRIKE

In this pull play, two or three handlers are up front working a give-and-go—running a two- or three-player mini-game up the field—until one of them has beaten her defender out into one open lane or the other (either side of the stack). After the give-and-go movement has advanced the disc to that lateral position, a deep cutter breaks downfield from the middle of the stack while the last cutter bolts in for an underneath cut for the

shorter option (see figure 5.18, a-b). As with any long cut offered, if the big throw does not go up, the downfield cutter must return to the stack in a hurry. Not only has the deep cut expired, but the defender may have been so worried about being beaten long that his defensive assignment is now wide open coming back in. Whoops!

Other Offensive Sets

Teams want to create space and fluid movement, giving cutters more lawn in which to cut and providing throwers with a greater number of low-risk options early in the stall count. Two of the offenses that have developed from the straight stack are the horizontal, or H-stack, and the split stack, called a spread. Each offense strives to attack a defense by opening different areas on the field and by isolating cutters in those spaces with one-on-one matchups. Both formations are most effective when the disc is located in the middle third of the field, and both formations employ one or two backfield reset cutters to reduce the number of players (both teammates and opponents) in the passing lanes. The result is more options for throwers and cutters alike, thus making the defenders' tasks tougher. Bingo!

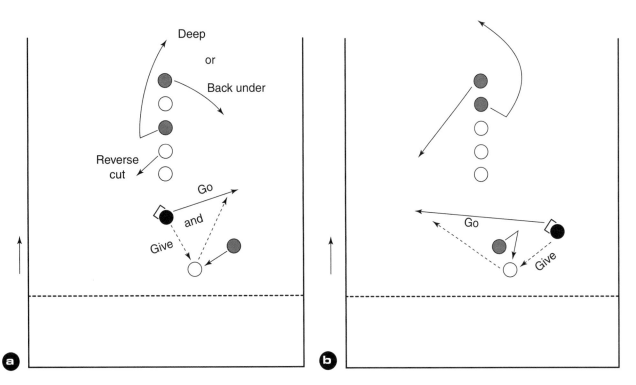

Figure 5.18 Give-and-go strike play: *(a)* force side; *(b)* break side.

Spread Formation (Split Stack)

A commonly used spread formation, sometimes called a split stack, divides the stack of receivers in two so that the cutters are lined up on either side of the field about 5 yards (meters) from each sideline, and roughly 10 and 15 yards (meters) downfield from the thrower (figure 5.19). This orientation opens favorable space in the middle third of the field, in contrast to the vertical stack, which opens space on the outer thirds. With the spread, a cutter can attempt to get open in the middle or be isolated when on her side of the field. The two reset cutters set up as follows.

One reset takes position on the open side, at about a 45-degree angle from and 10 to 12 yards (meters) behind the thrower, while the other sets up level with the disc on the break-mark side, again 10 to 12 yards (meters) away. This takes two more players and their defenders out of the downfield cutting action. If the thrower is unable to get a throw off to a downfield cutter, he commits to one of his resets by a stall count of five and must hit one of them. This timing is vitally important to the success of the spread. Practice cutting for and throwing to backfield and short upfield resets. The spread formation recycles well and can still run with precision, gobbling up huge chunks of yardage.

A team can number the four spread cutters according to the side that they occupy, such as #2 and #4 on the right side of the formation and #1 and #3 on the left side, as depicted in figure 5.19.

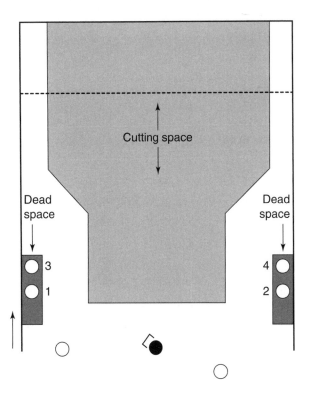

Figure 5.19 Spread (split stack) formation.

Before receiving the pull the call might be odd, in which case either #1 or #3 cuts, followed by the other odd-side cutter, and finished by the even-side deep, #4.

Four-Person Play Out of a Spread

A four-person pull play can be run out of the spread offense. Begin by designating the side to which the play will be run. For example, the call on the line might be to run the play to the left side. As with the straight-stack four-person play, whoever catches the pull is #1. After hitting #2 in the middle of the field, #1 remains on the pull side and sets up as a lateral or backfield reset for the teammate to whom he just threw. Now the orientation has been set, and #2 is viewing her teammates in a spread setup. Because the call was to run the play on the left side, #3 and #4 must decide whether to set up their cuts from the front position of the spread or the rear. (This is usually a matter of preference and can be ironed out in practices and team scrimmages.) If #3 chooses to cut from the rear position, as in figure 5.20a, then #4 is already setting up the next cut, ideally downfield for a score, or at least a sizable gain. As in the straight-stack version of this play, the cutters on the opposite side of the formation fill the roles of short and deep fill, while

the reset cutter who did not catch the pull—and has set up on the opposite side of the pull—is the seventh person. That way the short reset is available immediately, and the play still runs as called. Again, if #3 is stymied on his cut, then #2 calls for and hits her short fill, who throws to the deep fill as in the straight-stack version. The fills are isolated on the opposite side from the original call and are prepared to cut as needed. Players should remember to hit one of the resets if options look slim downfield or movement stagnates. This reset will buy time and help the cutters to set up again. Figure 5.20b shows another example of this play, called Cross.

The spread may be somewhat less effective if the disc is located on or near a sideline. The team must either strive to keep possession in the middle third of the pitch or make use of the isolated nature of the cutters, because they are only in pairs on each sideline. If this is a struggle for your team, falling into a straight stack might be best in these situations. A defense may also choose to employ a zone to thwart a spread offense. In this case, your team must alter its attack.

Be patient with this offense and resist bailing out of it if things do not go exactly as you planned. The spread can be improvisational in nature and still be quite opportunistic. Keep working with it.

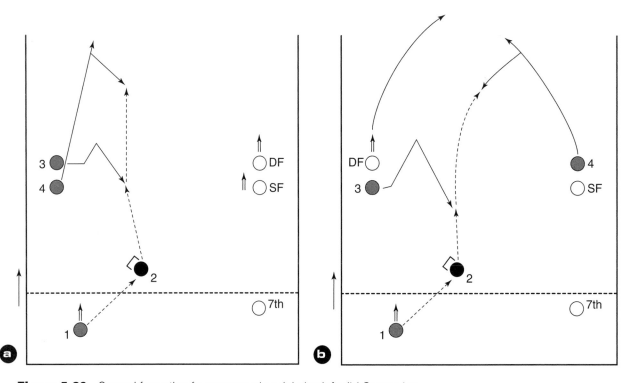

Figure 5.20 Spread formation four-person play: (a) play left; (b) Cross play.

Horizontal or H-Stack

Some time ago Ultimate teams began to experiment with configurations like the H-stack. Most Ultimate players have played in vertical stack offenses, but then someone came up with the idea of situating downfield cutters in a line perpendicular to the sidelines (figure 5.21). The idea, of course, was to find a new way to create and attack the green space. Positioning the cutters about 20 to 25 yards (meters) away from the thrower gives the offense the ability to gain yardage by cutting in or away downfield. This formation also sets up cuts that play off out-of-position defenders who are victimized while trying to help (or to obtain help from) their teammates. Figures 5.22 and 5.23 illustrate two plays or patterns that are effective using the H-stack.

You should choose an offensive plan that maximizes your team's skill set. If your team lacks accuracy on long-range throws, then an offense designed to advance the disc downfield with shorter change-of-direction and break-mark cuts might be the best choice. Likewise, if your team has tremendous speed or height, you will want to choose a plan that makes use of this advantage. Of course, you should work on your individual and team weaknesses while exploiting strengths. Do not give up. Learn to work together as a team to create new wrinkles in your offense. As with any strategy, you must

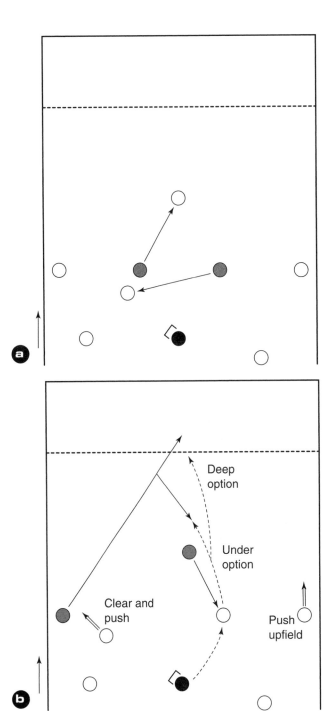

Figure 5.22 H-stack standard (middle) play.

practice what you hope to accomplish. Be willing to use live matches or tournaments to employ your new offense while learning it and be prepared for the frustration you may experience at first. To bring it together at game speed for the entire team, you must try it against another team, head to head. Working against yourselves at practice isn't enough.

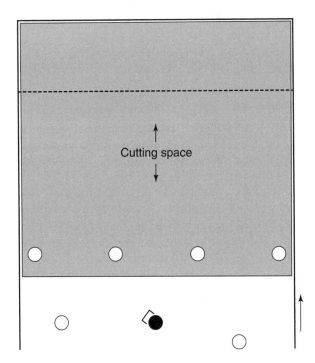

Figure 5.21 Horizontal (H-stack) formation.

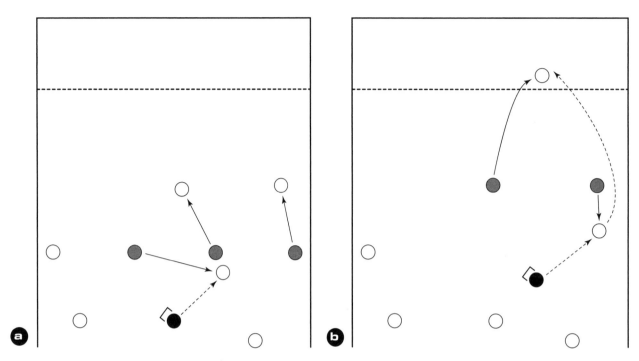

Figure 5.23 H-stack sweep play.

End-Zone Offense

Any of the offensive plays and sets discussed earlier can be effective in helping your team score goals. One major obstacle to scoring, however, comes when a team has to punch the disc in from close range, especially if flow has stagnated. As in American football, when teams run out of length of field, scoring can become more difficult. And, as in football, the area of the field from the 20-yard line through the end zone is referred to as the red zone. This name suggests not only how difficult it is to convert there but also how critical it is to find a way to do just that (see figure 5.24).

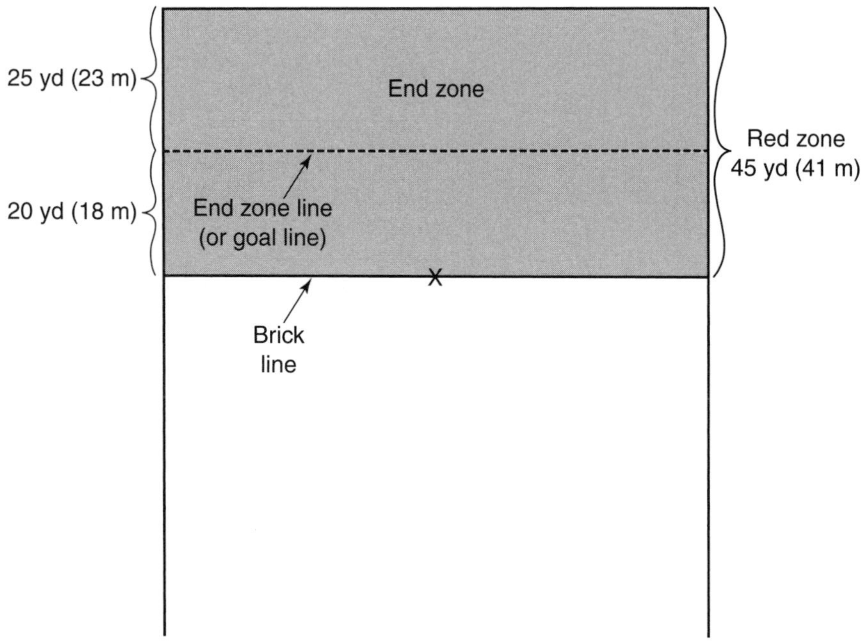

Fluid and well-conceived pull plays will go for naught if your team has a weak red-zone plan. The defense always stiffens when defending near their own goal, aided by the smaller space that they have to defend. Moreover, if your defense is pulling well and causing turnovers deep in the opponent's end of the field, you will find your team starting its transition offense near your opponent's end zone. All these situations demand that your team develop a sound red-zone plan.

Specifically, the red zone covers the 20-yard line, and beyond. That provides 45 yards (41 meters) of length, a distance that feels much shorter when, unlike in football, you can only pass it in to score a goal. This restriction is another aspect

Figure 5.24 Identifying the red zone.

that helps the defense. As a result, retaining possession, let alone scoring, can be difficult, but your team must keep the disc moving. Consider keeping statistics that chart your team's conversion rate in the red zone. Each time you enter this area, put a tally mark in the denominator of a red-zone efficiency ratio. If your team scores, regardless of whether it was forced back outside the red zone before doing so, enter a tally mark in the numerator. An effective red-zone team will place a priority on achieving a very high percentage.

Similarity to Full-Field Offense

The objective of your offense in the red zone is the same as it is when you have the full field to work with. You must have good spacing and make disciplined cuts according to the team plan, maintain fluid movement and clear quickly, and, most important, make wise choices with the disc. In other words, retain possession of the disc. As stated earlier, the reduced space makes this task more difficult. As with your full-field flow, a few simple principles will help your cause.

MENTAL APPROACH

Your team has worked the disc downfield and is primed to score. Because you were able to move your offense into the red zone, converting should be simple and straightforward, right?

The defense is on edge, determined to defend their territory at any cost. Anytime a line is drawn, in this case literally, between you and your opponent, the stakes go up, as does the anxiety level of the offense. What can your team do to overcome this negative, performance-diminishing emotion and remain focused? While chapter 9 offers several excellent mental toughness-training exercises to prepare your team psychologically, we offer here a few tactics that your team members should keep in mind and use when simulating red-zone situations in practice (see sidebar on this page).

Adherence to a solid plan does wonders for your mental game and yields positive red-zone results. Devote a significant amount of practice time to both. Try a best-of-five red-zone competition between two squads at practice.

SPACING

Placement of players is a concept that does not change in the red zone. Positioning, in fact, becomes more critical as field dimensions shrink. Similar to full-field offense, your team's aim is to

Essential Team Offense Tips

- ▶ View every red-zone appearance as an opportunity to succeed, and expect success.
- ▶ Have a well-conceived plan that your team will follow with discipline.
- ▶ Rather than forcing the disc into coverage, reset the disc, reverse the field, and if there is not a good scoring opportunity, repeat.
- ▶ Be aware that the defense is on edge and use that to your advantage. Throwing fakes is particularly useful in the red zone.
- ▶ Take a collective deep breath and focus confidently on that team plan.
- ▶ Most important, do not force it! Just complete the next pass and you will eventually convert.

isolate cuts, affording solid choices, and for Pete's sake, not to cut all at once. Having too many options can overwhelm a thrower and is nearly as bad as when no one is cutting.

Some teams like to run set plays with everyone except the thrower in the end zone. Others prefer to pull one or two players out of the scoring space, placing them as reset or weak-side (opposite side from the disc) swings or bail-out cutters.

What you choose to do with spacing also depends on the variety of disc skills that your team possesses. If your team is just beginning to develop the basic throws, the best approach is to keep it simple—a straight stack in the center, with the last cutter placed at the back of the end zone and one reset positioned as a safety valve if the initial cut is not open. If, on the other hand, you are able to break the mark readily (whether inside, around, over the top with a hammer, or through a reset and reverse) and accurately, you will be hard to thwart in the red zone because the defense will be responsible for more area.

CLEARING

Hard, purposeful clearing is crucial to red-zone success. When not cutting, remain in the stack, keeping your defender busy, wondering if you are the intended receiver. Sometimes a simple glance one way, a shoulder fake, or a single step is enough to freeze the defender; no one wants to be the player who gave up the score. On the other hand, everyone would like to be the defender who got the D, so if you are in the play, you will have to work hard to get open. If your defender, or another defender who is helping, denies your efforts, you must clear quickly to create space for a teammate to cut or to put yourself in position to do so again.

Often, when your cut is looked off, you are rewarded moments later by receiving the disc because you have cleared vigorously or have set up in a favorable reset slot. This may occur when a defender thinks that he has done his job and can relax as you clear or set up a reset. The thrower may release the disc over the shoulder of your defender and beyond you when you are on an "away" (or downfield) clear. The thrower may also throw the disc to a location that makes your clearing movement effectively a cut, or puts you in an advantageous position to cut again. So, by clearing out away from flow as hard as you cut into it, you will greatly help your team.

Specific Red-Zone Plays (Cuts)

There are many permutations on end-zone formations and the plays you can run from them. Here are several fundamental plays that your team will find useful.

Note: Most Ultimate teams have run versions of several of these. Take care not to blurt out the more obviously named plays, like Red Sea. You don't want to make the job easier for the defense by tipping your hand. Give unique names to any plays that you use or develop, with inside meaning that only players on your team will recognize.

CONE CUT

When the stack has efficiently set up in the red zone or has been able to set up following a time-out call, one of the most challenging spots to defend is at the front cone. The cone cut is a simple play that brings the last cutter or next-to-last cutter diagonally to the force-side front corner, as quickly as possible (see figure 5.25). It's a race to that spot, and the thrower's job is to hit the receiver in stride. You can run the same play to the break side as well. This option is more challenging for the thrower than it is for the cutter, who will most certainly be open, with the defender trailing from force-side positioning. Choosing someone from the middle of the stack to offer this cut unfolds it more quickly and provides an easier angle and increased margin for error for the break-mark thrower. If the cutter is not open, reset, reverse, and try again

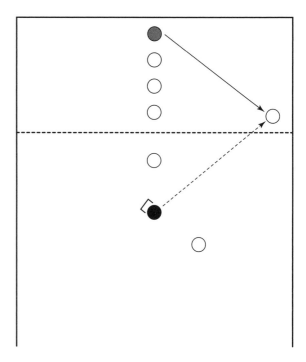

Figure 5.25 Cone cut.

on the other side of the field. Keep repeating this action until the cone cut is open. If playing off flow, calling any word that begins with a *C* will alert your cutters. Adding a word beginning with *B* communicates that the cone cut is to go to the break side. Teams can have fun creating oral cues like this to increase communication in critical and spontaneous situations.

GUT CUT

Adding an option to the cone cut just afterward and to the inside (thus the name) is the gut cut (figure 5.26). As the next-to-last receiver sees the cone cutter pass her shoulder, she sprints on a similar line to a spot 3 to 5 yards (meters) inside the cone cut. This cut is often open because the defense is paying so much attention to the cone cutter that the gut cutter's defender is taken off guard. Here, teammates have presented two quick options to the thrower, which is often all that is needed.

MOSES OR RED SEA

This play works best with the disc in the middle third of the field (figure 5.27). The first and second receivers in the stack cut simultaneously and convincingly in opposite directions. The third cutter then bolts in toward the thrower. That cut can come straight on or flair slightly force or break side, depending on the defender's position.

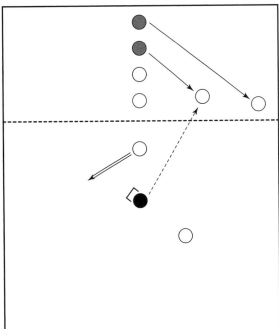

Figure 5.26 Gut cut.

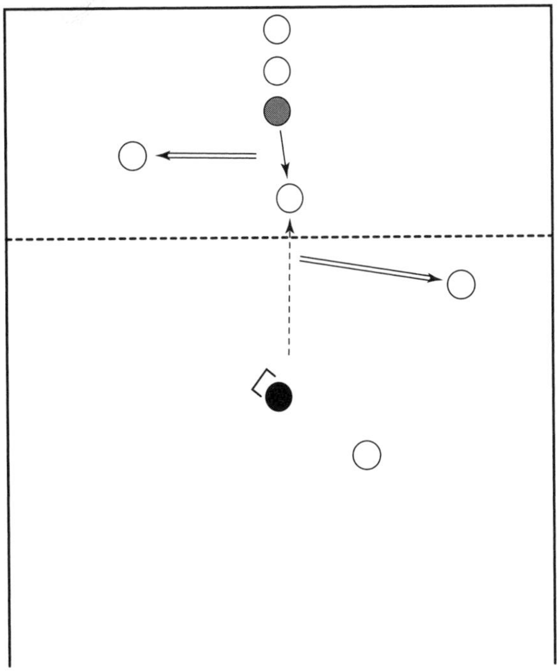

Figure 5.27 Moses or Red Sea play.

ISO CUT

There are several methods to set up isolated cuts in the red zone. One is to place a lone cutter out in the lane, hoping to draw a one-on-one situation for the iso cut. This receiver has 4 to 5 seconds to juke his defender until he is open for a pass. Another is to send a cutter streaking into the open lane from a backfield reset position. A third is for the thrower to hit the backfield reset or a swing cutter and then cut immediately for the give-and-go to score. One more suggestion is a misdirection play (figure 5.28). All the receivers in the stack cut in the same direction except one, who bolts in the opposite direction and is now isolated in a larger cutting lane.

RESET REVERSE

If, for any reason, a red-zone play fails, your team must retain possession to secure another opportunity. The reset reverse will do just that. This sequence can set up cutters for easy scores as the disc sweeps back and forth, reversing the field. Run cuts off the reset reverse sequence from various positions in the stack to keep the defense guessing. A reset reverse approach at the end zone makes the defense's job much tougher and will help to open break-mark possibilities as well. Do not discount its effectiveness as a primary red-zone strategy. Finally, red-zone cuts can open in a

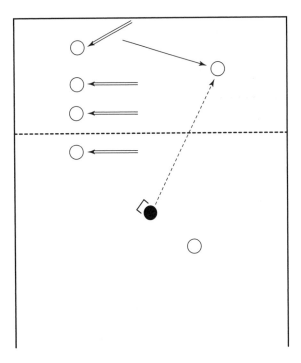

Figure 5.28 Iso cut play (misdirection).

flash. Work hard to keep lanes open and maintain focus, while patiently and actively creating the next opportunity. The end zone reset reverse drill will help your team gain confidence and proficiency when in the red zone.

End Zone Reset Reverse Drill

PURPOSE

This is an extension of the reset reverse drill and a fundamental drill to practice reversing the field and red zone offense.

EQUIPMENT

1 disc

SETUP

▸ Line at the front center of the end zone, extending into the end zone (see figure 5.29a).

▸ Line at the back center of the end zone, extending into the end zone (as shown).

▸ Handler with disc 10 to 15 yards (meters) out of the end zone and midway between the centerline and the backhand sideline.

PROCEDURE

First player in the front line makes a reverse cut to the forehand side of the field and receives the disc from the thrower. First player in the back line makes a cone cut and receives the disc. Second player in the front line makes a cut back out of the end zone, simulating a backfield reset cut, and receives the disc (as shown in figure 5.29b). Third player in the front line makes a reverse cut to the backhand side of the field and receives the disc. Second player in the back line makes a cone cut and receives the disc. All players clear to the line to which they just threw (may be in front line for several throws). Drill continues until you reach a goal—the passage of a targeted length of time or a number of successive scores without a turnover.

EMPHASIS

▸ Throwers should place the disc out in front of the cutters.

▸ All players should throw the correct throw to their receivers. For right-handed players this means forehand as the disc moves left to right and backhand as the disc moves right to left.

▸ All players must pivot in the direction that continues the current motion of the disc.

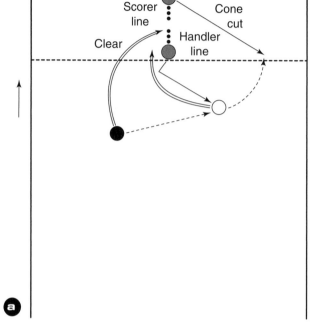

a

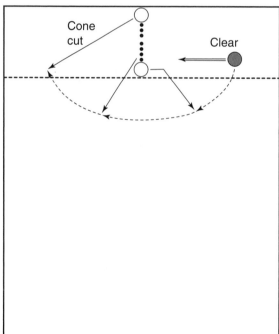

b

Figure 5.29 End zone reset reverse drill.

▶ After throwing, all players clear fast and wide.

▶ Reset, reverse, repeat!

VARIATIONS

▶ If upwind or downwind, run drill in both end zones to practice different throws in the wind.

▶ Thrower that throws the goal immediately cuts to the sideline to receive a straight back pass and next front line cutter sets up a reset cut for that thrower.

▶ Add a gut cut and give thrower the choice to hit either.

▶ Second player in the back line plays defense on the back line cutter, then sprints back into position to provide cut on other side of field.

Transition: Defense to Offense

You have just gotten the block for your team. Besides now finding yourselves on offense, what changes for you and your teammates? Because Ultimate is a game of keep-away and your team has earned possession, you must have a plan in place to transfer all that pumped-up defensive energy into a productive, efficient offensive composure. Do not give the disc back. What is the benefit of playing strong defense if you cannot make the transition to offense and convert on the hard-earned turnover?

Develop a strategy that your team can effectively implement, depending on the following:

▶ **Disc location.** Did the turnover occur out of bounds or near the middle of the field? Did your team gain possession in the opponent's red zone or in your own?

▶ **Opposing team's transition defense.** Has the opponent set up a one-on-one defense, trapping the disc on the sideline, or are they forcing the thrower toward the middle? Did they transition to a zone defense after turning over the disc?

▶ **Personnel on field.** Does your team have strong break-mark throwers in the point, or just solid possession players? Do you have a player who can dominate fast and deep on the field and an accurate thrower who can put the disc in his hands?

▶ **Wind, weather, and field conditions.** Is there a strong head-, tail-, or crosswind? Is rain causing poor footing for cutters? Is it cold, leading to poor circulation and reduced sensation for

throwers gripping the disc, making your transition offense more cautious?

Work hard to recognize the opportunities presented and practice making an immediate change from a defensive to an offensive mind-set.

This latter point is critical. Following a fine effort, it is all too common to see a defense that just forced a turnover give the disc right back because an overexuberant player is still in a defensive frame of mind and unfocused on the task of throwing, cutting, and catching. Successful teams work hard to overcome this tendency. The following principles will facilitate your team's ability to do the same.

Change of Mentality

The mental approach needed to play offense is in some ways drastically different from what is needed to play defense. Offense is quiet and in control of the situation. Offensive players know what they plan to do with the disc and are able to adapt to defensive pressure. Defense is reacting, aggressive, and on edge, sometimes nearly frantic in its effort to force a turnover. That mentality often spills over and spells disaster for a defense trying to convert on a turnover. Players need practice in turning the switch to an offensive mind-set.

▶ Take a collective deep breath, get in position, and think possession—just complete the next pass. You must switch from a state of frantic excitement and anticipation to an attitude of calm and poise. Keep in mind that in each cut is a race and the offense has the luxury of being the one who gets to say, "Go." That is a big advantage, allowing a head start.

▶ If you did not catch the disc while making the block, clear away from the area to allow a teammate to put it in play. This action allows you a moment to change focus before you become involved in the offense. Do not clear near the disc!

▶ If you did catch the disc, make a conservative choice by throwing to the first open receiver available. Then clear vigorously to your planned position in the offense.

▶ If you gain possession on or near the sideline, make your first look toward the center of the pitch, unless a teammate is providing a wide open and easy choice downfield near the sideline.

▶ The whole offense should keep their heads up, particularly the player who is approaching the disc to put it in play. Much on the field can change the instant you look at the disc on the ground. A defensive player might slip or a miscommunication might occur, leaving a teammate alone and uncovered. The defense may be setting a zone, which would change your whole plan if you were expecting a one-on-one defense.

▶ Take advantage of the opportunity to communicate with your teammates if the disc is turned over deep in the end zone or out of bounds. You have a few extra seconds to scan the field and convey your intentions or to react to what your teammates are suggesting. Keep your head up as you approach the disc and call one of the audibles that your team should have in its arsenal, even if it is simply the name of the teammate to whom you expect to provide the first cut.

▶ Move the disc quickly but without forcing it. The opponent is often vulnerable while in transition. The more rapidly your team can make the transition from defense to offense, the more your team increases opportunities for quick strikes.

Offensive Plan for the Defense

Determine roles for each player, whether fast breaking or taking a deliberate approach to your team's transition. You want to know who is attacking deep, filling the middle, and working the disc. Practice situations in which the opportunity to score quickly is available. For instance, set up game-simulated placements of the players on the field and set the disc on the ground in various spots. Say, "Go" and run past it to set the stack, taking your position in it. Or, recognizing that some players have outhustled their defenders downfield, you may choose to pick up the disc and reward them. Be certain that the receiver has ample separation or you may regret the choice.

In most cases, when the disc is turned over out of bounds, you want to get it off the line, toward the middle third of the field, so that more options are available. Putting the disc in play from a standstill on the sideline makes the defense's job much easier. And throwing up the line from the line leaves little room for error and plays into the defense's hands, particularly if several of both teams' players are on that strong side. Again, keep your head up to anticipate opportunities that may present themselves.

Your defense should be able to run all your offensive sets. If you obtain possession in your own red zone, you will be running a full-field offense. On the other hand, if you get your block in the opponent's red zone, you must be able to run an efficient end-zone offense. Simulating these situations is helpful and so is the Five- or Ten-Pull drill. Try it. Some teams devote significant blocks of practice time to this type of drill.

Five- or Ten-Pull Drill

In this drill one team is all-time defense and pulls every point, whether or not the offense scores. If the offense does score, they get a point and switch sides, and the defense pulls again, nine more times. If the defense forces a turnover, they get one chance to convert. If successful, they score one point and stay at that end zone and pull. If neither team is able to score, the play is dead, no one receives a point, teams switch ends, and the defense pulls again. After a set of 10 pulls the score could be 5-3, with the offense scoring on 5 of the 10 pulls that they received, while the defense forced 5 turnovers, converting 3 of them. This drill helps to emphasize that the offense must maintain possession to score, whereas the defense must not only take the disc away but also make an effective transition to offense and convert the point.

Deliberate Start of Offense

Some teams prefer to proceed deliberately to the disc after they have forced a turnover, determined to set up a structured attack to convert. This approach allows you to start your offense with a reserved, structured plan. For instance, you can have your team's best thrower on the field pick up the disc to begin the attack. This method also buys your team time to communicate while getting into position on the field. If your team has a solid break-mark thrower or great speed and cutting ability, this is a logical way to start your offense.

Fast Break

On the other hand, your team may like to fast break, striking quickly in the hope of catching the opponent flat footed. If the opportunity to fast break is available, by all means, push the pace, but never force a throw. The first look in a fast break could be a short one, just enough to get the disc moving and to adjust the angles that the defense is anticipating. As always, keep your head up and scan the entire field, taking care to survey as much movement as possible before picking up the disc. The opponent may have reacted swiftly to get into good defensive position and take away any chance of a quick, easy strike. Be vigilant and prepare to slow the pace if a measured approach is best for the situation. And whatever you do, do not send everyone breaking past the disc. That tactic will only clutter the downfield area and reduce the effectiveness of your fast break. One option is to use a pattern called Four to Score, in which no more than four players race wide past the disc to finish the point. This plan is most effective when your team has gained possession at midfield or beyond. Keep two players behind the disc as resets to open up the remaining space for the four downfield cutters. Those four are responsible for completing the score.

Following a turnover, your opponent desperately wants possession back to avoid being broken (scored on by the defense) on that point, and will be working extra hard to regain it. Take care of the disc and be prepared for your opponent to be gambling defensively. Young teams often become sloppy with decisions after forcing a turnover. Stress to your team how important it is to avoid this pitfall. If the offense gets it back from your squad, they will likely be more frugal with it this time around, making it less likely that you will gain possession again on that point. To be successful, your team must convert a high percentage of turnovers that it forces.

Zone Offense

Before we explain how to pick apart a zone defense, we need to discuss how a zone offense is decidedly different from a one-on-one offense. The entire team's mind-set and offensive plan must change, often in the middle of a point. No longer is a thrower looking for the cutter streaking in or out. No longer is the offense stacked up in the middle of the field. Throwers and receivers always need patience and poise, but these attributes are especially important when playing zone offense.

"It's a zone!" is a cry that is heard often on an Ultimate field, particularly on a windy day, when throwing precision and deep options are diminished. This phrase should immediately signal the offense that they need a new strategy. If your team has been anticipating a zone, then positions have already been assigned and everyone just falls in. If the zone is a surprise, then all players have to scramble into position, shouting to each other which spot they are taking.

Mental Approach

Breathe and relax. Because you are playing zone offense, you will be running less. You and your teammates will spread throughout the field to play a game of keep-away and wait for the zone to become tattered. But you cannot be lazy; you still must move and attack the zone with precision. A zone defense means that a specific person will not be covering you. As you go in and out of certain areas, different players will defend you. This situation can give you an advantage if you know exactly how your duties as a thrower and receiver have changed.

Positions and Responsibilities

Offensive players play at four different positions against a zone: handler, popper, wing, and deep. These terms and the names of various zone defenses may vary from region to region. For simplicity, we are going to describe how to beat a standard 3-2-2 zone (see figure 5.30), using a basic three-handler offense.

In this particular zone, described in more detail in chapter 7, three defenders form a cup, two wings beyond those players guard the flat areas toward each sideline, and the last two players are the short-deep and the deep-deep. The offense spreads out (see figure 5.31). The handlers work

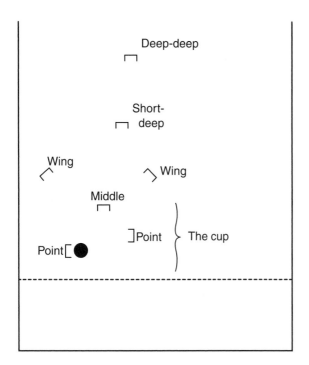

Figure 5.30 A standard 3-2-2 zone defense.

the disc near the cup; the offensive wings dance with the defensive wings on the sidelines; the popper torments the short-deep in the middle of the field; and the offensive deep plays mind games with the deep-deep. All offensive players work together constantly to create and exploit holes in the zone.

HANDLERS

These players are in charge of setting the disc in motion. Their basic job is to tire out the cup, making the front of the zone move back and forth and in and out. The more the cup moves, the more ragged it becomes and the more likely it is that an opportunity to strike downfield will develop (see figure 5.32).

The reset reverse is the tried-and-true method for getting around this type of zone. One side-handler receives the disc and looks downfield briefly, then turns toward the center handler, called the pivot (a second handler), and throws the disc to him. The pivot may also look briefly downfield, but almost immediately pivots to throw to the other side-handler (the third handler), fully reversing the field. If this tactic is not successful in pushing the disc upfield, turn back toward the center of the field and repeat the process.

The offense loses crucial time if a handler hangs on to the disc too long, hoping for something bigger and better, or tries to finesse the disc through the cup. The cup then has time to set up again and rest while the wings and short-deep move in. The defense is hoping for this to occur, so offensive players must

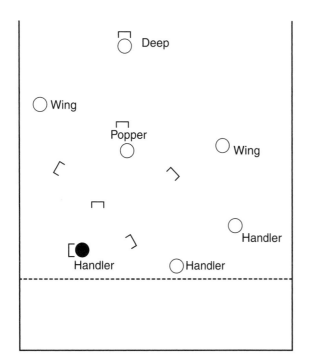

Figure 5.31 Basic three-handler zone offense.

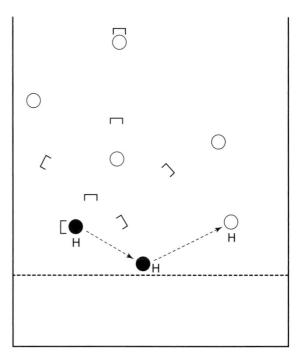

Figure 5.32 Three-handler movement (back and forth) across the field.

keep the disc moving. Openings will eventually appear, so the offense must not get anxious to force the disc downfield.

WINGS

The same basic rules for cutting apply to the wing position. As the handlers reset and reverse, the wing is already setting up his cut. By the time the side-handler pivots to throw the continuation, the wing will have arrived ahead of his defender, ready to receive the pass. If the wing arrives too early, the side-handler will not be ready to throw. If the wing arrives too late, the defenders will be able to stop the pass. Timing is critical (see figure 5.33).

The wing will most likely receive the disc near the sideline, and the defense will be hungry to put on a trap. The wing instantly looks to continue the disc to the deep or his opposite side wing for a long strike. If this cut is not available, the wing needs to get the disc off the sideline immediately. A brief glance toward the popper, who should be hitting a gap toward the middle, might provide this. If the popper is not open, the wing throws back away from the line to a handler. He should not allow the defense to trap him!

An error that often diminishes the effectiveness of the wings is an overeager popper. As the handlers reverse the field, clearly intending to get

the disc to the wing, the popper cuts off the wing's opportunity, effectively reducing the number of offensive players to six. The popper needs to stay out of the way, and the wing needs to tell her to do so. Dragging another defensive player into the area isn't helpful, and if the popper is patient, the disc will be coming to her shortly.

POPPERS

The duty of a popper is to make himself a huge target for the handlers. He is the preferred receiver after the zone shows some holes. The popper needs to be aware of where the short-deep is at all times and when to move to a hole in the cup. A handler will see the popper standing beyond the hole and zip the disc to him (see figure 5.34). After the popper becomes the thrower, "Katy, bar the door!" The team has a fast break opportunity and should be able to score. The popper must instantly continue the movement of the disc, preferably to the deep. Either wing is also a target for a quick pass. The last thing a popper wants to do is allow the cup to reset around him; any delay nullifies the offensive advantage. At the same time, the popper must not force the issue if neither of the wings nor the deep is open.

Novice poppers, as well as novice deeps, often make the mistake of running too much and moving

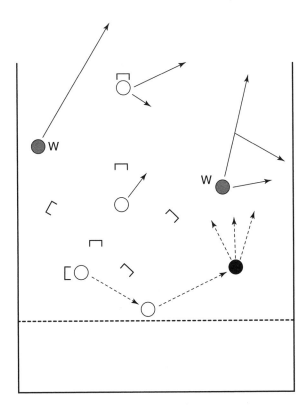

Figure 5.33 Wing positioning and movement.

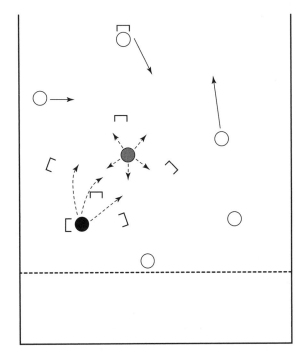

Figure 5.34 Popper positioning and movement.

with the defense rather than opposite the defense. As the disc advances downfield, they often move with the zone and do not look for holes. Although standing relatively stationary while the defense is moving may seem counterintuitive, the savvy popper knows that holes will eventually appear and that she needs to be ready for a quick catch and even quicker continuation. This technique often works because the cup's responsibility is to pursue the disc wherever it goes, allowing the stationary and patient popper to find openings.

DEEPS

The deep is often the scorer against a zone, particularly if a fast break occurs. Most of the time, however, the deep receiver's main job is to keep the defensive deep-deep away from action while looking for an opportunity to come in toward the disc or strike long. The deep will thus be moving in, toward the zone, and back out. The deep will want to receive the disc from the popper or a wing, and therefore needs to set up his cut in anticipation of doing so (see figure 5.35).

The deep should not hang around too close to the popper, however, because doing so allows the defensive deep-deep to pinch in and help out the

short-deep. The deep receiver should not hang too far downfield either, because the deep-deep will know that he is not a threat and will also be able to pinch in. If the offense is heading into a strong wind, the deep-deep may split the field side to side with the short-deep or pinch in considerably. The defenders know that getting off a long throw is almost impossible, in spite of where the offensive deep is playing. If you find yourself positioned deep downfield in this situation and no one is covering you, you are in trouble. You must make yourself a threat to the defense, because if you don't, the zone has succeeded. Figuring out when and where to move comes with experience. The more your team rotates players in and out of the various offensive roles during practices, the stronger each player and the team will become.

Movement

Movement in zone offense should be constant. Experienced players should never be stalled in a zone. If they are, the fault probably lies with the failure of teammates to make the correct move to help them out. Players must constantly spread the defense out, creating and hitting gaps in the zone and moving dynamically as a group. As an offense and the disc advance, strive to ensure that multiple options are always available for the thrower. Your team will make many more throws against a zone than it will against individual coverage, so all players have to be smart about their throwing choices.

Wind is often a factor, so you should choose the throw that has the highest chance of completion. Facing a zone defense often reveals which players have worked hard at perfecting a full range of throws, as well as those who are lazy or limited. Work hard to limit mistakes, not the possibilities.

Throwing fakes continues to be an important skill when facing this type of defense. A quick fake can move part of the cup, and you should have a split second to throw right by them. Remember that you want the disc out of your hand quickly. There is no point in faking repeatedly through the cup in hopes of shooting something by to the popper. If everyone is patient, moving and repeatedly hitting gaps in the zone, throwing opportunities will continue to present themselves, and a calm, poised offense will likely prevail.

See table 5.1 for team offense troubleshooting tips.

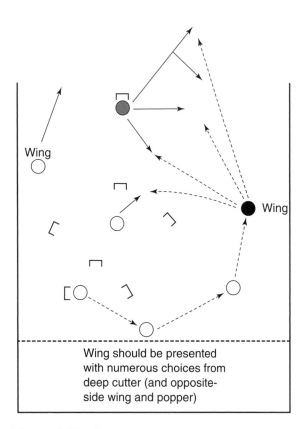

Figure 5.35 Deep movement in zone offense.

Table 5.1 Team Offense Troubleshooting Tips

Common Mistakes	Solution
The passing lanes are cluttered with both cutters and defenders.	Be sure cutters clear swiftly to your offense's designated dead space once their cut expires.
Your offense frequently turns the disc over when it is near the sidelines.	Reset and reverse the field whenever your offensive flow stagnates along the sidelines. Teams should greatly value the reset and reverse.
Your offense has an unreliable deep game.	Strive to set up deep cuts from placements on the side of the field opposite the thrower.
You have little trouble moving the disc downfield, but you struggle in the red zone.	Remember the three R's—reset, reverse, and repeat—if your offense does not score. Also keep in mind the three P's—patience, pivot, and "phake"!
The team has a difficult time transitioning from defense to offense.	Take a deep breath, do not rush things, and call one of your team's audibles to get players and the disc in motion.
Your zone offense has difficulty getting the disc beyond the cup.	The popper and wings need to coordinate to overload the defense midfield and strive to create and exploit gaps in the zone.

Summary

An effective offense requires the teamwork of everyone on the field as well as those on the sideline. All players need to commit to improving their skills and fitting into the team's overall offensive plan. The time for working on personal development is on your own and at practice. The time for showing that you are one part of an offensive machine is during competition.

Almost any plan will work if everyone agrees to it. No plan will work, no matter how skilled the players, if everyone is not on the same page. Some strategies will work better than others, depending on your personnel, the opponent, and the weather. The leadership of the team must determine which strategy to use, and each player must trust and strive to carry out those decisions.

6

Defense: Individual Skills

Key Terms

backing

biting

core (trunk) musculature

coverage sack

defender

dictate

foot block

fronting

hand block

layout block

marker

poach

point block

pre-act

reaction cushion

stall count

triangulate

Players new to Ultimate typically spend most of their time and effort developing the disc skills unique to the sport. This focus is understandable. No one would expect to have much success playing basketball without having developed some skill in dribbling, passing, and shooting. But as Ultimate players learn to throw, cut, and catch, they must also learn how to impede opponents from throwing, cutting, and catching. Effective defense plays an enormous role in Ultimate, and capable, knowledgeable defenders are essential to team success. Many teams at the top levels of play employ specialized lines as a strategy; that is, players go in only on offensive or defensive points. Elite-level teams may carry on their rosters twice as many defensive specialists as they do offensive players so that they can throw fresh players out there on every defensive point, aiming to wear down the opposing team's offense.

Although elite teams, stockpiled with highly skilled athletes, may have several lines available, this approach is not appropriate for developing teams whose players are learning how to play both offensive and defensive points. For middle school, high school, and newer college and club teams, every team member must learn to play effectively on both sides of the disc. Regardless of a team's level of play, if the offense loses possession, it must make the transition to playing sound defense to get the disc back and have a chance to score.

This chapter will teach how to play shutdown, dictating one-on-one defense. Besides discussing the psychological aspects of playing defense, this chapter will cover physical skills such as marking the thrower, gaining and maintaining position on a receiver, and many other principles. Finally, we will provide drills and exercises that focus on developing these critical skills.

Mental Approach

. . . .

Offense takes precision, patience, and poise, whereas defense requires proper positioning, relentless pressure, and persistence. The defender is at a disadvantage, because the offensive player determines when, and largely where, the cut begins. Consequently, a successful defensive player is acutely on edge, vigilant, and aware of movement all over the field, anticipating the action to come. At any given moment a receiver may suddenly and explosively cut, change direction, and sprint toward the end zone. An active, alert defender works hard to be in position to foil any cuts that the receiver wants to make, essentially taking away that player as an option to the thrower. If each defender can effectively deny the thrower easy options, the chances of forcing a turnover increase dramatically.

Attitude

The first mental characteristic of an effective defender is an aggressive and relentless attitude. The offense tries to dictate the pace and create space to secure the disc as they progress down the field. Defenders, then, must work hard to turn back these advances, striving to force a low-percentage pass by placing the offense in a vice—squeezed between the marker, denying the thrower one side of the field, and the downfield defenders, covering the other side—narrowing the choices available.

What you hope will result is that covered receivers are scattered and clogging the passing lanes and the thrower's choices are limited to throwing into coverage, punting a Hail Mary pass downfield, or being stalled (a violation of the 10-second stall count that is counted aloud by the marker). And no one ever wants to be stalled.

Awareness

Another mental characteristic of a successful defender is having awareness of the action around her. Paying attention to the offender to which she is assigned is not enough. Much can change in an instant in Ultimate, and these changes can pull a defender quickly out of position. The defender must be aware of more than just her assignment. She should be in position to see the player currently in possession of the disc, as well as the teammate marking that player, and check in frequently, because the disc changes hands and location on the field at least every 10 seconds. Defenders must sustain their vigilance.

Anticipation

An alert defender is thinking more than one pass ahead, aware of the various choices earned for the thrower, and ready to help other defenders, if needed. Such anticipation requires thinking more like an offensive player—recognizing patterns of flow, seeing the possibilities unfold, and then playing percentages (anticipating the higher percentage options that an offense is likely to choose). In a corner of the field in the red zone, for instance, a thrower has fewer choices and wants easy ones offered to her. A defender knows this situation well and can anticipate where the thrower is likely to go with the disc, thereby more effectively denying a cut by the receiver whom she is covering. Such anticipation also enables players to switch (trade) cutters whom they are guarding or poach (briefly step into the cutting lane) to get a block or, simply and momentarily, help take away another immediate choice from the thrower. Because offense often has the advantage, knowing when and where the race (a receiver's cut) begins, the defense must do all they can to negate that head start. Rather than just react, defenders should *pre-act,* a playful but useful term coined by Seattle middle-school teacher and area youth Ultimate developer Joe Bisigano. Joe uses this term to emphasize an important concept of seeing and thinking ahead—being in position and prepared physically before actually needing to be—so that an offensive player's explosive movement is preempted by an equally explosive anticipatory action on the part of the defender. Defensive players must think ahead and prepare ahead.

Taking this preemptive posture to defense a step further, to a proactive extent, we introduce the concept of dictating on defense. Offense has obvious advantages. On defense, however, a player and a team can do much to dictate the course and pace of a point and of a game. Later in this chapter we offer techniques and strategies that can swing the balance of influence back in favor of defense.

A defender's mental approach requires a zealous and hungry attitude, awareness of all players on the field, not just the player for whom he is directly responsible, and alert anticipation of the possibilities at that moment and beyond. Defenders should study opposing teams, their strengths and weaknesses, as well as their tendencies. Effective defense is a secondary skill of primary importance and is vital to a team's success.

Marking the Thrower

Throwing a disc accurately in Ultimate can be a challenge, but for those proficient at the skill it can be fairly easy to complete seemingly difficult passes, even with a defender applying pressure. If the defender guarding the current thrower, the marker, is not effective in reducing the thrower's choices, her team probably won't be playing long because the opponents will be scoring easily and often. The marker should strive to maintain the force she and her teammates decided on and not allow the thrower to break her mark. As mentioned previously, a break mark occurs when a thrower is able to get a pass off to the area on the field that the marker is taking away (figure 6.1). Preventing the thrower from breaking the mark can be a formidable task. For this reason, markers should strive to give up the least harmful break-mark pass. This is usually the flat (lateral) around-the-mark pass which does not gain much ground and allows defenders time to recover and reposition.

Fundamentally solid marking is a vastly underrated and often overlooked defensive skill, one that players and teams will be well served to spend considerable time developing.

Physical Fundamentals

An effective marker invests considerable time developing an athletic position that will allow explosive lateral movement. As figure 6.2, *a* and *b,*

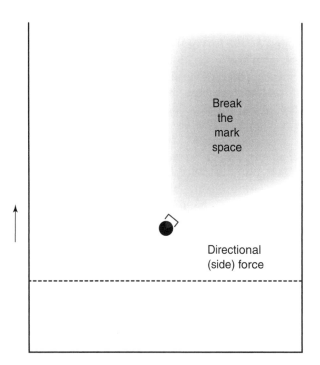

Figure 6.1 Areas of the field the mark is establishing as the force side (allowing) and the break space (the area being denied).

shows, marking a thrower requires a low, balanced position, with the feet underneath the body, slightly more than hip-width apart. The marker should be on the balls of the feet, with weight evenly distributed. She should be sure to bend at the knees more than she does at the hips. That way the torso

is upright and the leg muscles are activated, like compressed springs, ready to explode into action. Bending at the knees and "loading the springs" will drop the center of gravity and allow quicker, more responsive movement on the mark. Along with keeping the torso upright, the marker must keep the head up to maintain awareness of the thrower's intentions and options, be ready to pre-act to the thrower's pivots and fakes, and be able to distinguish a fake from the authentic release. The hands should stay low, because most throws are released below the waist, particularly the more dangerous break-mark throws (figure 6.3). Furthermore, from a hands-low, palms-facing-the-thrower position, the

Essential Physical Tips for the Marker

▶ Keep weight on the balls of the feet, with the feet just beyond hip-width apart.

▶ Load the springs by bending at the ankles and knees, less so at the hips.

▶ Keep the head and torso upright.

▶ Position the hands near or below knee level.

▶ The palms face the thrower to permit quicker reactions.

Figure 6.2 An effective marker's stance: *(a)* front view; *(b)* side view.

Figure 6.3 A marker must keep her hands low.

marker can raise her hands and body to stop a higher release more quickly than she can drop to stop a lower release. This position is most effective when offenses are facing a strong wind and must release

from lower points. We will discuss the occasional exceptions to the rule of maintaining a low level on the mark more extensively in the chapter on team defense. In most cases, however, whether facing novice throwers or seasoned veterans, marking low is most effective.

Movement Fundamentals

As mentioned earlier, to be quick on the mark, the center of gravity must be low. This stance flexes the leg muscles, effectively activating them. To dictate the action on the mark, a player will need to be able to slide quickly from side to side, drop step fluidly, spring up, and lunge low and slide wide. All these actions require strength and flexibility in the leg and hip complex and a well-conditioned core. A player's core body muscles (upper legs, hips, gluteals, and all muscles up through the trunk and shoulders) are the relay center for explosive extremity movement, regulating the rate and intensity of action and reaction. A wise Ultimate athlete will rigorously train these areas. When forcing a thrower straight up, for instance, in a chest-to-chest position, allowing her to throw to the sides but not downfield, the marker must keep her body upright and hands wide to obstruct direct downfield shots (figure 6.4, *a-b*). When forcing to one side of the field (forehand or backhand) or when forcing middle (always forcing back to the weak, or wide, side of the field), the force-side hand should be low and the stance a bit open (figure 6.5). This

Figure 6.4 Marker's position for forcing a thrower straight up.

Figure 6.5 Open position of the marker when forcing to one side of the field or forcing middle.

positioning can narrow the thrower's choice to one side of the field. The marker must focus on making the thrower throw only to that force side. This skill takes both practice and conditioning.

One fun activity to build specific muscular strength and endurance and to work on the skill of pre-acting is called mirroring. In this drill one player pivots and fakes all sorts of throws from various release points without releasing the disc. His partner acts as the mark. He is responding to all throwing motions and release points, striving to be in position to prevent or block any attempt to release the disc. One repetition may last from 15 to 20 seconds. Partners then switch roles. Extend this drill further by having markers hold their arms behind their backs or grip medicine balls at the waist. Keep in mind that this is only a drill to improve reaction time, body positioning, and quick

Essential Movement Tips for the Marker

► Keep the force-side hand low.
► Keep the legs underneath the torso when shuffling.
► Do not lunge out of position.
► Condition the core and use lateral explosion exercises (see chapter 8).

changes in levels. A marker's responsibility is to reduce the thrower's number of choices, never to prevent every one of them. The rest is up to his defensive teammates.

Vision Fundamentals

The marker must be ready to prevent all throws to the side of the field that she is responsible for defending, but she must not fall for the thrower's fakes. Players should study opponents' throwing motions to know their tendencies, their range of effective release points, and the difference between their fakes and the real deal. By watching the thrower's eyes, the marker can get an idea about which cutters the thrower might be looking at and what throw he may be considering. Furthermore, the marker should not be afraid to glance briefly back over her force-side shoulder for a quick update on the movement of the cutters and defenders. A defender may have lost her footing or been part of a defensive switch on cutters and find herself suddenly out of position. On the mark, then, it can pay off to scan the field swiftly in an

Essential Vision Tips for the Marker

► Don't bite on fakes.
► Observe the thrower's tendencies.
► Watch the thrower's eyes.
► Occasionally scan the field with brief glances over the force-side shoulder.

anticipatory (pre-acting) manner, providing timely help, if needed, by briefly hindering the offense's sudden advantage. But the marker should not go so far as to switch the direction of the force from what the team decided on before the point in an effort to help an out-of-position teammate. If every other defender is in position, switching the force to help one will cause all the others to be suddenly out of position. Markers must avoid doing this.

Maintaining a Disciplined Force

Above all else, defenders must know and remember one thing—the force, the direction in which the team plans to funnel throws. Although doing this sounds easy, it can be a challenge for some players to accomplish, especially when fatigue sets in. One mental lapse can cost a team dearly. The sideline players should remind those on the field, especially the player who is marking, by repeatedly calling out the predetermined force throughout the point. This prompt is especially helpful if the force is middle, because the direction of the defensive force will change frequently, as often as every throw. Teammates can help the mark considerably by alerting her where a break-side cutter might be open for the thrower. Shouting cues such as "No inside (the mark)!" or "No around!" allows the marker to shift her position without having to look. These sideline teammates essentially function like eyes in the back of the marker's head. This effective team skill will be discussed further in chapter 7. The main point here is that merely remembering the force makes it easier to maintain.

A good thrower will pivot and fake, trying to pull the marker out of position to get off the desired throw. The marker, therefore, must be disciplined and alert to the best options available, quick, and yet careful not to be fooled by the thrower's fakes. The marker must work hard to allow only a force-side throw. If this occurs, the open space on the pitch is significantly reduced for the cutters, putting the offense in the vice and tightening it! And if the mark is broken, the defender on the cutter now in possession is out of position and must overrun the play to stop the offense's break-side flow and reestablish the original force. If able to break the mark, the offense has a sizable advantage, because throwers and cutters have newfound space, angles, and lanes where defenders are not initially present. For this reason, maintaining the force is a high priority for defenses.

The list in the sidebar on this page offers some techniques to help prevent break-mark throws.

Using these techniques will go a long way in establishing a team as a strong marking squad. That objective should receive considerable focus and effort at practices.

Getting a Point Block

A marker's primary responsibility is to establish and anchor the defensive force and prevent throws to the break side. Ensuring that alone can be a tall task. As a result, the block of a throw on the mark, referred to as a point block, is rare, but it can and does happen. A far more frequent occurrence is a downfield block, interception, or errant throw resulting from a trustworthy mark forcing throws into coverage. Markers should take great care not to give up a break-side throw in an effort to get a

point block. For this reason, our discussion of the point block will be brief.

Point blocks may result when a thrower telegraphs her intentions, lacks variety in her release points, does not reach far enough or wide enough to get around the marker's reach, or fails to pivot or fake the marker out of position. However, point blocks most often occur when a thrower attempts to break an effective, reliable mark. Players with accomplished disc skills and multiple release points are hard to force into coverage, let alone point block. But against less skilled players—and every team has them—anticipating the timing and release point of a throw can be helpful. Teams have break-mark throwers as well as those who simply want to make or are expected to make an easy force-side pass. Astute defenders will assess the ability level of the player with whom they are matched. A point block can be devastating to the opponent's offense and can change the momentum of a game.

HAND BLOCKS

When hand blocks occur on the mark, they suggest an awareness of the thrower's movement, fakes, and release points; either that, or the marker simply guessed right! Hand blocks can have a detrimental effect on the offense's confidence. To attempt a hand block, stay well balanced, distribute your weight evenly on the balls of the feet, just beyond hip-width apart, and have the knees comfortably bent. In this athletic position, shuffle laterally with the thrower's fakes and pivots, being careful not to overcommit and give up the force. Keep the hands low and palms facing, while reaching for a point lower than appears necessary. This position is more advantageous for making a block. Watch the thrower's eyes, take a quick peek over the force-side shoulder, and listen to verbal help from defensive teammates (see figure 6.6). Those

---

Essential Tips for Preventing Break-Mark Throws

▶ Take a step back on the mark or move in closer to the thrower.

▶ Use a drop step on the force side, stepping back from the thrower.

▶ Listen carefully to teammates who are providing useful cues (e.g., "Inside!", "Around!", "Strike!", or "Last back!").

Figure 6.6 Note position of sideline teammate, who is able to see downfield and is giving verbal cues to the marker.

on the field, as well as those on the sideline, can be instrumental in effective marking, including getting the rare point block. A point block is a defensive team effort.

FOOT BLOCKS

Blocking or preventing a throw on the mark with the feet can be effective on occasion, but it can also be costly to your team and potentially dangerous to the thrower if not done properly. Although reaching out with the foot affords greater range, doing so compromises the "springs loaded" explosive athletic position required on the mark. Recovering your balance after attempting a foot block can be awkward and time consuming if the throw does not occur. And the thrower will be able to pivot away from the fake and release an uncontested pass.

To kick one leg out to get a block or a prevent (an act that causes a thrower to pull back on a throw), a marker must shift her whole weight to the other leg. For that reason, you should rarely attempt this maneuver early in the stall count. The foot block can help a shorter player overcome a reach advantage by a taller thrower. Nevertheless, if using this method, keep on balance but narrow the stance a bit and straighten the legs slightly to allow a quicker weight shift to the plant leg. When going for the block or prevent, be certain to reach out *and* back slightly, not forward toward the thrower's hand. Reaching forward, particularly on a backhand release, can create contact with the hand or arm, which is swinging rapidly forward, and can potentially cause injury. For that reason, many in the Ultimate

community frown on foot blocks. If done sparingly, such as at a very high stall count, and properly, by extending the leg out low, below the hips, back somewhat, and with a quick recovery, foot blocks or prevents can be both safe and effective. Note that the key word here is sparingly.

Studying a thrower's strengths, weaknesses, and tendencies, as well as fakes and release points, will enable the marker to anticipate effectively in her effort to prevent and occasionally block a throw. Again, though, we cannot stress enough that markers should never bite on fakes in an all-out attempt for a point block. This is rarely the best choice, especially at higher levels of play, and will result in being pulled out of solid marking position. A good fake will be followed by a break-mark throw. By using reliable marking principles to maintain the force on which the defense has decided, favorable things should happen. Fundamentally sound and explosive marking in tandem with effective coverage on cutters will raise the anxiety level of any offense, providing many opportunities to create turnovers.

Covering a Cutter

In one-on-one coverage, a defense hopes to create individual matchups that benefit defenders and cause turnovers, whether by an interception, block, or forced throwaway. If marking is strong and players guarding the cutters maintain solid fundamental position, these athlete-versus-athlete matchups become tougher for an offense to win, placing considerable pressure on throwers. This pressure increases the likelihood that the defense will force a coverage sack, in which no one is open and the offense is left with nothing but low-percentage choices.

Triangle Positioning

To be effective in guarding a cutter in a one-on-one strategy, a defender must not only get into appropriate position but also maintain or recover it throughout a point. Establishing this position is simple, but keeping it as an offense is in motion is hard work and requires plenty of practice. As with marking, good individual body position helps in this effort. Defenders are most effective when in position to see the cutter whom they are guarding while keeping an eye on the current thrower and marker. Figure 6.7 shows the triangle created by these three points.

The defender sets up in the force-side passing lane so that she can see both the cutter and the thrower peripherally or with a slight turn of the head. This position also provides a reaction cushion for the defender to "absorb" cuts on the force side. It allows her extra time and space to react and be in position for a block or interception should a throw come her way—or even to eliminate the threat the cutter poses. This cushion helps defenders neutralize the head-start advantage of cutters while remaining close enough to recover if a cutter instead goes to the break side. Defenders strive to maintain and reestablish the triangle throughout the point, although they may change its shape somewhat. Two suggested approaches to establishing a defensive triangulating technique are fronting and backing.

FRONTING RECEIVER

Figure 6.8 exhibits a fronting position, in which the defender positions herself between the cutter and the thrower, providing a slight head start in taking away any underneath cuts back toward the thrower. This position negates the cutter's advantage of surprise by gaining time and space to read the cutter's jukes and actual cuts. This positioning is effective against an offense whose cutters often cut back in for the disc from downfield,

Figure 6.7 The triangle formed and maintained by the downfield defender.

Figure 6.8 Demonstrating a fronting defensive position.

and particularly on a team's main throwers. The fronting defender also has the ability to see other cutters beyond hers, permitting greater awareness of teammates' responsibilities and allowing her to offer help vocally or by switching with a teammate—that is, by picking up the open cutter while her teammate inherits responsibility for the cutter the original defender had previously been covering. Playing too far off the cutter on the force side, however, can make breaking the mark easier, even when throwers are being marked effectively. Although the break side is the primary responsibility of the marker, defenders can help by staying close enough to the cutter on the force side to be able to cover a short, inside-the-mark break throw or close in quickly on a receiver cutting to the break side.

Defenders should also front when attempting to deny backfield reset cutters short lateral options. These resets (dumps) are already a high-percentage choice for an offense. To stop this, defenders guarding the backfield resets must take measures to get between the thrower and these cutters, working hard to maintain this positioning.

The disadvantage to fronting is its susceptibility to deep shots downfield and overheads to the break side, away, as figure 6.9 illustrates. Effective deep help and defensive switching can overcome this drawback. The defender who is covering the last cutter in the stack can quickly leave her assignment (switch) to help defend an open cutter streaking deep downfield, while her beaten teammate inherits responsibility for the cutter the helping teammate left uncovered. As for stopping break-side throws, that responsibility falls largely on the shoulders of a hardworking and fundamentally reliable marker.

BACKING RECEIVER

Playing behind a cutter is more prudent in some situations. In this technique, called backing, the defender keeps the cutter in front of him, sandwiched between him and the current thrower. By standing behind the cutter's force-side shoulder (figure 6.10), the backing defender makes the prospect of cutting deep more difficult, because that cutter would have to get around the defender's position, a sufficient deterrent for many offensive players. If the cutter sprints in and successfully catches the disc, the backing defender will be right there to stifle a continue pass by promptly containing—closing in and setting a mark with the appropriate force following a reception underneath. The vantage point presented to the backing defender allows him to see all the action involving those in front of him, providing him with the opportunity to help. This method offers several advantages:

▶ Keeps faster or taller cutters from getting downfield as easily

▶ Forces cutters less skilled in throwing to go in to receive the disc

▶ Gives the defender the ability to set the mark from a "containing" approach angle

▶ Puts the defender in a position to help teammates who may have been beaten deep

Although backing is often used as a preventive measure—to keep cutters from going deep, thereby necessitating more (defendable) cuts back to the disc—it can also be effective when a team is forcing flat on the mark. A flat force (figure 6.11) allows lateral throws toward either sideline, throws that will gain little downfield yardage. The increased number of lateral throws needed to take advantage of a flat force provides the defender more opportunity to race past the cutter for a block. When the

Figure 6.9 Fronting defender will be out of position, trailing the cutter if she heads deep downfield.

Figure 6.10 Defender in backing position.

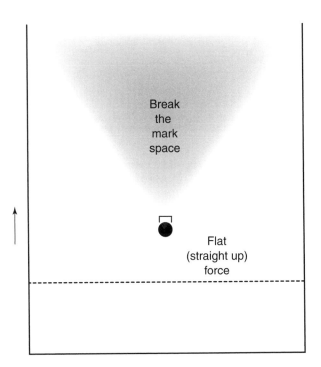

Figure 6.11 Flat force denies the middle of the field and deters hucks.

offense faces a headwind, the effectiveness of this tactic may increase because the wind will cause the disc to fly slower and may cause it to hop up and down en route. By itself, a headwind makes the thrower's and cutter's jobs difficult. Add to this a hardworking defender, and conditions are promising for a one-on-one defensive play. When the offense is throwing with wind at its back, touch is affected, and discs fly faster and lose altitude more rapidly. These conditions can also be favorable for backing and marking flat. Defenders must strive to maintain this downfield position on cutters and reestablish it after a thrower they are marking has released the disc and cleared downfield to again become a cutter.

Coverage Tactics

Cutters typically have an advantage over their defensive counterparts, so constant triangle positioning bolsters a defender's effectiveness in negating that advantage. A few suggested tools —or tricks of the trade—can, however, reinforce the plan.

BACKPEDALING: DO NOT COMMIT THE HIPS

When positioned in the lane, a triangulating defender will be able to see both the cutter and the thrower as long as she maintains this placement,

which is essential to cluttering the passing lane and denying throwers easy force-side options. The ability to backpedal fluidly as the offender attempts to set up a cut is crucial. The cue here, though, is to stay in balanced athletic position, with body weight split equally on both legs and on the balls of the feet. The defender must work hard to keep body weight slightly forward to avoid backpedaling onto the heels. Backpedaling onto the heels makes changing speed or direction with explosion difficult and puts the defender at the mercy of the cutter. Defenders must keep arms close, with elbows at the sides and flexed slightly. A visual cue is to picture an Old West gunfighter, hands open and close to the hips with the upper body leaning slightly forward, weight evenly split between the boots. From this position the backpedaling defender can "draw" quickly and drop step (step backward) off either foot, depending on the movement of the cutter (figure 6.12). This quick movement at the correct time turns the hips in the same direction as the cutter, allowing a seamless transition from a backpedal to a straight-ahead sprint.

Quarter (90-degree), half (180-degree), and full (360-degree) squirms are agility drills that help develop backpedaling skills and fluid, explosive hip turns out of that movement. See page 102 for a description of how to administer these drills.

Figure 6.12 The defender is backpedaling but on balance and able to change direction readily.

Squirms Drill

PURPOSE

This agility drill is useful in developing good footwork, fluid hip turns, and explosiveness transitioning out of changes of direction.

EQUIPMENT

5 cones

SETUP

5 cones in a line, each 10 yards apart.

PROCEDURE

Athlete begins backpedaling at first cone. At second cone turn 180 degrees (half squirm) to the right and sprint to the third cone. At third cone turn 180 degrees to the left returning to a backpedal, decelerating as little as possible. At fourth cone turn 180 degrees again to the right this time and sprint through the fifth and final cone. On next repetition, turn to the left to sprint (at cone #2), turn to right (at cone #3) to return to backpedal, and then to the left (at cone #4) to sprint through the finish (cone #5).

EMPHASIS

▶ Athletes should stay in a low, springs-loaded position when backpedaling.

▶ Encourage athletes to explode out of turns and decelerate just enough to facilitate a quick and concise turn (squirm).

▶ Remind athletes to utilize their arms vigorously to aid in fluid squirms and explosiveness coming out of breaks.

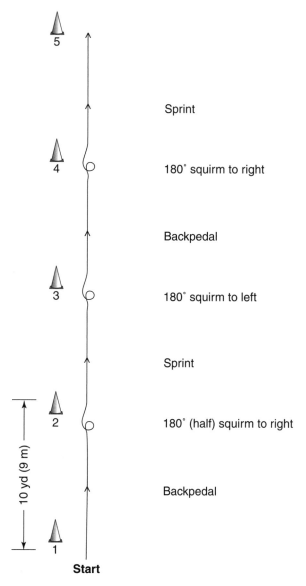

Figure 6.13 Squirms drill.

VARIATIONS

▶ Athletes begin drill in a sideways shuffle (right shoulder leading) and at second cone turn 90 degrees (quarter squirm) to the right and sprint straight ahead to third cone, turn 90 degrees to the right again, returning to a now left shoulder-leading side shuffle; at fourth cone, squirm 90 degrees, this time to the left, and sprint through fifth and final cone.

▶ Athletes begin with sprint, turning to the right a full 360 degrees (full squirm) at the second cone, trying not to slow down as they complete the full turn and returning to a straight-ahead sprint; then complete a full squirm to the left at third cone and sprint through a fourth and final cone. This variation is great for developing proprioception and dynamic balance.

▶ Vary the distances between, or the layout of, the cones (for example, use a zig-zag pattern).

▶ Athletes squirm on stimulus like coach's whistle or teammate's "Up" calls.

The defender must not commit to turning the hips in transition out of a backpedal until the cutter has committed to a direction. If the defender does this properly, the cutter may choose to bail out of his attempt to get open on the triangulating defender. In this case, the defender may never have to commit her hips in any direction. She can maintain her positioning, hips and all, yet keep tabs on her assignment and the disc. Working hard on this skill allows a defender to maintain a triangulated orientation longer and recover more quickly if juked out of position. At some point the cutter will decide either to accelerate to try to pass the defender, to head for a break-side reception, or to clear out of the desired passing lane to open things up for another cutter. At these pivotal moments the defender must make a decision to commit the hips to a transition (half squirm) out of the backpedal to win the race to the disc or to maintain a triangle cushion (with a quarter squirm) if the cutter heads break side or clears downfield.

KNOW THE THREATS

Each team has its featured players, and some are tough to contain no matter how well they are defended. An intelligent team will be aware of such athletes and how best to neutralize their strengths. A player whose strengths are tremendous disc skill, quickness, and cutting ability, and who likes to operate at the front of an offense, will require a different defensive approach than a player whose superior deep speed or height is the primary weapon. Scouting the opposing team's personnel and how they typically use them is important. Most squads choose to stick with what works for them offensively. The defense should formulate a plan to match up with, position for, and defend the most dynamic playmakers on the opposing team.

PLAY THE PERCENTAGES

A team will be well served to work hard at maintaining the agreed-on defensive position on offensive players while using the tactics suggested earlier—occupying the cutter's desired space and backpedaling—and knowing who the primary threats are and how best to lessen their influence. If all these strategies are in place, denying the desirable higher percentage choices can further increase the effectiveness of individual defenders. If the skilled thrower mentioned earlier is forced to go downfield as a cutter but does not possess the speed or height to be a deep threat, the odds are that he will be less of a factor and will be cutting back in toward the front of an offense in an attempt to get the disc in his hands. A defense knows this and will position on that offensive player accordingly. To take this illustration a step further, if that player is the offense's main downfield thrower, he will be even less likely to have a well-thrown pass come downfield in his direction. This, in turn, will allow the defender assigned to him to take an aggressive fronting position, because that cutter is likely to return to bail out his lesser-skilled teammates.

At times players cut to undesirable places on the field, as when hanging out too deep or offering a long, downfield, break-side cut that reduces their legitimacy as a threat. When offensive players go to such areas on the field, their defenders may have opportunities to play off or poach, enabling them to help teammates whose opponents are in a more immediate and threatening field placement.

On offense, a less experienced squad may insist on forcing the disc upfield along the sideline, causing the passing lane to become progressively narrower. In such instances, the defenders' jobs become easier. The lane has become more like an alley, reducing the cutting space, thus shrinking the area that defenders have to cover. In addition, each defender has the luxury of waiting for the incoming cutter and taking full advantage of lowered offensive percentages. A similar situation arises when a team does not break the mark well or does not possess good disc skill in windy conditions. Such an offense is less likely to overcome the combined effect of the wind, good marking, and effective force-side defense. All these situations enable defenders to maximize one-on-one positioning, play off assigned cutters, and help other defenders in the process.

Generating a Downfield Block

A team made up of skilled and hardworking defenders will create many opportunities to make plays on the disc. Effective one-on-one defense ranges in appearance from basic (force middle) to bold (trapping sideline), from dull (coverage sacks) to dramatic (diving blocks), depending on the team's approach and its athletes' abilities. Ineffective defense, on the other hand, results from poor technique and a lack of conditioning, continuity, and trust in one another. The probability of producing an off-the-mark turnover increases markedly if the team is consistent and diligent in how it marks and defends downfield. Gaining and keeping possession of the disc *is* the object of play, and individual defenders will be more pleased with their efforts if they work together as a team.

COVERAGE SACKS

If each member on defense is doing everything possible to foil the opponent's efforts, coverage sacks result. A coverage sack is similar to what occurs in American football when a quarterback looking to throw has no open receivers and chooses either to take a sack or, perhaps unwisely, try to force a pass into coverage. Unlike taking a sack in football, however, failing to make a throw within the 10-second stall count in Ultimate always results in a turnover. The choice instead is to try to sneak the perfect throw into coverage or heave the disc long downfield (as when the quarterback throws a long pass that might be caught but is more likely to be intercepted, thus effectively serving as a punt). If marking is strong, limiting throwers primarily to force-side options, the effective downfield defender will be in position to get a block or interception, regardless of the thrower's choice. Although this task is easier said than done, solid marking and coverage fundamentals will support the defense's cause.

LAYING OUT ON DEFENSE

If you were to poll Ultimate players, many would say that the most exciting play in the sport is the diving, or layout, block. Although solid coverage skills lead to easier, more effective defensive play, the cutters' head start still makes the task of denying every pass unrealistic. But defenders who are willing and able to leave their feet to dive horizontally at top speed can get to the disc before the cutter does if they are one or even two full steps behind the cutter. This type of block generally occurs more frequently at elite levels of play and can shift the momentum of a point or an entire

Figure 6.14 The stages of a defensive dive in Ultimate: (*a*) the forward lean; (*b*) the forceful launch; (*c*) the flat landing.

match. Figure 6.14, *a* through *c*, demonstrates the stages leading up to getting a block. Refer also to the concepts discussed in chapter 3 on laying out for catches.

We repeat here our warning about laying out: There is a right way and a wrong way to do it. Bad technique and carelessness can lead to shoulder, wrist, finger, knee, or even rib injuries. Players should not lay out until they feel comfortable with the demands of the skill. No player should attempt to lay out if she is not ready to do so.

See figure 3.11 for help developing proper layout technique.

Furthermore, it is unwise to lay out for a block just because you can. If you are too far behind the cutter to have a legitimate shot at the block, do not leave your feet. If you do, the new thrower you should be marking has 2 or 3 seconds without any mark present while you are on the ground applying no pressure. If that player immediately makes a throw and strikes downfield as a cutter, he will be a wide-open threat as you struggle to recover from lost defensive positioning. This circumstance can be extremely costly to a defense, so, while learning *how* to dive, learn also to discern *when* diving is appropriate. You accomplish the latter through experience and by observing others who are effective at the skill. If no one on your team is modeling proper layout form and timing, watch DVDs that highlight high-level play and specific skills, including diving. Refer to the appendix to find sources for suggested products.

JUMPING ON DEFENSE

Winning the jump balls in Ultimate is important, given that the flying disc sometimes hangs in the air longer than the thrower intended. Practice the skill of reading the flight of the disc. Strive to increase vertical jumping ability. Finally, work hard on positioning for these overhead plays on the disc. If height is equal, relative positioning and reading the disc are the difference makers. If playing behind (backing) a faster or less skilled cutter, you will be able to maneuver into good position should a floating disc approach. But as discussed in chapter 2, a tailwind causes a disc to lose altitude, so a backing position may not allow the best play on a high throw. In this case, the player with inside positioning will more likely be able to make the play. Assess the wind and the angle of the rim in relation to the spin put on the disc. Was the throw a flick or a backhand? Did it have an inside-out or outside-in release? Is the wind facing the disc or chasing it? Or is it crossing the spin? Learning how these nuances affect disc flight takes time, and experience is the best teacher. In baseball, an outfielder must learn to recognize the pitch, bat speed, and velocity and spin imparted to the ball as it soars through the air to determine whether to break back or in, right or left, to make the play. You should throw in windy conditions as much as possible, changing position in relation to your throwing partner to discover the subtle influences of wind on the disc. Just developing knowledge of flight characteristics will make you more effective at winning those jump balls. Add to that better positioning skills, and positive results will often follow.

Dog and It's Up, two drills introduced in chapter 3, will improve reading and positioning skills for plays overhead, whether alone in space or battling an opponent for the disc. To increase vertical jumping ability, see chapter 8 for several specific exercises.

POACH BLOCKS

As already mentioned, poaching is the act of temporarily playing off the cutter to whom you are assigned to get a block or help an out-of-position teammate by preventing an easy throw to her open cutter, allowing time for her to catch up. Sometimes you can accomplish this by simply darting from the stack into the force-side passing lane as an open cutter breaks in or by lingering briefly in the lane as your cutter clears out. This can be enough to deter the thrower, causing him to look off that cutter and choose someone else. By that time, the beaten defender has recovered, as have you, having located and gotten back in position on the momentarily uncovered cutter, sometimes without that player even knowing what took place.

Defenders must be on the same page so that the poach will surprise the offense, with little or no consequences. A team that poaches effectively will be able to switch on assigned cutters throughout an offense's flow, essentially handing off cutters to one another and thereby spoiling opportunities earned by the offense.

As with laying out for a block or interception, poaching involves some risks. Cutters are briefly left uncovered, and good teams will recognize and exploit such opportunities. Do not overdo it on poaching. A player who decides to do too much will put excessive demands on teammates, who must cover for their poaching comrade. In addition, teams that poach liberally have the tendency to relax on one-on-one coverage, leading to sluggishness in that tactical area and out-of-position defenders. They basically slack on fundamentals. Do not fall into that trap! Furthermore, while some offensive strategies are vulnerable to poaching, other strategies will prey on players who take this risky approach, making blanket use of poaching unsound. Finally, careless poaching can be dangerous, leading to blind collisions because the cutter and the poaching defender may not see one another. Above all else, play safely!

Still, poaching can catch an offense off guard, causing it to have to reason and process more rapidly, disrupting offensive rhythm and flow. Raising this cognitive (thinking) demand often heightens the anxiety of the offense and impairs their performance, resulting in more blocks for the defense. But be prudent. There is no replacement for solid one-on-one coverage. If a cutter defended by a teammate is open for little gain early in the count, poaching off the opponent's best cutter, who may streak long for a big gain, makes little sense.

Along with fundamental and disciplined one-on-one defense, judgment about when to poach is a skill that takes time to develop. Put in the time, and the result will be blocks and coverage sacks rather than easily exploited poached cutters. Use the Macon drill to help develop individual coverage skills. See table 6.1 for individual defense troubleshooting tips.

Table 6.1 Individual Defense Troubleshooting Tips

Common mistakes	Solutions
Marks continue to be broken, even when your team knows the force and works hard to keep it.	Remember to load the springs early. Bending at the ankle and knees puts you in a lower, more explosive marking position.
You want to get a point block but cannot seem to pull it off.	Keep in mind that a point block is much less likely to occur than a downfield block on a throw into coverage. If the throw is released into your defense's force side, you will be doing more for your team if you are in position to block it, not focused on getting the rare point block when marking a thrower.
You work hard on the mark, but are called often for fouls.	Stepping back a foot or so on the mark and using a drop-step with the force-side leg reduces the chance that you will foul and also helps prevent inside breaks.
Your team has trouble preventing deep cuts.	Try backing cutters, dictating all cuts in toward the thrower. This tactic is especially effective when used on a team's best deep cutters or weakest throwers, because it forces them to handle the disc.
Several of your defenders keep getting beaten on cuts back to the disc.	Practice triangle positioning and try fronting cutters when they are in the front half of the stack. Front a team's handlers.

Macon Drill

PURPOSE

This drill focuses on establishing and maintaining a dictating triangle defensive positioning throughout a cutter's movement. This task is more difficult as cutters are moving rapidly toward defenders.

EQUIPMENT

▶ 3 cones

▶ Approximately 10 discs

SETUP

Place 3 cones in a V shape, with each side of the V about 15 to 20 yards (14 to 18 meters) long. Line athletes up behind the point of the V. The thrower stands with a stack of discs roughly 10 yards (meters) away from and in the middle of the two ends of the V (see figure 6.15).

PROCEDURE

The first athlete in the line steps out to the backhand side of the cone, establishing a triangle position on the second athlete in the line, who is the first cutter. That cutter runs

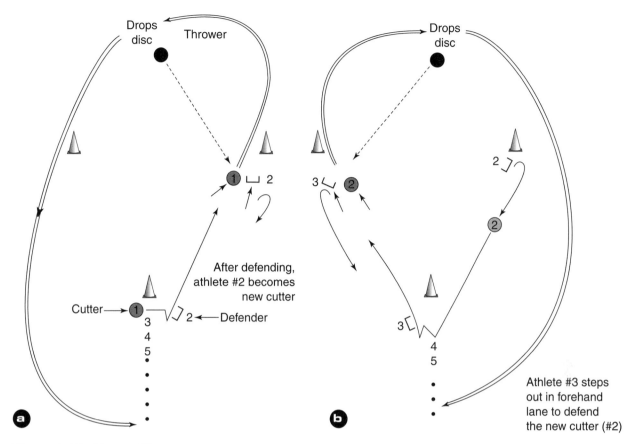

Figure 6.15 Macon drill.

at and jukes once or twice to try to maneuver the defender out of position or off-balance, then breaks in toward the thrower's backhand. The defender strives to maintain triangle position throughout the cutter's movement, trying to make a block or interception once the disc is thrown to the cutter. The thrower tosses the disc to the cutter once she has committed in a direction toward the front cone on this backhand side of the drill. Regardless of whether the disc is caught, intercepted, or blocked, the defender reverses direction back toward the line, becoming the next cutter, now to the forehand side of the V.

Meanwhile the third athlete in line has stepped out into the forehand lane to establish triangle position on this new cutter, who is arriving soon to attempt to juke her out of position or throw her off-balance and then will cut in toward the front cone on the forehand side. If the cutter catches the disc, or the defender blocks it, the cutter runs the disc back behind the thrower and drops it at her feet and clears around the drill to the back of the line. If the defender intercepts the disc, she drops it or flips it to the cutter, whose job it is to deliver it to the thrower on her clear to the back of the line.

EMPHASIS

▶ Defenders should establish triangle position that allows them to see both the cutter and the thrower.

▶ Defenders should work hard to stay on the outside (force side) of the cutters as they approach and cut in to get the disc.

▶ Defenders must load the springs early, in preparation of the arriving cutter, who is already in motion and running swiftly at them.

▶ Stay low and balanced and focus on the rapid foot strikes needed by defenders to dictate the cutter's options.

(continued)

VARIATIONS

▶ Add a downfield cone to each side of the drill, giving the cutter a deep cutting option, which increases demand on the defender.

▶ Give the thrower the choice of whether or not she throws the disc, perhaps announcing, "No!" instead of throwing to the covered receiver.

▶ Place drill near one sideline and set up to run to only that side (i.e., backhand or forehand side) to focus on trapping defense.

▶ Set drill up to go away from thrower, focusing more so on defending downfield throws.

Summary

One-on-one defense is a demanding skill that requires diligent practice. Players can learn the required mental toughness, physical techniques, and fitness through discussion and vigorous drilling. Defense should receive as much, if not more, attention as offense does. Solid and disciplined marking in tandem with good downfield positioning and coverage tactics can lead to defensive success. Everyone loves to see high-flying horizontal layout blocks or skying Ds. Although having teammates capable of such momentum-changing plays is comforting, mastery of individual technique and a sound team plan for defense is more practical and will lead to greater success. The next chapter will show how to incorporate these individual skills into an overall team defensive context.

Defense: Team Skills

Key Terms

An experienced offense clearly has a big advantage on the Ultimate field. If a team is composed of strong, quick, competent throwers and cutters, they most likely will score. The defensive team will find it difficult to create turnovers, and the best chance they have of creating one is by working together. An individual defensive player may think that she has her person shut down, but if the entire team is not playing the same defense at the same time, the offense will often prevail.

How does the average team achieve this goal? The basis of good defense is excellent communication. A coach or captain must do more than just assign a player his defensive responsibility and then walk away. Every player on the team has a role to play.

Playing team defense is a noisy enterprise. Players must constantly talk to each other on and off the field. Sideline players are essential to making a team's defense work well. The most experienced teams have players on both sides of the field constantly barking instructions specific to the situation at hand. Creating a turnover is not easy, and the entire team should relish its occurrence because all are responsible for making it happen.

Like many other sports, Ultimate uses a variety of defensive sets. The most common is individual coverage, historically called man-to-man and which we refer to as one-on-one. At the beginning of a point, a defensive player chooses an offensive player who appears to be a comparable matchup in height, speed, and ability. The defender is mainly responsible for the actions of the player whom she is covering, while also watching the developing offense of the other opponents.

In a zone defense, a defender is responsible for guarding an area of the field rather than a person. This area changes as the disc moves around the field. The defender is responsible for the offensive players that intrude into his area as well as the disc if it flies through his space. Ultimate teams use a variety of zones to stymie various types of offense. We will explain the basic cup defense, usually called the 3-2-2, as well as some variations.

If you combine the concepts of individual coverage with the basic premise of the zone, you end up with the clam. This form of defense is called junk. A team that understands the essentials of the clam can modify the principles of this defense to suit itself.

Finally, an experienced team may want to develop a transitional defense, which is a combination of any of the defenses discussed earlier. A team may play a cup zone for five passes and then switch to individual coverage. This switch forces the offense to reevaluate its offensive choices, and turnovers may result. Regardless of the type of defense a team uses, each player must understand the intricacies of the overall defensive set as well as the role that she is expected to play.

Communication

Ultimate is not a silent sport. A team playing strong defense should be in a state of controlled frenzy. While the offense is patiently trying to develop its flow, the defense should be on its toes, yelling and listening, trying to force a turnover. Effective defense requires the cooperation of every member of the team. The main purpose of communication is to provide additional information to the players on the field, thereby making it much easier for them to do their jobs.

Common Commands

So what exactly must players communicate when playing defense? This, of course, depends on what type of defense you have chosen. A command that works for a zone will not make much sense in other instances. Here are some of the most common calls that players will use and hear throughout a game of Ultimate.

▶ **"It's up!"** Players yell this phrase whenever the disc leaves the hands of an offensive player on its way to another, and it could mean that the disc is headed for the end zone. The purpose of this call is to alert all defenders that the disc is airborne and that a completed pass or score could be imminent. All defenders should immediately locate the disc in the air and do their best to attempt a block if they have a chance at the disc. Even if they don't have a chance for an immediate block, the "up!" call warns defenders that the disc is moving to a new location and enables defensive teammates to reposition accordingly. They may have a second opportunity to make a play on the disc, even if they are trailing the play.

▶ **"Home!"** This command indicates that the force on the field is toward the sideline the defensive team has designated as its own, or the home side. This means that, regardless of where the offense would like to throw the disc, each marker will be forcing the throw to go toward the home sideline. The concept of team forcing will be covered later in this chapter.

▶ **"Away!"** This call is the opposite of "Home!" The force will be toward the opposite sideline, away from the defensive team's sideline. The defenders will receive further instruction from the teammates on the far sideline.

▶ **"Strike!"** Assume that you are the defender near a sideline, marking the person with the disc.

Your defensive assignment is to force the offensive player to throw a forehand. You are completely focused on preventing a throw to the middle of the field when suddenly you hear the call "Strike!" This call means that, just for a second or two, you should jump around in front of the thrower to prevent a throw to a receiver coming up the sideline. Most often, the player who yells this command is on the sideline, sees the developing cut, and knows that a momentary switch of force will not disable the defense. A defender who can see that a long throw is about to go up or is likely to occur may also make the call.

▶ **"No big!"** This call is similar to "Strike!" except that it is intended solely to stop a long throw. It is most often used when the disc is in the center of the field and the thrower appears to be winding up to throw it far.

▶ **"No break!"** This cue lets the thrower's marker know that a cutter is making a break-mark cut behind him. It indicates that the marker is in immediate danger of being broken and should continue to mark strongly. A more precise way to impart this information is to use the phrases "No around!" or "No inside!" These calls let the marker know exactly in which direction the thrower would be most likely to break his mark. "No around!" means that the thrower is going to pivot around the mark and try to release the disc over or under the marker's right (outside) shoulder. "No inside!" indicates that the thrower will most likely launch an inside-out throw and that the marker needs to shift to block that release point.

A team may also develop its own series of verbal cues that will meet the specific needs of its defensive squad. They can use any phrases they choose, as long as everyone understands them. A team that develops a strong, consistent system of communication will benefit in many ways, from creating more turnovers to playing a more efficient brand of Ultimate.

Role of the Sideline

Players in any sport rarely enjoy being on the sideline. The traditional view of bench players is that they are inferior and useful only when a match is out of reach, for transporting equipment, or for bringing out water during a time-out. Nothing could be further from the truth on an Ultimate team. Each player has a role to play, whether on or off the field. Those who sulk about playing time should probably be playing an individual sport.

Ultimate has not developed to the point that an entourage follows an individual team around, unless you count parents, children, and significant others. At this point, many teams do not have a coach, so the coaching usually falls on the shoulders of the captains, who are also trying to run subs and play well themselves. Performing well in this combination role is almost impossible. The strongest teams are those that delegate responsibility and rely on everyone. Whether by providing information, maintaining intensity, or supporting individual teammates, an active, engaged sideline is crucial to competitive success.

APPEARANCE OF SIDELINE

What does a sideline of active players look like? First, let's look at a sideline that is not doing its job. The off-field players are sitting or lying down, clearly not engaged in the game. They may be eating, gossiping about the night before, or lazily stretching. All of this is going on while their teammates are a short distance away, doing their best to prevent a goal! If any players happen to be on the far, or "away," sideline, they usually are stationary, perhaps tossing the disc around or wondering when they are going to get a chance to play. A team like this is headed for divisiveness, conflict, and defeat.

But sideline players who understand their power and importance are spread along both sidelines. They are following the action up and down the field and are as close as possible to their teammates without stepping on the field or getting in the way. They congratulate their teammates vociferously and often. They do not get into conflicts with the sideline players of the other team, because they know their job is important. These off-field players always know what the defense is, they know what each player is expected to do, and they provide the commands to help their teammates do their jobs.

PROVIDING INFORMATION

Every sideline player should become familiar with the common commands and use them appropriately. Players can practice using the commands during drills, because they are the verbal component to what players are attempting to do physically. For example, during a break-mark drill, the players waiting to do the drill should shout, "No around!" or "No inside!" to provide more information to the marker. Anything that becomes a habit during practice transfers more easily to the field of competitive play.

Although all on-field players should know when a turnover has occurred and that they are no longer

on offense, this does not always happen. A focused sideline knows that the first few seconds of the transition from offense to defense are crucial. In this case, the sideline looks immediately to see who has become the offense's most dangerous threat and what the defense can do to neutralize her. For example, let's say that your team has turned it over near the middle of the field. One of the opponent's most skilled handlers runs to pick up the disc, and one of their strongest and swiftest cutters starts to break long. Both offensive players are anticipating a fast break score. The teammate marking the handler needs to hear "No big!" immediately, and the deepest teammate needs to take off after the streaking cutter, even if he has to leave another person. Properly executed, these responses will prevent the quick throw for a goal, and your defense will have a few seconds to regain its composure.

Players watching Ultimate from off the field have the advantage of being able to recognize patterns that players on the field are unable to notice. If the opposing team is consistently breaking a zone by going through the middle, perhaps the cup needs to tighten up the holes or maybe the defense needs to use a different zone. If a certain offensive player clearly relies on her long flick for scores, the team may want to switch the force at the next break in play. If a newer player is experiencing difficulty marking one of the opposing team's veterans, a switch should probably be made.

Having many pairs of eyes on a game is always an advantage, although having everyone offer strategies at the same time in the next huddle can be confusing and frustrating. Each team should have a system for relaying new information and observations. An experienced team will have one or two people listen to input and then decide which, if any, new strategy the team will implement. If the team does not take a player's suggestion, he should get back to the sideline and help his teammates. The player will likely have another chance to make suggestions, whether later in the day or at the next practice.

DEVELOPING AND MAINTAINING INTENSITY

Intensity means that the team is working as an integrated defensive machine. Every part supports the others, and every part is essential. Intensity does not always come easily. Teams need to develop and practice intensity, just as they would practice an important strategy or skill.

Players may use a variety of excuses not to communicate from the sideline. Several are particularly toxic:

"This game doesn't matter anyway."

"I'm really tired. They can do it without me."

"No one helped *me* out when *I* was on the field."

Obviously, all these excuses are counterproductive and divisive. A dedicated player will find it within herself to do what she is supposed to do, whether it is running an extra sprint or yelling for her team.

Sometimes intensity comes easily to a team. A spectacular layout block by a teammate makes it effortless for everyone to be focused and intense. But what about those days when the sideline is simply down? At those times your team just has to "Fake it 'til you make it." Go through the motions of being intense. Choose a specific player on your team to help, perhaps one that you can see is visibly struggling. Give him instructions that you know will improve his game. Look for opportunities to offer small rewards. Not everyone is going to achieve a spectacular block, but the player who doesn't get broken or who prevents a pass by a two-second poach has also earned a compliment. By working hard at developing your intensity, it will eventually become more genuine. And if everyone on your team is "faking it 'til they make it," your team will soon be back on the right defensive track.

SUPPORT

Every player needs to support her teammates to the best of her ability. Providing support may mean bringing out water during a time-out, helping someone warm up on the sideline, bandaging an injury, or providing feedback during a practice or game. This last part can be tricky, because everyone hears advice differently. A player who can accept advice from one teammate may not want to hear the same thing from someone else. Few people are fired up by negative feedback.

Most players want to hear support from their teammates, whether they are playing well or playing poorly. A compliment for a good play is easy to give. The wise player waits for the right opportunity to criticize a teammate. For example, let's say that a player is continually being scored on. What he doesn't need to hear from his teammates is "You need to shut him down!" or "Don't you know what the force is?" or "You need to know where the disc is!" The player already recognizes that he has made an error, and confirmation from his teammates is unnecessary. He will probably get burned again on defense after hearing comments

like these, because he is not focusing on the job that he is supposed to do. Instead, teammates should make suggestions for improvement when he is off the field or perhaps even well after the game. An experienced player can make it a point at the next practice to work with the player having difficulty and offer suggestions then.

Think of how you feel when you play well. You most likely feel focused on the right things and supported by the rest of your team. Your legs feel light, and you can run all day. You have no difficulty breathing, and you can see the field clearly. This positive mental attitude translates into strong play on the field. Don't you want all your teammates to feel that way too? Thinking that your team can achieve this all the time is unrealistic, but a team that commits to only saying positive things during a competition clearly understands the connection between individual support and team success.

Individual Coverage

New teams will likely defend with individual coverage. This type of defense is easy to explain because it translates readily from other sports. Each player lines up across from an opponent before the pull, choosing someone of about the same height whom she thinks she can cover. The defender tries to prevent her opponent from getting the disc. If the opposing player does get the disc, the defender stays with her and marks her.

As in other sports, a team can employ different types of individual coverage. Experienced Ultimate teams use forcing, trapping, and switching to stymie the offense. The more a team plays together, the more adept they become at different types of individual defenses and the more easily they can force a turnover.

Forcing

The pioneers of this sport figured out early that the easiest way to create a turnover was to allow a player to throw the disc where a defender had a chance at a block. This strategy has developed through the years. The four major forces used nowadays are force forehand, force backhand, force middle, and force straight up. The common thread is that the marker wants to induce the thrower to make a throw where the rest of the defenders are positioned.

FORCING FOREHAND

This is the most common force because, for many throwers, the forehand, or flick, is the most recently learned and therefore the most vulnerable throw. The marker sets up on the left shoulder of the thrower, as shown in figure 7.1. The marker's responsibility is to make the thrower choose a forehand to throw into the open throwing lane. The marker is determined not to let the thrower choose an inside-out forehand or any kind of backhand to the break side.

The other defenders set up so that they are between their opponents and the open throwing lane, also shown in figure 7.1. Look at this illustration carefully. You will see that the thrower's easiest throw is into the open throwing lane. The marker wants the thrower to make that throw. But each potential receiver has a defender directly in his way. The forehand is now a difficult throw to make safely, so the offense has to reevaluate their options.

This basic force works well as long as all the defenders understand their duties. The marker on the thrower cannot be broken, because all the defenders would then be on the wrong side and the offense would be off and running. The defenders

downfield must make sure that they are positioned correctly and that they prevent any viable cuts into the throwing lane. If they allow an opponent to make an uncontested cut for a forehand, the defense has failed.

FORCING BACKHAND

This defense is simply the mirror of the force flick. The marker stands on the right shoulder of the thrower and forces her to throw into the backhand passing lane. The other defenders are now set up on the opposite side from where they were forcing forehand, to prevent any cutters from using the new open lane.

Although switching from a forehand force to a backhand force would appear to be relatively easy, teams need to practice making this change. Because most teams force flick, markers and defenders are used to setting up on their opponent's left shoulder. For that reason, setting up on the right shoulder may feel strange. A momentary hesitation about how to set up the force can result in an uncontested pass or score, so teams must go over both of these forces in practice.

FORCING MIDDLE

This strategy is a combination of forcing backhand and forcing forehand, depending on where the thrower is on the field. The defensive team has decided that it is going to force the offense to throw toward the middle of the field, always. They will never allow a throw toward the sideline. This force can be a useful ploy against spread formations (split and H-stacks) and give-and-go offenses.

If the throw is near the sideline, the marker puts his back to that sideline and forces the thrower toward the middle (figure 7.2). This strategy becomes tricky only when the disc is near the middle of the field and the other defenders cannot tell which way

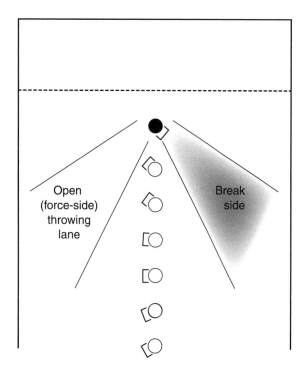

Figure 7.1 Forcing forehand. The marker forces the thrower into using the open throwing lane. Other defenders prevent cutters from going into this lane. Forcing backhand is simply the reverse.

Essential Forcing Tip

When someone yells, "Force forehand!" the force does not change according to whether the thrower is right-handed or left-handed. The defense will end up forcing a lefty's backhand even if they are forcing forehand, because the command designates which way the force should go. A more precise way to state this is to use "Force away!" or "Force home!" because the terms apply the same way to marking both right-handed and left-handed throwers.

the force will go. The marker on the thrower then has the obligation to decide instantly which force to put on and to yell either, "Home!" or "Away!" This call lets the other defenders know which side they should set up on. The sideline players are crucial in this type of defense. After the thrower has established which way he is forcing, the sideline must loudly echo what he has yelled.

Downfield defenders have an even tougher job in this kind of defense. Because the force is often switching, they must constantly be evaluating whether they are in the correct position to make it difficult for their person to get to the disc. Teams must practice all defenses to be successful, but forcing middle probably needs more focused teamwide attention if it is to work well.

TRAPPING

This strategy is the opposite of forcing middle. The defense has decided to force the thrower toward either sideline, by using either a force forehand or a force backhand when near the appropriate sideline. When the marker has determined that the thrower is close enough to the sideline to put on a trap, she yells, "Trap!" and the sideline echoes her. Figure 7.3 illustrates the clear advantages to a trap. The playing field has now shrunk to the width of a bowling lane. The job of the downfield defend-

ers has become much easier, because they know that most of the receivers will be cutting into that narrow area. If the offense tries to use a backfield reset to get it off the sideline, the reset's defender can try to take away that throw.

A good trap often results in a turnover, or at least a short pass up the sideline that can continue to be trapped. The defense still has a strong advantage here, and if the wind is blowing, this defense becomes difficult to beat.

FORCING STRAIGHT UP

This was the defense of choice at the beginning of the sport. The defender stood in front of the thrower and tried to prevent him from releasing either throw. If the thrower pivoted, the defender tried to mirror his movements, moving actively from side to side.

The straight-up force, or flat mark, is slightly different today. Because players' throwing, pivoting, and faking skills are more advanced, defenses use a flat mark sparingly. Any experienced player nowadays should easily be able to get a throw off to either passing lane. The straight-up force is also a difficult strategy for downfield defenders, because they have no idea which side of the receiver to cover as she makes her cut toward the disc.

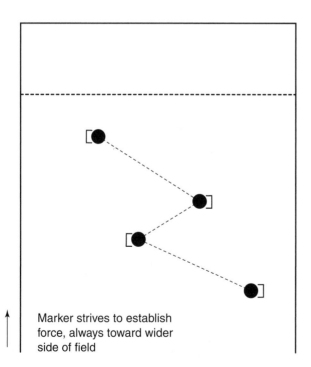

Figure 7.2 Forcing middle. As the disc moves back and forth across the field, the marks always force the throws to the middle of the field.

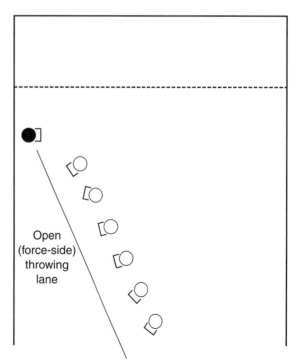

Figure 7.3 Trapping. If the offense continues to throw the disc down the sideline, the trap should continue to be held.

But this force can be successful in stopping a long pass. In this version, the defender moves little with the thrower's movements. He stands in front of the thrower like a brick wall, hands moving from low to high and extended out, and feet moving slightly side to side. If the thrower does get off some kind of long throw, chances are that it will be a loopy, arcing throw that a defender has a chance to block.

Switching

Switching occurs when two defenders exchange offensive players during a point. The switch should happen quickly because any miscommunication can leave a player open and uncovered. Experienced teams use switching as a defensive strategy, but novice teams should use it sparingly. To switch effectively, each defensive player must be aware of the entire field and be able to communicate immediately and clearly.

Let's say that you are a defender and are fronting your player. Fronting means that you are playing on the force side of the cutter, between her and the disc and are denying cuts in toward the thrower. Suddenly your player breaks long and is wide open for a long pass. You cannot easily make up the distance between the two of you.

An aware teammate farther downfield sees what is happening. She shouts, "Switch!" and is now covering your original player. You quickly look around to find her player, the one whom she has let go. You respond verbally and start covering that player. You have averted the danger with a perfect switch, and both of you are covering new players.

Some teams play a switching defense for most or all of a game. This usually means that the person covering the back of the stack will pick up any cutters streaking downfield. This defense is also called last-back defense. Sometimes the defenders at the front of the stack will then cover any players who are cutting in toward the disc. Again, communication is key. Teams who play this kind of defense are constantly talking, identifying the players whom they are covering and whom they are letting go. The danger in playing this kind of defense is that a smart offense will flood either the front or back and make it impossible for the defenders to cover multiple cutters.

Teams should use a switching defense sparingly. This kind of defense can upset a team's offensive rhythm, but after the offense adjusts, the defense should replace it with a variety of individual coverages or perhaps a zone.

Zone Defense

A zone is a defensive set in which the defense covers an area and the opponents who are moving through that area. Unlike in individual coverage, a defender does not stay with one person in a zone. He is constantly anticipating who will be moving into and away from his space and whether the disc is going to travel through this space. This area is always shifting, depending on where the disc is, the thrower's skill level, and where the offense is trying to go.

Teams typically use the zone when it is windy or when the opposing team does not have strong throwers. Many throwers become rattled when three defenders surround them, and the zone can often cause a turnover. One of the best reasons to play zone is that after a turnover occurs, the other team must scramble to mark up. In those few seconds of chaos, a savvy team can usually move the disc quickly and have a chance for a fast break or quick score.

The basic zone in Ultimate is a 3-2-2, or cup, zone. Teams employ a variety of zones, but the 3-2-2 is the foundation of all of them. The team that masters the 3-2-2 zone will have an easy time learning others.

Positions and Responsibilities

Each person is assigned a certain position in the zone. The positions are cup, wings, and deeps (see figure 7.4). Determining who should play where in a zone is up to each team, but the relative strengths and weaknesses of each player should be considered. The quicker players should be up front, either as members of the cup or as wings. Taller players, or players who have good vertical leaps and the ability to read the disc, should play deep.

Each member of the zone has a number of duties to fulfill, depending on what the offense is trying to do. Other variables include the type of zone being played, the weather, and the skills of the throwers and cutters, so players' responsibilities may change throughout a point or game.

CUP

The cup is made up of three quick players who love to run, because those three will be running the most in a zone. The first two members of the cup are the on-point and off-point. The on-point marks the thrower directly, forcing her toward the off-point, who is at least 10 feet (3 meters) away from the thrower. If the off-point is closer than 10 feet,

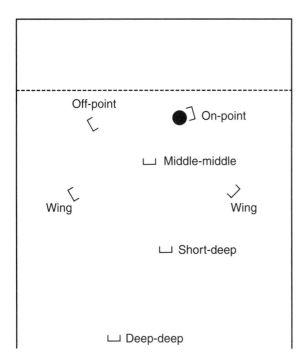

Figure 7.4 Positioning of players in the 3-2-2 zone.

Essential Zone Tip

Players should not become too comfortable playing a certain position in a zone. During practice, players should switch positions so that each player can experience a different set of responsibilities. By practicing in this way, players will see the challenges that their teammates face and perhaps improve communication and strategy.

this is a double-team, which is against the rules. The on-point's main responsibility is to avoid being broken. The off-point must stop a swing pass or a pass to the offensive wing. The third member of the cup is the middle-middle, who is slightly farther downfield, between the other two players in the cup. He tries to prevent the disc from penetrating the middle of the cup.

The players in the cup do not want the disc thrown through it in any manner. The cup has done its job if the offense continually resets the disc or throws it over the cup, where the wings or short-deep have a chance to make a play on it.

WINGS

The wings' highest priority is to guard the sidelines as well as the area beyond the cup toward the centerline of the field. They should have their backs toward the sideline, positioned so that they can see where the disc is and where an incoming cutter may be. Because many offenses rely on the reset reverse strategy to move around a zone, the wings should pay particular attention when the disc is swung to their side of the field. But they should not push upfield toward the swung disc in an attempt to put on a mark. That is the job of the point who is closest to the new thrower.

The wings' job is to prevent the next throw up the line, so they must always be aware of the sneaky defender who wants that long sideline pass. The wing is successful if the disc is swung but no opportunity is available for a pass into his area. If the offense has to turn back to the pivot, or center handler, for a reset and try to attack the other sideline, the wing has fulfilled his responsibility in the zone.

DEEPS

The two deeps in the zone are called the short-deep and the deep-deep. The short-deep is situated in the area a bit downfield from the cup and is responsible for stopping anything over the cup or into the middle of the field. She does not have primary responsibility to stop throws through the cup, although she should be aware of any receiver in her area who might be anticipating such a pass and must communicate with, direct, and reposition the cup defenders in front of her to rebuff such a threat.

If a throw does get through the cup, the short-deep must not try to mark the thrower. She must immediately get back into position, allow the cup to reposition around the new thrower, and listen to instructions from the deep-deep.

The final line of defense in the zone is the deep-deep. He is often the person who has the last chance at a block before a goal is caught. For that reason, he usually should not allow anyone behind him who might be a deep threat, or at least not play too far off of him in case a huck goes up. The deep-deep must constantly assess how close he can play to the back of the zone without getting burned deep. If the wind is directly in the thrower's face, reducing the likelihood of a long throw, the deep-deep can move in quite close. If the conditions are right, he may be able to split the field lengthwise with the short-deep, a setup that sometimes makes the zone much more effective.

If the throw does go up, the deep-deep has a chance to be the hero. As the last defender, he has the opportunity and obligation to prevent a long pass or a score. He must be adept at reading the disc, positioning himself well, and jumping for the disc, if necessary. If he has not pinched in too far, he should be in position to make the downfield block.

Common Commands in Zone Defense

A zone defense has a set of commands that are sometimes different from the ones used in individual coverage. Because communication is a vital part of any team's defensive strategy, it is important for all players to familiarize themselves with some common terms:

▶ **"Drop!"** This means that the zone defender needs to move downfield quickly, away from the disc. Teammates usually yell this to the deeps and wings to stop a fast break.

▶ **"Pinch in!"** This is the opposite of "Drop!" The call means that the defender, usually a wing or deep, should move toward the disc, because there is no offensive threat in his area.

▶ **"No dump!"** This command is intended for the on-point, who should then prevent the thrower from throwing the disc to the dump, that reset receiver who is behind the disc. This command is used when the stall count gets high and the thrower becomes fixated on hitting that reset.

▶ **"Crash!"** This signal lets the cup know that another offensive player is coming into the cup and that the defender should follow her in and perhaps prevent her from getting a pass. Note that a double-team does not occur if two defenders are near the disc and each is covering an opponent. The second defender has to stay 10 feet (3 meters) away only if no other offensive player is in the cup.

▶ **"Trap!"** This command is yelled out when the thrower moves close enough to the sideline that the on-point switches the force from middle to sideline. The off-point covers the resetting dump pass, and the middle-middle stops the short easy sideline pass while also being ready to stop the inside-out flick intended to get it off the line. The near wing moves right along the sideline to stop the arcing pass up the line, and the far wing pinches in to stop any type of crossfield pass.

▶ **"Right!"** and **"Left!"** These calls let the off-point and middle-middle know whether they can slide either right or left to prevent a completed pass. The short-deep may yell this command, but the sideline often has this job.

Variations in Zone Defense

A team that has become adept at playing the 3-2-2 zone may want to explore other options. Having a variety of zone defenses makes it difficult for the other team to anticipate which defense they will be facing. Here are brief descriptions of some other zones:

▶ **1-3-3.** This zone has only one mark, who forces the thrower toward either sideline, depending on which side of the field he is near. (When the thrower is near the middle of the field, the marker determines which way he is going to force by calling, "Home!" or "Away!") The two lines operate like two umbrellas, trying to contain the offense toward the nearer sideline (see figure 7.5).

▶ **Box-and-one.** This zone uses only six players because the other defender is covering a player one-on-one. Teams use the box-and-one when the opponent relies heavily on one player for its offense. The short-deep position is eliminated from this zone. If the strong thrower does get the disc, a four-person cup is used temporarily until the disc is passed on.

The Clam

As mentioned earlier, the clam is a defensive strategy that combines aspects of individual coverage

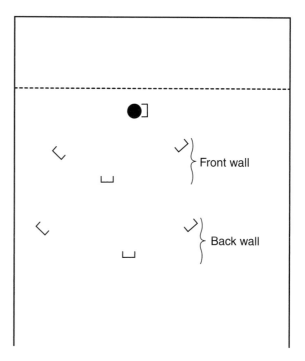

Figure 7.5 1-3-3 zone.

with concepts from the zone. Most teams use the clam sparingly. It is most effective when used as a surprise weapon. If the offense has been able to slice their way through a 3-2-2, the defense may want to come down in a clam on the next point. The offense may think that they are still facing a regular zone and throw the first quick pass away or directly to a defender.

In the clam the three players closest to the disc match up on cutters individually as they run toward the disc. When the cutters leave their areas, the defenders release them to one of their other four teammates, who form a zone behind them (figure 7.6). The clam can look confusing when a team first plays it, which often means that the team is playing it correctly. The purpose of the clam is to create chaos in the area immediately in front of the thrower, but that does not mean that defenders run around randomly. The confusion created by the defense has a definite pattern to it. Each player has a specific position to play as well as important responsibilities.

Positions and Responsibilities

In this defense, the positions are numbered instead of named. These numbers correspond roughly to the names in a regular zone:

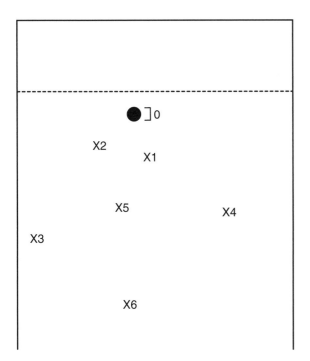

Figure 7.6 The clam. The positions 0, 1, and 2 are constantly switching on and off the mark.

Zone	Clam
Cup	0, 1, 2
Wings	3, 4
Deeps	5, 6

The first three numbers cover the area near the disc, as they would in the cup. The 3 and 4 are on opposite sides of the field and are responsible for passes toward the sidelines. The 5 is a combination of the middle and short-deep, and the 6 is analogous to the deep-deep.

0, 1, AND 2

In the basic clam, the force is always forehand. The force does not change throughout the point, even if a backhand trap seems inviting, because the rest of the team is set up to stop any kind of forehand throw. Occasionally other forces can work well with the clam, but most teams start with the forehand force until they are comfortable with this defense.

Three players are assigned the numbers 0, 1, and 2. None, however, has the specific assignment of playing point in this defense. Another difference is that all these defenders are positioned sideways so that they can see the disc and any incoming cutters. Either 0, 1, or 2 can become the marker, depending on who is closest to the disc. Let's assume that 1 is marking the disc. The responsibility of 0 and 2 is to prevent any cutters who are coming under from getting the disc. They are constantly talking, telling the other whom they are covering, and then releasing the cutter when he leaves their areas. Suppose that the cutter whom 2 is covering manages to get the disc. Because 2 is now the closest defender, she becomes the marker, and 0 and 1 stop the incoming cutters.

In this quickly switching defense, communication is essential. If you look again at figure 7.6, you'll see that the worst place (for the defense) for the disc to go is on the weak side, where 4 is positioned. After the disc is on this side of the field, the clam is broken and a score may easily result. This means that the forehand force absolutely cannot be broken. To ensure this, the first threat that 0, 1, and 2 have to cover is the thrower. Then they need to stop the incoming cutters, and finally they should cover the backfield reset. The players at 0, 1, and 2 must understand this system because the clam can break down if they are confused about who is the most dangerous threat.

3 AND 4

These positions are similar to the wings in the 3-2-2 zone because both 3 and 4 are covering the area from centerfield to their respective sidelines. The responsibility of 3 is to stay out of the way of 0, 1, and 2, yet be close enough to stop a forehand throw to his side of the field or up the sideline. Again, he cannot get pulled in too close to the disc, because the biggest threat to his position is the long forehand throw arcing over him and up the sideline. The 3 also should talk to 0, 1, and 2 because he will be able to identify the most dangerous incoming cutter.

The player at the 4 position has a very difficult job to do, because she is covering the largest area with only marginal help from 6. After the disc is swung to 4's side of the field, 4 should not be tempted to move too close to the disc; that is still the job of 0, 1, and 2. Instead, 4 should be looking for deep threats behind her or hammers in front of her and try to stop those. She should not drop back as far as 6, but she should do her best to stop the disc from advancing deeper into her area.

5 AND 6

The duty of 5 is to stop the long pass up the middle. A common mistake that 5 often makes is playing the position like a short-deep, thinking that he has to hang back and help out 6. Or, sometimes 5 thinks that he should try to help near the front and gets pulled too far forward, thus leaving the middle wide open. Instead, this position is more of a combination of the middle of a cup and the short-deep. This means that 5 should be closer to the disc, behind 0, 1, and 2, and try to sew up the middle so that no disc gets through. He should also be talking constantly to the three players in front of him, identifying incoming cutters.

The player at the 6 position has the weight of the world on her shoulders. She is the last line of defense in the clam. If the clam is working well, her main job is to stop the frustrated forehand huck that often happens when the thrower can't get off anything up close. Because this is the expected huck, 6 can often get the block. If the clam is broken to the break side, however, and 4 is panicking because there is too much space to cover, 6 has a much more difficult job. This defender must instantly identify and cover the most dangerous receiver. If 4 and 6 can shut down the long throw on this side, the front of the clam can reset, the forehand force will be reinstated, and the clam has yet another chance of forcing a turnover.

Defensive Options

So now that you have seen some of the essential defensive formations, how do you decide which one to use and when? Before trotting out any of these defenses during a game, you must fine-tune them during practice. Your team does not need to have strong knowledge of all these defenses; often a team chooses to refine three or four to form their entire defensive arsenal.

Evaluating an Offense

Before deciding which defense to use, you need to analyze the offensive weaknesses and strengths of the other team. Do they all have strong forehands? Do they rely on one or two players to keep their offense moving? Do they have the patience to move the disc through a zone? Do they rely on their long game? After you understand what the other team likes to do, you can decide which defense will be most likely to stymie them.

Your team must also understand that a failure of the defense may be the fault not of the defensive strategy you chose but rather your team's execution of it. For example, if your team chooses to force forehand but the other team manages to work it up the force side to a score, the fault is not with the strategy. The fault lies with the players who keep getting beaten to the force side. They need to improve their defensive positioning, or run harder, or lay out, before you abandon this defense.

Transitional Defense

A team that is confident with a variety of defenses may want to try a combination of defenses, called transitional defense. Rather than sticking with one defense the entire point, the team can switch defenses in the middle of the point. The most common form of transitional defense is switching from zone to individual coverage after a predetermined number of throws (other signals include using a code word to initiate the switch, or a landmark, such as midfield).

If a team has decided to make this switch, defenders must first cover the deep receivers. A defender should then mark the thrower. Finally, defenders should cover the rest of the players at center field. To make this switch happen quickly and effectively, a team must rehearse its transitional defense repeatedly during practice.

The advantage to transitional defense is that it disrupts the offensive rhythm of the other team. The disadvantage is that some teammate may be playing one kind of defense while others are playing something else. A poorly executed transitional defense is clearly vulnerable to a quick offensive strike.

Choosing a Defense

Now that you have evaluated the other team's offense, developed a group of defensive sets, and understand how to switch from one to the other, how do you make the final choice? Table 7.1 gives some options that you may want to consider when confronting certain offenses.

Table 7.1 Choosing an Effective Defense

What the offense is doing	What the defense could do
Throwing only backhands	Force forehand; zone.
Relying on one or two handlers	Zone; box-and-one; force forehand; clam; let a weak thrower get the disc and try to force a turnover.
Scoring long on forehand hucks	Force backhand; force straight up.
Scoring long on backhand hucks	Force forehand; force straight up.
Working it easily through the zone	Switch from zone to one-on-one; play only one-on-one.
Spread offense	Transitional defense, starting in zone or clam.
Calling a time-out to figure out how to beat the defense	Change to another defense.

Summary

Although most players start playing Ultimate because they love to throw and catch the disc, the Ultimate players who distinguish themselves are those who learn to love defense. Playing on a team that makes defense a priority can be more exciting than playing on an offensive juggernaut. A team's offense is expected to score; a team's defense that prevents a score takes the game to another level. From forcing a team to throw 50 passes against a zone to making a huge layout block in the end zone to prevent a goal, defense is what separates the good teams from the great ones.

part II

Your Ultimate Program

8

Ultimate Fitness

Key Terms

absolute speed

acceleration

body-weight exercises

deceleration

dynamic stretching

external weight exercises

frontal plane

functional strength training

manipulative skills

movement portfolio

multiskill development

plyometrics

sagittal plane

speed endurance

static stretching

transverse plane

Many Ultimate players rely on natural ability and mistakenly believe that their bodies will consistently perform well for them as long as they play and practice the sport itself. Players do themselves a disservice if they adopt such an approach to training and performance preparation. Overall athletic formation and successful performance requires attention to all aspects of physical training, not the least of which is proper movement preparation.

Overall Movement Portfolio

A conditioning program should be appropriate for the athletic age (physical maturity) of the players. For younger athletes of middle-school age, early specialization is not as important as multiskill development (or multilateral skill development, that is, training in a variety of activities and sports to promote a broad, more comprehensive range of physical development). As Tudor Bompa asserts in his book *Total Training for Young Champions,* studies have suggested that training young athletes for sport specificity earlier than 14 years of age at the expense of developing overall movement quality is not beneficial to long-term success or devotion to any given sport. Many young athletes who specialize before reaching an appropriate age (age 14 to 16) report high rates of injury and burnout, with either leading to the other. For this reason, practice and training sessions should be fun and include various instruction formats.

Athletes who are more mature—those in high school and beyond—and can train specifically for their sport will find it beneficial to take a comparable approach. This approach is wise, not only to combat injury and burnout but also to develop the explosive movement patterns and unique manipulative skills (e.g., throwing and catching the disc) required by Ultimate. Having variety in training tactics, regardless of age and physical maturity, makes clear sense.

Logically then, while practicing the skills of Ultimate, players should employ various physical training methods and approaches to preparation. We cannot stress enough how important it is that athletes, young and old, build an overall movement portfolio—a more comprehensive approach that allows success in all sorts of activities. This may appear to run counter to the idea that we must emphasize instruction of the skills specific to our unique sport, but it is the logical way of promoting lifelong physical activity and will increase the chances that an athlete will not only choose a sport most akin to her skill set but also devote a career to training more specifically and zealously for that sport (Brown & Ferrigno, 2005).

Several elements are essential to a comprehensive Ultimate conditioning program:

- ▶ Warming up and cooling down
- ▶ Flexibility training
- ▶ Training for speed, agility, and quickness
- ▶ Functional strength training

Warming Up and Cooling Down

Warming up is a critical aspect of proper physical training. If an athlete does not devote appropriate time and attention to preparing the body for strenuous activity, lackluster performance and even injury will result. Jogging around the field to "get the blood pumping" is not enough. Whether a team is preparing for practice, a scrimmage, a day of tournament play, or simply a skills training session, all players should adequately prime themselves for the physical work that lies ahead. Athletes should have broken a sweat following a thorough warm-up. Likewise, the activity should end with a cool-down period to decompress the body's muscles and joints, as well as the mind, from the demands of training or competition.

Key Warm-Up Principles

An effective warm-up should include the following components to prepare for the broad array of movements involved in the transitional sport of Ultimate:

1. Perform low-intensity activities that use major muscle groups, the prime movers (arms, legs, and trunk), for no less than 5, and up to 10, minutes to increase circulation and core body temperature. Athletes should be freely perspiring following the warm-up.

2. Do an assortment of exercises to warm up the muscles, tendons, and ligaments that are engaged in cutting and lateral movement.

3. Gradually add exercises incorporating movements that are more explosive, but of medium intensity.

4. Always follow an adequate warm-up with flexibility training, preferably of a dynamic (active) nature.

Suggested Warm-Up Exercises

The warm-ups that follow incorporate and build on these four key principles.

Players should jog at a slow to moderate pace for 3 to 5 minutes and then perform several of the following activities. Exercises should incorporate forward, backward, lateral, and diagonal movement patterns.

- ▶ Follow-the-leader runs—weaving, zigzags, skips, and so on.
- ▶ High knee walks—using the hands at the top of each movement to grasp and squeeze the knee to the chest while rising up on the toes, for 15 to 20 yards (meters).
- ▶ High heel walks—using the same-side hand to grasp the foot and pull toward the glutes at the top of each movement, rising up on the toes, for 15 to 20 yards (meters).
- ▶ Linear (forward and backward) active movements—regular skips, backward skips, skips for height and distance, backpedals, straight-legged bounds, and walking lunges for 20 to 25 yards (meters).
- ▶ Lateral (sideways) active movements—lateral slides, carioca, crossover steps, and so on for 20 to 25 yards (meters).
- ▶ Low-intensity interval runs—walk 15 yards (meters), jog 15 yards, stride 15 yards, jog 15 yards, and repeat several times.
- ▶ Medium-intensity accelerators covering 40 to 60 yards (meters)—from a jog at 50 percent of sprint capacity, gradually accelerate to 65 to 75 percent, and eventually to 85 percent, of sprint capacity.
- ▶ Medium-intensity linear agilities—high knee drives, high heel kicks, straight-legged bounds, and retro-runs (running in reverse) over a distance of 20 to 25 yards (meters).
- ▶ Straight-legged dead-lift walks—stand on one leg and bend forward at the hips, simultaneously raising the free leg in back to form an upper-case T with the plant leg as the trunk, while the free leg, upper body, and outstretched arms form the cap, dynamically stretching the hamstrings (6 to 8 repetitions on each leg).

▶ Wheelhouse lunges—performed in all directions, like the spokes on a wheel of an old covered wagon (forward, forward diagonal, sideways, backward diagonal, and backward), two complete sets on each leg (figure 8.1, *a-b*).

Sample Tag Game

Monarch is a dodging tag game that works on teamwork skills, passing, moving without the disc, and pivoting when in possession of the disc. Use an end zone or a smaller space as the boundaries for this game. If the space is too big, the game will not be as challenging. One player, the Monarch, begins with a soft disc (the Fun Gripper Flyer from www.usgames.com is our favorite). When the game starts, the Monarch can run after anyone and tag or hit him with her disc. Once the Monarch has a partner (that player just tagged or hit), whichever one of them is holding the disc cannot run. Only those tagged player(s) without the disc can run, trying to get in position to receive a pass close to would-be victims. From the original "it"—the Monarch—the number of players who are tagged or hit increases, until the last player is tagged. This last player "captured" becomes the "it" who will start the next round.

▶ Backward and forward lunges with trunk twist, four times on each leg.

▶ Scramble-ups—from all fours, lying prone (face down), and lying supine (face up) positions, two repetitions each for 5 to 10 yards (meters) (figure 8.2, *a-b*).

▶ Medicine ball throws with partner—chest push passes, two-handed overhead, side-to-side, and underhanded high throws to develop core strength and stability (2 to 3 kg ball recommended).

▶ Light games such as Monarch (see sidebar) or other tag games to raise kinesthetic awareness and provide a fun, refreshing break from the routine.

Cooling Down

A proper cool-down is as essential as the warm-up. Ending a physically demanding session abruptly, without taking proper care to slow down the body to a relaxed and restorative condition, is harmful for several reasons. Athletes should allow the body and mind to recover from the significant exertion just experienced, reduce lactic acid pooling and the natural shortening of muscles and tendons that occurs following vigorous work, and gradually calm the body and neuromuscular system to enter a period of relaxation, regeneration, and adaptation between training or competitive sessions.

Figure 8.1 *(a)* Forward lunge; *(b)* forward diagonal lunge.

Figure 8.2 Scramble-ups: *(a)* starting position; *(b)* sprinting through the finish line.

Cooling down can be less exhaustive then warming up, because the goal is simply to engage the muscles just used in the activity or competition at a lower intensity. A light jog, a follow-the-leader run, low-intensity agilities or accelerators, or even a light tag game for 3 to 5 minutes is an effective way to decompress the tissues from the strenuous activity and add a fun component to closing a practice session. Keep in mind that the intent is to calm the same tissues that were stimulated in the warm-up phase. This is why some conditioning specialists refer to the process as a warm-down.

Athletes should take advantage of the opportunity to lengthen soft tissues while in a warm and relaxed state by finishing with a thorough stretch routine. The most beneficial approach is to follow the active segment of the cool-down with static stretching, as discussed in the following section. Adequate hydration and sound nutrition habits should always follow hard work to aid the body in its process of recovery and help build stronger tissues.

Flexibility Training

The most effective method of preparing for an intense activity is to use movements similar to those that will be demanded during live action. For this reason, both the warm-up and the flexibility exercises that precede practice, training, or competition should mimic movement patterns required in the sport. Two approaches are recommended for developing flexibility in athletes—dynamic (or active) stretching and static stretching.

Stretch routines are meant not only to lengthen muscles and tendons to increase range of motion in a joint but also to ready those tissues for the vigorous activities ahead. Dynamic stretching is more effective for preperformance, to prepare the body for explosive effort, whereas static stretching routines are most useful after a practice or competition to restore the muscle to its preevent length, calm the nervous system, and reduce muscle soreness.

Dynamic Stretching

Dynamic stretching involves moving the joints through an ever-increasing range in an active manner that prepares the muscles and tendons for explosive concentric (shortening of the muscle belly) and eccentric (lengthening of the muscle belly) contractions. The best way to describe these two types of muscle actions is to think of concentric contractions as those involved in force production, like pushing off with the foot when accelerating. Eccentric contractions, on the other hand, lead to force reduction. For example, this action occurs when a player rapidly decelerates to set a mark or in preparation to cut. Clearly, both muscle actions occur constantly and repeatedly, which is why a dynamic warm-up and dynamic stretching are more conducive to the demands of transition sports. Besides, because this type of stretching is active in nature, it is fun for children as well as adults!

Moving the body in multiplanar (sagittal, frontal, and transverse; see figure 8.3) patterns at various levels (high, medium, and low) and with increasing intensity more closely simulates the specific movements of the upcoming work. Begin at the feet and progress upward through the body's kinetic chain. We present suggestions from which to develop a progression in three groupings: flexibility exercises for the lower extremities, trunk, and upper extremities. In addition, sample movements are shown in figures 8.4 through 8.8.

Lower Extremities

▶ Ankle circles—standing on one foot with the toe of the other foot pointing at the ground, make circles in both directions for counts of 10 seconds each.

▶ Calf push starts—in push-up position, push forward off each foot, rocking forward and then back, repeating in both knee-bent and knee-straight position.

▶ Heel-raise circles and figure eights—rise up on the toes and imagine drawing circles and figure eights with the heels, trying not to let the heels touch the ground at any time during the movements.

▶ Toe walks and heel walks—forward, backward, side to side, and diagonally.

▶ Knee circles—clockwise and counterclockwise, with knees bent and hands on thighs.

▶ Leg swings forward and back—with a partner or holding a pole and so on (figure 8.4).

▶ Leg swings side to side—with a partner, one at a time, or holding a pole and so on (figure 8.5).

Trunk

▶ Hip circles—both directions, with knees straight to isolate hip muscle complex (figure 8.6).

▶ Lateral trunk flexion and extension—leaning first to the right, then to the left, for several repetitions (figure 8.7).

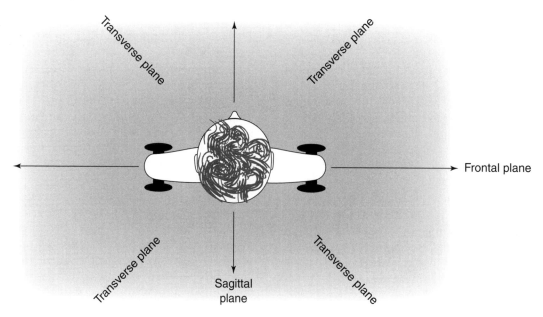

Figure 8.3 Planes of movement. The vast majority of movement—all that lies in between sagittal and frontal plane movement—is transverse planar movement. This is the least trained and where the most can be gained.

Figure 8.4   Partner leg swings, forward and backward.

Figure 8.5   Partner leg swings, side to side, one partner at a time.

▶ Trunk circles—bending from the hips to the right and making a complete circle, moving down toward the waist and then upward on the left side to the starting position (figure 8.8, *a-b*).

▶ Trunk rotation—with feet parallel and then with staggered stance, arms bent, with upper arms held parallel to the ground at chest level, twisting the upper body from side to side.

Figure 8.6 Hip circles

Figure 8.7 Lateral trunk flexion.

Figure 8.8 Trunk circles.

Upper Extremities

- ▶ Arm circles—both forward and backward, from small to large.
- ▶ Arm crossover—hugging yourself, progressing to arm swings toward the opposite side of the body, then to pats on the back of the opposite-side shoulders.
- ▶ Wrist shake—with loose wrists and floppy hands, shaking both wrists and hands vigorously.
- ▶ Wrist circles and figure eights.
- ▶ Neck flexion (tilting forward) and extension (tilting backward), lateral flexion and extension (tilting side to side).

To gain the most benefit from the active warm-up, follow a dynamic flexibility progression with an activity like a skill-building drill or conditioning exercise rather than a discussion. At this point the athlete's body and mind should be well prepared for vigorous, focused work.

Remember to close the training session, practice session, or day of tournament play with an appropriate cool-down, followed by static stretching.

Static Stretching

Follow the cool-down with a static stretch routine, taking care to address all major muscle groups. In this technique the athlete maintains a gentle stretch, at less than maximum exertion, for 45 to 60 seconds, repeating with each muscle group. Holding a stretch for 12 to 15 seconds may be beneficial to the muscle belly but has little effect on the tendons largely responsible for range of motion and flexibility. About 30 seconds must pass for a stretch to progress from the muscle belly to the tendon. Thus, static stretching of 45, but not more than 60, seconds (and repeating) not only relaxes the muscle belly but also allows the tendons to lengthen, which is vital to increasing dynamic mobility (Foran, 2001).

Training for Speed, Agility, and Quickness

Like many court and field sports, Ultimate is a game of transitions that requires explosive movements. Players strive to run fast, accelerate and decelerate rapidly, and change direction quickly, all with great frequency and intensity. The development of these skills is essential to boosting on-field performance. For more information, refer to *Training for Speed, Agility, and Quickness* by Brown and Ferrigno.

Speed

Children become faster runners by running, and a natural progression occurs as they grow and gain strength. But focused work can significantly enhance this process for athletes of any age. Athletes can improve their speed, first, by emphasizing good running form. To become a faster runner, a person must become a more fluid runner. For young athletes who are passing through an awkward stage of growth—with lengthening limbs not matched by increases in coordination and strength—concentrating on proper form will help develop movement patterns that will elevate performance later in the maturation process. In the same manner, the more athletically mature player will realize increases in speed by focusing on proper technique to develop fluid running form.

There are two types of speed: acceleration and absolute speed, and speed endurance. Acceleration and absolute speed refer to how rapidly a athlete gets up to his greatest pace, whereas speed endurance is the ability to run fast and do it repeatedly. In Ultimate, seldom does the athlete play at 100 percent of sprint capacity or absolute speed. More often, the ability to accelerate (and decelerate) quickly and repeatedly defines physical success. Clearly, both accelerative speed and speed endurance have application in Ultimate. The following examples of exercises focus on each. Also see figures 8.9 through 8.13.

Acceleration and Absolute Speed

- ▶ Arm action drills—standing or sitting, block arms by bending 90 degrees at each elbow, pump arms back and forth, terminating in front with one hand at chin level and the other in back, just past the hip (figure 8.9, *a-b*).
- ▶ Running on balance—balancing on one leg, posing in absolute top-end speed position, stepping and repeating on the other leg (figure 8.10).
- ▶ Falling starts—alone and with a partner (figure 8.11, *a-b*).
- ▶ Straight-legged shuffles—running on toes with the legs straight, keeping ground contact at a minimum.

- Scramble-ups on a stimulus for 5 to 10 yards (meters)—forces position of acceleration (as shown in figure 8.2, but more explosively).

- Flying starts—striding out, speed up to a cone, and then kick into a top-end sprint for various distances.

- Accelerators—run 40 to 70 yards (36-64 meters), beginning at 70 percent of sprint capacity, gradually increasing to 85 percent, and then run at up to 100 percent of capacity for final third of the distance.

- Sprint loading—inclines, stadium stairs, weighted sleds, or partner resistance (figure 8.12 a-b).

- Assisted running—declines on a surface with no more than a 2 to 3 percent grade (crown of football field to sideline is a grade of about 1 percent) and partner towing.

- Contrast training—resisted sprint followed by release or assisted sprinting.

- Stop-start sprints—on coach's whistle or with cones placed at intervals of 5 or 10 yards (meters), sprint from and stopping at each cone.

- Skipping for distance and height.

- Bounding—exaggerated running, elongating stride and forcefully bouncing like a running antelope (figure 8.13, a-b).

Speed Endurance Exercises

Perform distances common in the game, between 10 and 70 yards (9 to 64 meters).

- Interval runs—stride and then sprint, repeating for a predetermined time or number of repetitions.

- Team relays—several repetitions at various distances, with small teams (two to four members) to increase endurance demand.

- Pickup sprints—changing gears from cone to cone, say from jog to stride to sprint to jog, and repeating for number of reps or length of time (6 to 12 minutes, depending on conditioning level).

- Skill drills that incorporate functional endurance components to keep athletes moving with little or no down time between individual touches on the disc.

Figure 8.9 Arm action drills. Also try in sitting position on the ground to isolate arm action.

Figure 8.10 Running on balance, hold each position for count of 2 or more, concentrating on balance and form, then cycle to the other leg.

▶ Track workouts—Many college and elite teams work out on a track, running repeat 200s, 400s, and 800s to push back the anaerobic threshold (e.g., running a series of three 400s, each in under 80 seconds, resting 90 seconds after each rep, then resting 3 minutes, and then doing another set of three 400s). After the conditioning level has been raised, the time allowed for each repetition or the recovery time between repetitions can be reduced. Focus on maintaining good form.

Agility

In Brown and Ferrigno's *Training for Speed, Agility, and Quickness,* the editors describe agility as an athlete's "ability to decelerate, accelerate, and change direction quickly while maintaining good body control and without decreasing speed." An athlete should be able to move well in all planes of movement and switch readily from one to another. The planes of movement are *(a)* the sagittal plane—movement forward and backward, *(b)* the frontal plane—lateral movement, and *(c)* the transverse plane—all diagonal movement between the others, comprising the majority of the 360 degrees of direction in which a person can maneuver. If you picture standing in the center of a plus sign, the intersecting lines represent the sagittal and frontal

Figure 8.11 Falling starts, alone.

Figure 8.12 Partner resistance. Catch partner and provide resistance for several strides, then release (contrast training).

Figure 8.13 Bounding; also called bionic running.

planes, while all the space between represents the transverse plane (see figure 8.3 on page 130). Transverse planar movement is the area of sports training in which the athlete can realize the greatest gains: No transverse plane, no great gain! Balance is also a key in sport-specific movements, and agility training is additionally effective in boosting dynamic balance.

To enhance the development of agility, employ various motor movements (skips, slides, carioca, and so forth), allow recovery between repetitions, and do the following activities:

▶ Crossover skip—skipping with one leg crossing over and in front of the other.

▶ Backward skips and then transition into another movement—slides, carioca, short directional sprint, and so on.

▶ Twenty-yard (18-meter) shuttle using assorted motor movements—carioca, slides, backpedal, on all fours, and so on (see Twenty-Yard Shuttle drill below).

▶ T drill—see page 138.

▶ Agility box drills—see pages 138-139.

▶ Full, half, and quarter squirms—refer to drill on page 102.

▶ Rope jumping—both legs, single leg, and alternating legs.

▶ Single and double-leg pattern jumps—see page 139.

▶ Zigzag sprints—in zigzag fashion, change direction explosively every 5 or 10 yards (meters).

Twenty-Yard Shuttle

PURPOSE

Improves starting and stopping, short area quickness, and change-of-direction ability.

EQUIPMENT

6 cones

SETUP

Place 3 cones 5 yards apart in each of two parallel lines, as shown in figure 8.14.

PROCEDURE

Start by straddling the middle line, with the other two lines 5 yards to the right and to the left. On "Up" call, make a quarter turn and sprint 5 yards to the right line, plant the right foot on the line and cut back (left) in the other direction. Sprint past the middle to the left line, plant the left foot, and cut back (right), sprinting *through* the finish at the middle line. On next repetition, begin by sprinting to the left, then to the right. Be sure to face the original (starting) direction when planting to cut in order to train both sides equally.

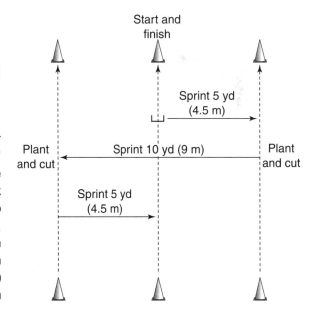

Figure 8.14 Twenty-yard shuttle.

VARIATIONS

▶ Try racing a teammate, facing each other at start to practice the mirroring skill needed in defending.

▶ Challenge athletes by having them perform other motor movements, such as sideways shuffles or carioca, or by having them start in sitting or lying positions.

T Drill

PURPOSE

This drill develops short area quickness, acceleration, and deceleration, focusing on straight ahead and backward (sagittal) and lateral (frontal) movement skills, which are helpful on the mark and in maintaining defensive positioning.

EQUIPMENT

4 cones

SETUP

Place the 4 cones to form a T shape, with the bottom being 10 yards long, while the top of the T is 10 yards wide (see figure 8.15).

PROCEDURE

Begin at the bottom of the T. Sprint 10 yards to the middle cone. Side shuffle 5 yards to the right cone and touch it. Side shuffle left 10 yards past the middle cone to the left cone and touch it. Side shuffle right to the middle cone, plant the right foot, and transition into a backpedal to the starting cone. On next repetition, shuffle left 5 yards, then back right for 10 yards, and 5 yards back to center cone (alternate each repetition) before backpedaling to start.

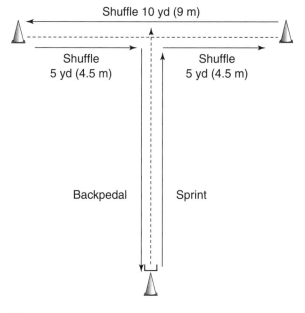

Figure 8.15 T drill.

EMPHASIS

▶ Athlete should stay low and balanced, focusing on quick and shorter foot strikes as she decelerates to change direction.

▶ Keep the weight over the feet, in a springs-loaded position, when backpedaling.

VARIATIONS

▶ Vary the dimensions of the T.

▶ Have athletes perform different motor skills, such as carioca, instead of shuffling across the top of the T.

▶ Alter the shape of the drill (e.g., A, Z, N, or W shapes) to change or increase the rotational demand when the athlete is changing direction.

Agility Box Drill

PURPOSE

This drill improves agility, change of direction, footwork, and short area quickness.

EQUIPMENT

4 cones

SETUP

Place the 4 cones in a square with sides 5 to 10 yards (meters) long (see figure 8.16).

PROCEDURE

Start at front right cone. Sprint to back right cone, plant right foot, and cut left and sprint to back left cone. Plant left foot and turn 90 degrees to the right, transitioning into a backpedal to front left cone. At the front left cone, decelerate and plant left foot, turning another 90 degrees, this time to the right, and sprint to the starting (front right) cone. On the next repetition, start at the front left cone and reverse the sequence. Alternate on each repetition.

EMPHASIS

▶ Stay low and balanced, focusing on quick acceleration and *even quicker* deceleration.

▶ Springs-loaded positioning allows for quicker transitions out of each chance of direction.

VARIATION

▶ Vary the dimensions of the box.

▶ Vary the movement skills asked of the athletes.

▶ Alter the shape of the drill, demanding more diagonal (transverse plane) movements and changes of direction.

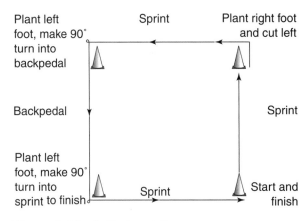

Figure 8.16　Agility box drill.

Pattern Jump Drills

PURPOSE

Improves agility, quickness, and strength in the ankles, knees, and hips.

EQUIPMENT

6 cones

SETUP

Using the 6 cones, form a hexagon with each side approximately 2 feet long (see figure 8.17).

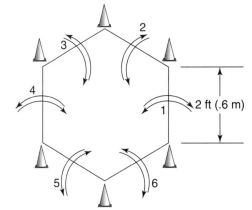

Figure 8.17　Pattern jump drills.

PROCEDURE

Start in the middle, facing the same direction throughout the drill. Jump out to the right and immediately back inside the hexagon. Jump diagonally forward outside the hexagon and back inside. Continue this pattern in a counterclockwise direction until athlete has jumped each side of the hexagon. Finish inside the hexagon. On next repetition, do the same sequence, but in a clockwise direction.

EMPHASIS

▶ Keep the legs close together, shoulder width or narrower throughout the drill.

▶ Try to minimize time spent on the ground.

(continued)

▸ The cue to listen for is "soft and spongy" landings, rather than "loud and slappy."

▸ For most athletes, the backward diagonal jumps (transverse plane) tend to be most challenging. Note why these may be tougher. What feels different?

▸ Focus on the quality of these repetitions.

VARIATIONS

▸ Vary the shape of the drill (e.g., box, plus sign, or X shape) and the patterns asked of the athlete.

▸ Raise the height of the sides of the hexagon, using small plastic hurdles (or other objects).

▸ Follow the final landing with a short sprint.

▸ See how many foot strikes (using the plus sign or an X drawn with chalk on the cement) the athlete can complete in 30 seconds.

▸ Do the same drills bounding from one foot to the other and back inside the hexagon.

▸ When strong enough, try hopping (take off and landing on the same foot) the entire drill; then do same on other foot.

Quickness

Like a car in a drag race, an athlete must start explosively, but quickness is more than that. The successful Ultimate athlete must also be able to stop abruptly, rapidly change direction, and explosively accelerate again. These actions are critical to overall performance. One of the greatest measures of success in a transition sport like Ultimate is the ability to perform explosive sport movements with great rapidity and without losing that explosiveness during any point in a game. The player who can initiate and react to movement in a shorter time interval will outperform her opponent, given equal technical ability in skills such as throwing and catching. After a player learns a skill, the pattern for repeating it is in place. The next step is to decrease the time that it takes to complete the same skill. Using repetition and striving for quickness will result in rapidity with control.

Begin quickness training by emphasizing deceleration and change of direction to accompany the development of explosive starts. The athlete who is able to stop the quickest will win most battles on the Ultimate field. This is because deceleration training also develops eccentric strength and the ability to use that stored energy to perform an explosive (concentric) movement. Plyometric exercises are effective here. This type of exercise trains the neuromuscular system to lessen the elapsed time between the stretching (lengthening

of muscle under tension, storing of energy, and force reduction) and shortening (shortening of muscle, use of stored energy, and force production) cycles of muscle contractions. Quickness and explosion result from training the body to reduce this stretching–shortening cycle.

The following drills can help develop quickness. The list progresses from simple to complex, and from medium to high intensity. During a plyometric training session, always rest at least 2 minutes to allow complete recovery before the next set. For more ideas and suggestions on how to use plyometric training effectively, see *High-Powered Plyometrics* (Radcliffe & Farentinos, 1999).

▸ Scramble-ups—from a variety of positions and over 5- to 10-yard (-meter) distances (refer again to figure 8.2).

▸ Lateral skates—8 to 10 repetitions on each leg per set, bounding sideways, from the right to the left leg, spending as little time on the ground as possible (figure 8.18).

▸ Rope skipping—incorporate different patterns to enhance results.

▸ Ankle jumps—bending the knee as little as possible, jump in place, traveling back and forth, side to side, or in diagonal patterns, 8 to 10 jumps per set.

▸ Rocket jumps—6 to 8 jumps per set (figure 8.19).

Figure 8.18 Lateral skates help develop lateral quickness and ankle stability.

Figure 8.19 Rocket jumps increase vertical explosion.

▶ Star jumps—jump up while spreading the arms and legs out and bring them back together at landing, 6 to 8 jumps per set.

▶ Split jumps—from stride split position, jump up and cycle the legs through to land with the legs in the opposite stride position, 8 to 12 total jumps per set (4 to 6 in each position).

▶ Long jumps—3 successive jumps, attempting to cover as much ground as possible, with rest before the next set of 3.

▶ Backward-forward-forward—4 repetitions per set. Jump backward, and on landing jump immediately forward, then forward again, covering as much ground as possible during this repetition and immediately following it with 3 more reps (figure 8.20).

▶ Zigzag jumps and bounds—attempting to cover as much ground as possible, take off and land with both feet (jumping) in a zigzag pattern for 8 to 10 jumps and then try the same number of jumps in reverse back to the start; next try alternate legs, bounding from right leg to left leg for 8 to 10 bounds and retracing bounds back to start.

▶ Zigzag hops—same as previous but one complete set out and back on the right leg and then one set out and back on the left leg.

▶ Depth jumps—drop from a box or bleacher 12 to 18 inches (30 to 45 centimeters) high and absorb the landing. This is 1 rep. Do 2 sets, with 6 to 8 reps per sets. This exercise is excellent for developing eccentric (deceleration) strength. After training for a period of 2 to 4 weeks, try jumping as high as possible immediately after the landing for the same number of reps and sets. Warning: These demanding jumps require prior strength and plyometric training.

▶ Plyometric exercises followed immediately by a sprint.

Figure 8.20 Backward-forward-forward jumps.

Functional Strength Training

Ultimate, of course, requires strength. Although spending a tremendous amount of time in the weight room to develop brute static strength is not necessary, it is beneficial to build a solid foundation centered on functional strength. This foundation not only provides protection for the body's muscles and joints but also augments the development of explosive power, particularly if athletes are also employing plyometrics properly in their training. Clearly, increased strength bolsters potential gains in agility and quickness. Also enhanced are sport-specific performance aspects, such as jumping and the lunging positions needed to throw or mark effectively. Given the often grueling length of tournaments, games, and even individual points, players should possess strength endurance.

While some of the more elite Ultimate players devote training time to lifting external weights, particularly in their off-season, the following body-weight exercises will do wonders for building the appropriate strength and endurance. Refer to the appendix for other resources that provide strength training ideas.

- Squats—regular and staggered stance (figure 8.21).
- Lunges—regular, diagonal, lateral, and reverse positions (called wheelhouse lunges earlier in this chapter).
- Squat thrusts—squat, place the hands on the ground, kick the legs out to assume a push-up position, do one push-up, explosively spring the legs back under the body, and finish by jumping as high as possible. This is 1 repetition. Do 8 to 12 reps per set. Have fun varying these exercises.
- Hip thrusts—propped with hands on bench or bleacher in a reverse push-up position, allow hips to sink and then thrust hips as high as possible. Repeat for 12 to 15 reps (figure 8.22).

- Push-ups—regular version, with staggered hands, with hands extended beyond head. Builds stability and specific strength to protect shoulders when body is extended on landing from a dive (figure 8.23).
- Crunches—regular (trunk moving toward legs) and reverse (knees moving toward trunk) (figure 8.24).
- Planks—regular and side positions (back straight in push-up position, but propped on elbows). Hold for 30 to 60 seconds per set (figure 8.25).
- Table tops—hold reverse push-up position (face up and propped on the hands with the heels digging into the ground) for 30 to 60 seconds or alternate lifting one leg at a time as high as possible (figure 8.26).
- Side-lying double-leg lifts—alone or with a partner (figure 8.27).
- Trunk hyperextension—lying face down with upper body extending off the end of a bench or bleacher, partner holding legs, lower and then raise the trunk as high as possible. Do 10 to 15 repetitions per set (figure 8.28).
- Reverse hyperextension—lying face down on and grasping a bench or bleacher, with legs extending off the end, lower legs and then raise them as high as possible. Do 10 to 15 repetitions per set (figure 8.29).

Figure 8.21 Body-weight squats, *(a)* regular and *(b)* staggered stance.

Figure 8.22 Hip thrust starting position. This exercise builds hamstring and gluteal strength.

Figure 8.23 Push-ups with (a) staggered hands and (b) one leg raised for added stability and core demand.

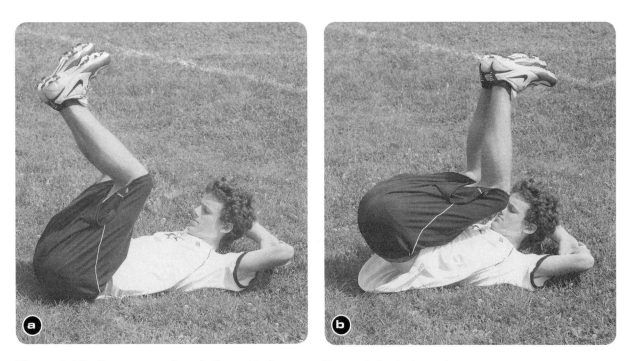

Figure 8.24 Reverse crunches challenge hip flexors and lower abdominal muscles.

Figure 8.25 Planking in *(a)* regular and *(b)* side position helps develop core strength and stability.

Figure 8.26 Table top, lifting one leg at a time as high as possible to strengthen hip extendors—the hamstrings and gluteal muscles.

Figure 8.27 Side-lying leg lift strengthens abductor and adductor muscles, important in lateral movement.

Figure 8.28 Trunk hyperextensions strengthen both hip and back extendors.

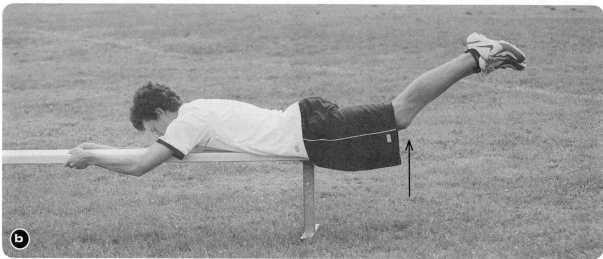

Figure 8.29 Reverse hyperextensions strengthen hip extendor musculature.

We highly recommend acquiring a bouncy medicine ball weighing no more than 2 or 3 kilograms (4.4 or 6.6 pounds) to help develop core strength and total body power. Rotational throws and movement drills are tremendously effective in building explosive dynamic motion and the ability to change direction quickly. Medicine ball work can be done throughout the season. Performing medicine ball routines one or two times per week will greatly enhance rotational strength and explosive transitional movements.

A team that practices four times per week should perform functional strength training on at least two of those days. In the competitive stretch of the season, strength training should occur once per week. Speed, agility, and quickness training should be part of the plan throughout the season. Establish a rotation, focusing on one of these three areas of performance at each practice session.

Summary

A comprehensive approach to fitness training promotes the overall development of the athlete. Setting fitness goals and objectives helps teams and individual athletes map out plans for the season and take advantage of the cumulative effect of proper training. A program that strives to train all aspects of athletic development—speed, agility, and quickness; flexibility; and functional strength—all coupled with proper warm-up and cool-down—will serve the Ultimate player and team well. A comprehensive, well-planned program will enhance the quality of performance, reduce the threat of injury, and enrich lifelong attitudes and approaches to fitness of all sorts.

9

Psychological Preparation for Competitive Performance

A team must look at mental preparation for Ultimate in the same way that it looks at physical readiness. Mental toughness is just as important as skill, strategy, and conditioning, and as the apex of the season approaches, it becomes the most important factor to success. The better-prepared team on the field will not be the one with the most complex offensive strategy, but the one that knows how to execute its plan with calm and focus.

This chapter will introduce some of the basics of sport psychology as it applies to Ultimate. Most of this information is from lectures and books by Dr. Alan Goldberg of Amherst, Massachusetts, a sport psychologist who wrote *Playing Out of Your Mind* and *Sports Slump Busting.* He has been integral to the success of the Amherst boys' varsity team and has worked closely with professional athletes from across the country. Any coach, player, or team that is serious about achieving competitive success should explore the world of mental preparation.

Mental preparation for practice is decidedly different from mental preparation for games. We will first look at how the athlete should mentally approach practice each day, from beginning to end. From arriving on time, ready to play, to working at maximum effort in every physical challenge, practicing well is the foundation for playing well. Practice is a dress rehearsal for a performance, which is, of course, the game.

An Ultimate game requires all that a theatrical performance does. When something goes wrong on stage, actors support each other and continue. If someone forgets her lines, another cast member comes to the actor's aid. If the production is falling apart, people step up to prevent a complete disaster.

Think about competitive debacles on the Ultimate field. Although team members may point to a single error as "the reason we lost," chances are that players were making mistakes much earlier in the game. This chapter will explain how to recognize and avoid disasters before they do lasting damage, as well as how to make the competition more enjoyable for all.

Practice

Why do teams practice? Think about it. Why does a player go to practice each day? For some athletes, practice and drills are a bore, and games and tournaments are the only reason they play. Some players go to practice to socialize with their teammates, do some individual conditioning, or find out when the next tournament is. And a few players go to practice just to complain about practice.

A team that practices hard will play well in games. Everyone knows this, yet few teams do it. One of the cliches in sport is that an athlete needs to have a "really big game" to succeed in that game. This idea is a myth. An athlete needs to have a "really big practice" to succeed in a game. And to have that big practice, that athlete has to figure out why he is there in the first place.

A Big Enough Why

Before athletes step out onto a field, they need to have a group discussion about why they are part of the team. Each player needs to articulate why she wants to commit the next few months to building the strongest team possible. Players do not need to have the same reason, but they do need to listen to each other. Teams can avoid many conflicts later in the season if each person honestly describes his level of commitment in the beginning. Look at a sample team conversation on this topic:

> Player 1: "I am on this team because I want us to make regionals this year for the first time. I am tired of being eliminated at sectionals. I've been training all winter."
>
> Player 2: "I want to work out three times a week, and chasing a Frisbee is the best way for me to do that. I hate drills."
>
> Player 3: "I quit track last year because I am *sick* of competition. I just want to have fun with my friends."

This team is clearly in trouble, and they haven't even stepped on the field! All these reasons for playing are valid, but that doesn't mean that these players can easily form a cohesive team. This team needs to work out some kind of group compromise, and here is where an experienced leader steps in. Several compromises are possible, such as holding tryouts, forming an A team and a B team, or starting an intramural league. Each group of individuals should do their best to meet the needs of all team members, although this is not always realistic or possible.

A player who wants to enjoy the experience of being part of a competitive team needs to figure out what her Big Enough Why is. Whether the player seeks advanced competition, a commitment to conditioning, or an alternative to other sports, a Big Enough Why is essential. The player who has it will cut no corners at practice, both figuratively and

When a team is firing on all cylinders, great things are possible.

literally, and will do her best to arrive on time and stay until the end of every session. She will show up at practice each day, ready to work her hardest. The Big Enough Why is her motivation for traveling on the weekends, for contributing to the team the best way that she can, and for making all the choices that she has to make, on and off the field, to help her team reach its competitive goals.

Practice will be a drag for the player who doesn't have a Big Enough Why. The player who constantly wishes that he were somewhere else other than practice will suffer the entire season. And if he isn't enjoying most aspects of being on an Ultimate team, why play?

Get Comfortable Being Uncomfortable

The coach's job is to push players out of their comfort zones. Because this means different things for each player, the coach must use various motivational techniques. Some players have no problem being yelled at; others want to meet off the field privately. Whatever the style, the coach must motivate players to play outside their comfort zones, and that starts in practice.

NO COMPLAINING

No team should allow anyone to complain—ever. Players must not verbalize their negative opinions about the weather, fatigue, field conditions, anything! Complaining is the surest way to deflate a team and ruin a practice. If someone starts complaining, another player will probably agree, although perhaps silently. The next thing you know, the whiners on the team have wasted two or three hours of everyone's time! Players must keep their misery to themselves while they are at practice. They can save it for later, if they must, but we suspect that if players put all their energy into the task at hand, complaining will soon fade into the background, where it belongs.

STRUCTURE DIFFICULT PRACTICES

Practices should be harder than games. A practice should be composed of a number of focused drills and structured scrimmaging, with plenty of sprinting. Down time should be virtually nonexistent, although the schedule should certainly include breaks for instruction and water.

Everyone needs to approach drills with energy and enthusiasm. Drills must have a clear purpose, and the coach or captain may need to make a connection for the rest of the team by saying something like, "Yesterday we had difficulty getting the disc off the sideline because few people were breaking the mark. This drill will help you learn to break the mark, and then we expect everyone to attempt this skill during the scrimmage."

If the team approaches any drill lackadaisically, stop the drill. Going through the motions does not build skills or team strength; all it does is teach the team how to go through the motions in a competition. Stop the drill and do something else. Sprints or push-ups usually help a team regain its focus. If these interventions do not work, do a different drill. Make sure to vary the drills each day, even if you are working on the same skill.

Everyone wants to scrimmage because playing Ultimate is more fun than drilling for Ultimate. But in practice, scrimmaging should not turn into a pickup game, in which players just throw it long to their buddies and no one plays D. Whatever the team learned during the first half of practice should be incorporated into the scrimmaging. If you want to work on zone offense, play a game to 3 in which players use nothing but zone. For some of the scrimmages, making mistakes must have consequences. For each drop or egregious throwaway, the penalty could take the form of extra sprints. It is fine if, at the end of practice, the players still want to play more. A hungry team at practice translates into a rabid team at game time.

Essential Mental Toughness Tip

If a team is having difficulty with a drill, various interventions may improve it. If that doesn't work, the team can revisit the drill later in practice or the next day. Chances are that the drill will be much better later because players will want to prove to themselves and their teammates that they can do it. Teams that learn to rebound from failure in practice are more likely to be able to do the same in tournaments.

MAKE MISTAKES

A smart team leader will not allow players to become comfortable in the roles that they usually play. A team should try new stuff in practice, not in a game. Someone who always handles should cut deep for an entire scrimmage. The team could play a game to 3 in which each player is allowed to catch with only one hand. Reduce the stall count to 5. Or play a game to 3 where one team is already ahead 2-1. When players try something new, even if it doesn't work, the team may benefit in the long run.

When players are in unfamiliar roles, they will make mistakes. They *should* make mistakes, because that's the only way they will improve. Let's say that a tall player is accustomed to playing a deep position in a zone. For this practice, she plays in the cup the entire time. Perhaps a shorter player breaks her at will, and she is unable to stop the thrower on the mark. She must keep trying—by getting lower, by running faster. Although she may not play this position in a game, the experience in practice will at least help her appreciate what her teammates have to do.

Practice Focusing

Teams often yell, "Focus!" during a tight game. What exactly does that mean? Everyone can interpret this command differently. The word is far too general to be an effective command. But working on the techniques of focusing during a practice makes sense. If players throw an inside-out forehand for 5 minutes, they should be able to allot 2 minutes to some mental focusing. Working on a physical skill is important, but developing the ability to focus mentally will save a player later, when his execution starts to falter.

There are many ways to practice focusing. All of them can work if they include deep breathing and a concentrated effort to relax the mind.

The purpose of the following exercise is twofold. First, players learn to breathe deeply and slowly, which will calm them down and prepare them for practice or a game. The second benefit is that players learn how to bring the mind back if it drifts away, an ability that all good athletes need to develop.

After the stretching portion of the warm-up, lead the team through this exercise. Ask each player to get comfortable. Some will sit, and some will lie down. Some may focus on a piece of grass. Others may close their eyes. Anything is fine as long as they are out of eye contact with each other.

Step 1: Begin with some deep-breathing exercises. Remind the players to expel all the air. Speak and count slowly. Have them breathe in and hold their breath.

Step 2: Ask them to think of the number 1. They should focus on the number 1 as they exhale.

Step 3: As they breathe in, something may intrude on their thoughts. They may start worrying about lying in the rain, or about finishing their schoolwork, or about what they will have for dinner. They are no longer thinking of the number 1. So, the next time they breathe out, they should focus on the number 2.

Step 4: They are now on their own. They should continue this drill for about 2 minutes. Every time they drift away and think about something else, they increase the number that they are concentrating on. At the end of the 2 minutes, some players will still be on number 1; others may be on number 23 or higher.

After this focusing drill, explain that it doesn't matter which number they reached. The important point is that they recognize when they are drifting and can bring themselves back.

As the season progresses, most players learn how to limit the number of times that they drift away. Players can also do the exercise at home. Like any skill, the more they practice it, the better they become.

And how do you know whether this drill is working? In the following section about game performance, you will see how a stronger mind leads to stronger performance on and off the field.

Game Performance

Everyone looks forward to games and tournaments because the team has a chance to see how they stack up. Yet teams often prepare poorly for games. From the moment that players arrive at the field, they should be mentally preparing for how they will play the upcoming game, and only that game. As they go through their physical routine, they

should also be going through some calisthenics in their minds. Dr. Goldberg believes that practice is 90 percent physical and 10 percent mental and that games are 90 percent mental and 10 percent physical. Well-prepared teams and players arrive at the field ready to rely on their mental strength *and* their physical readiness.

No Expectations

Let's start with the most difficult concept first. Every player, captain, and coach needs to approach each game with no expectations. Whether they crushed the same opponent last week, whether they have never beaten their opponent—it doesn't matter. The goal is to stay in the moment. Thinking about past and future games leads players into their heads and away from the moment at hand.

Why is staying in the moment so important? Players want to perform at their best in a game, and thinking too much will get in the way. If a player has practiced seriously and diligently, his body will take over and execute to its best ability. If the player starts thinking too much, and perhaps even panics, blood will rush away from his extremities and into his brain and lungs. With less blood in the arms and legs, he will drop the disc more often and

A little levity often works well before a stressful competition.

run more slowly. (The same response occurs if a player eats too much, except that blood rushes to the stomach. So players must never eat too much on the sidelines. Grazing on bits of food throughout the day makes the most sense.)

If players can stay in the moment and focus only on what they are doing right now, they will perform better. They should break each game down into small pieces, something that they may have done in practice. Instead of thinking about an entire game, they can think about short games to 3. If the team is pulling, teammates can race each other down to cover the pull and set up a mark before the opponent can get off a throw. If players are having trouble with drops, they should not think about throwing the disc until they have completed the catch. Some players even look at the disc to see that it has stopped spinning. Anything that players can do to break the game into small competitions will help them stay in the moment.

Warm-Up Rituals

Rituals are comforting and safe. Your team should perform the same ritual before each game. This approach will prevent outside forces or uncontrollable events from interfering with the players' preparation. Whether worked out beforehand or developed during practice, the ritual is an important part of mental preparation and should not be skipped.

An effective pregame ritual should include throwing, jogging, some light agility exercises, stretching, focusing, and a drill or two. The composition of the warm-up will often depend on the time available between games at tournaments, but the team must come together in some form before each game.

During the team's ritual, all players should be in game mode. Each should be focusing on what her role will be in the game, whether it is providing support from the sideline or shutting down the swing in the cup. Idle chatter should be at a minimum, although some players prefer a lighter atmosphere before a competition. No one should be watching the other team's warm-up or the game being played on a nearby field. The players should not be talking about the other team at all. Remember, it's all about your team and how you will perform that day.

Many players find visualization an effective way to prepare for a game. Visualization is a form of focusing. Instead of trying to clear his brain, a player will run a highlight reel of his greatest

Develop an effective warm-up ritual to prepare your team for competition.

offensive and defensive moments. He should try to remember the specific details of each highlight: how the disc felt, how quickly he was running, what the air and grass felt like. This sort of visualization will make it easier for him to replicate that feat in the upcoming game.

Some teams prefer to visualize as a team, whereas others decide that players should do this alone. As long as each teammate realizes that she needs to calm her mind before she plays, then it doesn't matter how she does it. Of course, the more she practices this, the easier it will become.

When your team is performing drills, at the end of your ritual, each player should be going all out. This means that players are now running at 100 percent and are cheering for each other as loudly as possible. A player who hears his name called when doing a drill receives an extra boost. And as the team brings it in for one final cheer before the game begins, everyone feels warmed up, calmed down, and ready to play!

Identify and Ignore the Uncontrollables

What factors influence how a team plays? Weather? Field conditions? Poor calls? A team could probably list 20 reasons that could help them or hurt them on the field, and a poorly disciplined team will focus on them relentlessly. How many times have you heard the following at an Ultimate competition?

"It's too windy."

"Why do we always get the worst field?"

"I still can't believe he made that call in the first half!"

"The tournament format is unfair."

"Look at how tall the other team is."

"The other team probably has a ringer."

"Our best player is hurt. We don't have a chance."

"I am so mad at myself for dropping that disc in the end zone."

Uncontrollables are traps. If you spend time focusing on what you can't control, you will not succeed. Uncontrollables, or UCs, suck all the energy and focus out of a team. We have witnessed players having long team discussions about UCs, such as tournament seedings or a bad call, when it is clear that they can do nothing to change things. Frustration is understandable, but the quicker you recognize that you or your team is obsessing about

something that can't be fixed, the quicker you can change your focus. For example, let's say that the weather has turned bad. The sun is gone, the wind is whipping up, and you can feel rain in the air. Instead of bemoaning the fact that the nice sunny day is gone, figure out how your team can prepare to battle the elements. Cover everyone's gear with a tarp or garbage bags and then get them on their feet to practice some short throwing. With the poor conditions, most teams will have to shorten up their offense, so players should practice throwing with lots of spin, set up behind each catch, and holster the fancy throws. Discuss which zone you want to use and in which direction you want to force. Determine from which direction the wind is coming and talk about what you have to do when moving the disc upwind or downwind. The more energy your team puts into controllables, the more easily they will be able to ignore the things that cannot be changed.

Support

Remember the analogy of the theatrical performance? Practice is like a dress rehearsal, and the game is the performance. This idea is helpful to keep in mind as you work your way through a game or tournament. Your team should work out any problems at practice or team meetings; problems must not be the focus during a competition. As angry and frustrated as some players may become, they need to stifle negative feelings until they are in another arena. This goes for coaches too.

Players must support their teammates throughout competition. Not everyone has to support every player, but the best way to ruin someone's

Essential Warm-Up Tip

Although many teams find it important to get really pumped up before a game, replete with screaming, jumping, and good-natured shoving of their teammates, maintaining this intensity throughout a game is impossible. Teams that rely too much on this tactic will often find themselves deflated after a few points. We suggest doing whatever you need to do to start a game with a strong sense of team unity and then committing yourselves to a focused presence on the sidelines. Cheering for your team when something spectacular happens is easy. The challenge is to be positive when bad things are happening on the field.

performance is to criticize her during a game. Few competitors can ignore criticism; most respond best to genuine praise. Remember that plenty of teams out there want to see your team stumble and fall. No one on your own team should contribute to a possible collapse.

Moving On

After the game ends, teams normally discuss the result. Whatever has happened, it is essential to allow a short time for processing and then move on. If your team has just experienced a crushing loss, talk about it and then get ready for the next game. If your team was surprisingly victorious over a tough opponent, celebrate it and then start warming up for your next challenge. A mentally tough team, in the middle of a weekend of com-

petition, knows that until the final curtain comes down on Sunday afternoon, there is no real reason to despair or celebrate.

Summary

Succeeding in Ultimate is not just about excelling in the physical aspects of the game. The individual athlete knows how important the mental game is and prepares for it throughout the season. A team that wants success on the field will focus on the mental strength needed to develop as a team. And a team of individual athletes who all commit to achieving mental toughness as a team will be unstoppable both on and off the field.

10

Starting a Program

Starting an Ultimate program, whether in a school, college, or recreation department, is often a challenge. Because Ultimate is a relatively new sport, less than 40 years old, many administrators have not heard of it. If they have heard about Ultimate, they most likely think it is a game played on a beach with a dog. In addition, many athletic directors or administrators already face the very real problems of little field space and a limited budget. They may have difficulty maintaining a mainstream sport such as football or basketball and cannot imagine adding one that they never played and do not understand.

Most Ultimate programs, therefore, have had a rocky start. Ultimate enthusiasts are often outsiders to the school or recreation department setting, and almost every organizer older than 30 has an anecdote about how they were actively discouraged. Some have been forbidden to talk to mainstream athletes; others have had funding and fields denied to them. Parents sometimes forbid their children to play Ultimate because college scholarships in the sport are not available. We assume that this will change as the sport increases in popularity and acceptance. The following strategies are based on the collective experience of these early advocates. This chapter is intended for the enterprising Ultimate athlete, teacher, or coach who wants to start an Ultimate program but doesn't know where to begin.

In spite of these roadblocks, Ultimate can become an essential part of many schools' athletic offerings. Whether you are trying to start an Ultimate program in an elementary or secondary school, or upgrade your college or university team, we offer the following advice on how to get what you want without chaining yourself to the front door of the gymnasium.

Types of Teams

First you must decide what type of Ultimate team you want. Let's start with a loosely organized school team. Several options are available to you. Do you have a group of friends who play Ultimate after school and only need a place to play? In that case, your best bet is to keep the gathering informal. Don't bother the athletic director. Simply meet at a local park. (Make sure that you treat the park well, of course!) As people learn how to play and improve their skills, they may decide that they want to play against someone else. Some friends may see this as a sign that you have become too serious, whereas others will view it as a natural outgrowth of learning a new sport. If you decide to take this next step, you will most likely have to come under the official jurisdiction of an adult.

But which adult? Do you need an advisor? A coach? A parent? You will have to answer these questions yourselves. If you and your group decide that you want to become a school team that plays an interscholastic schedule, you can't do it alone. There are simply too many regulations to follow. If you want fields and insurance, you must have an adult as your official representative. We have found that having a teacher or some full-time school staff member as an advocate makes the process much easier. Even so, players can still do the organizing. Young people can learn many life lessons by trying to establish an Ultimate team, and we strongly encourage all players to learn the ropes at an early age.

Club Status

Most likely you will start as a school club team, which means that you are not part of the varsity program. Club status usually means that you can get any field that a varsity team does not want.

These middle school players all went on to play for the United States at the 2006 World Junior Ultimate Championships.

When Tiina started her program at Amherst Regional, Tom Cullen, the football coach, gave the Ultimate team his field for the 45 minutes immediately after school, before his team was ready to play. The Ultimate players made sure that they were on that field as soon as the bell rang, and they were lucky if they could scrimmage for 25 minutes. They knew that practice was over when the army of football players lined the field, ready to charge forward as soon as they received the signal. Yet this worked for the Amherst team. They were meeting at an established place at an established time, and kids were able to get a taste of Ultimate. Michael's experience at Paideia was slightly different. Because this school has an urban campus, they had no fields anywhere near their school. They had to drive around to the local parks looking for some field space that local youth soccer teams were not using. Since then, Paideia has acquired some athletic fields, and Michael, along with his supportive athletic director, Marty Hays, is part of a group that decides how to allocate the fields.

Having club status also means that you can use the school for announcements, meetings, and fund-raising. Your advisor may receive a small stipend, instead of a coach's salary, although we know plenty of wonderful adults who volunteer many hours of their time. Being a club team will probably work well for a number of years. You should be able to play other schools, travel to tournaments, and get some coverage in your school paper. You may even be allowed to host a tournament. Most important, those in middle school and below will view Ultimate as a viable activity, which means that you are building a strong foundation for the future. Of course, you will probably not receive much money from the school, and Ultimate will not be considered a true varsity sport.

Varsity Status

Club status may be fine for you and your team. We know that achieving varsity status can be difficult. Tiina lobbied the Amherst Regional High School administration for years to make it happen. Every September, at her first meeting with the athletic director, she would ask that her

program become a varsity team. Every year the AD turned her down, until one day he finally gave up and gave in. Michael had it a bit easier at Paideia. A group of administrators who were impressed by his and his team's dedication offered them varsity status. We also know that in some school systems, players aren't even allowed to establish club teams. In any case, the benefits of being a varsity team are immeasurable, and we encourage the brave or foolish among you to seek varsity status.

Varsity status means that you should receive the same resources as all other varsity teams: good fields at good times, paid coaches, tournament fees, uniforms, transportation, a published athletic

One of the perks of gaining varsity status is that your team might be permitted to play under the lights.

There are three types of divisions: open, which is predominantly male, though both men and women participate; women's; and mixed, in which there are combined squads of men and women, with three or four people of each gender playing at a time.

their local recreational department, Andover Youth Services (AYS), and they have a town team. AYS provides them with a place to play, advertising, and insurance. Although most of the players are from the local high school, the team is under no restrictions from the athletic department. A strong program has developed, with a boys' and girls' team and a middle-school program. The players are motivated; they started a summer Ultimate league to introduce the sport to their friends and others. They achieved all this without any assistance from the local school system.

Types of Divisions

After you have your team playing regularly, you will have to decide which division to compete in. Ultimate offers open, women's, and mixed divisions. Open means that both men and women participate, although the teams are predominantly male. The women's division is obviously just for female players, and the mixed division is for combined squads of men and women. In this division, groups of three or four men or women play at one time. The offense usually gets to choose which gender combination they are going to put out on the field, and the defense has to match it.

The Ultimate community has been debating for years which division is the most rewarding to play in and which encourages the most growth. We will not revisit these arguments, except to say that you should talk to your teammates about this and other issues. Most of the conflicts on a team come from people making decisions without really listening to others or from people remaining silent because they don't want to cause problems. All divisions have strengths and weaknesses, and you and your teammates must find the right match.

schedule, coverage in the local press. These advantages, in turn, should lead to a level of respect that you did not enjoy as a club. There will always be critics who dismiss Ultimate because they don't know any better, but, for the most part, varsity status will bring your team and the sport more respect.

Other Types of Status

What should you do if school affiliation is impossible or undesirable? You want to play other teams, but you do not wish to be associated with your school. Perhaps you would like to include players from other schools and form a local club team, or you may simply want to be on your own. You still need a place to play regularly and some sort of adult support. And, of course, you must have insurance. Seattle has been extremely successful in establishing mixed school Ultimate leagues, from which a multischool club team has formed. Moho is a team composed of players from several schools, many of whom met when they were in middle school and played together in various youth Ultimate leagues. They travel to tournaments and represent the league and the city of Seattle, not an individual school.

We also suggest that you consider what the folks of Andover, Massachusetts, have done. Under the leadership of Tommy Proulx, they are supported by

Obtaining Administrative Support

Approaching an athletic director about starting an Ultimate team could be one of the most intimidating tasks you will ever face. Before we explain our strategies, you should first try to put yourself in the shoes of these administrators. Ultimate organizers often approach these adults with a combination of naïveté and bravado. Players may think that administrators can easily grant them everything they want, and they expect the administrators to embrace Ultimate immediately. Remember that, in many cases, athletic directors are harried people who are just trying to do their jobs. They have tons of paperwork to fill out, too many games to supervise, difficult schedules to coordinate, and numerous conflicts to resolve. The last thing they want is another sport to regulate!

First Meeting

Your first step is to meet with the administrator. Do not skip this step. Sneaking onto fields beforehand will show deep disrespect. Make an appointment a couple of weeks in advance. Do your homework by learning what you can about any local or state regulations. Before the appointment, have a brief planning meeting with the teacher, coach, or parent who will accompany you, as well as with some younger players to ensure that your program will live on after you graduate. We know of many high school and college programs that disappeared or foundered after their core group of seniors graduated. Make sure that someone takes notes at this and every meeting; a team archive is extremely valuable down the road.

Do not ask for too much. If you want a field, say that you will be willing to use any field any time, even on a Sunday afternoon. If you want uniforms, ask to borrow them from teams that are currently in their off-season. The Ultimate team from Northfield Mount Hermon in Northfield, Massachusetts, wore old soccer jerseys before they attained varsity status and, subsequently, new uniforms. If you need to rent a bus, you may have to do some fund-raising to pay for it. As your team becomes established, you can ask for more, but fields, uniforms, and tournament fees are the common obstacles that a new team faces.

Put everything in writing. The purpose of doing this is not necessarily to hold the athletic director accountable, but to document what has occurred. Probably the most important document you can write is the thank-you note. We are not kidding. After the meeting, take a minute to send the AD a quick note of thanks for considering your requests. This advice is not just for those in high school. If you are meeting with a college administrator or parks and recreation director, write a thank-you note. If you obtain fields, you may even want to splurge on a gift. The goal is to distinguish your team from others as one that is polite and appreciative.

Follow Rules

Follow every rule. Some administrators are just waiting for your Ultimate team to fade away or make a mistake so that they can send you away. The first mistake to avoid is ruining the fields. We have found that football teams, soccer teams, and lacrosse teams are often allowed to trash fields, but the same rules do not apply to Ultimate teams. Imagine that you have just gained permission to host your first tournament. You have spent hours preparing for the event. Two days before the tournament it starts to rain, and then it rains some more. Teams show up on Saturday morning clamoring to play, but if you want your program to have any longevity, you must tell them that the tournament has been canceled. Before the tournament, ask for help in coming up with alternative fields. Watch the weather reports conscientiously and make a decision as early as possible. Ask the athletic department to provide someone who will determine whether the fields are playable. But whatever you do, don't let the teams tear up the fields. If you do, it may be years before you can use them again. Athletic directors have many responsibilities and long memories.

Other Options

And what do you do if none of those tactics work? We know some players who can't even get their foot in the door of any athletic office. We have heard of students who have been turned down because coaches don't want to lose their athletes to Ultimate. This next suggestion may be scary, but if you really want to succeed, you may have to go over the administrators' heads and talk to someone with more power—the principal, superintendent, or school board. Parents or other adults must be involved with you at this point. They can write letters or make phone calls. They can help you write up a petition to circulate at school. They can contact the press. Most school systems respond when parents start making a ruckus. We even know of a college Ultimate team who received fields because some of *their* parents made phone calls!

Above all, never give up. Our motto is "Apply gentle and relentless pressure." You want a team, a program, a tournament? Be polite, anticipate problems, and do what you are told. Figure out ways that you can help the athletic director. Clean out a storage room or have your team patrol the fields for trash. Try to develop a partnership with your athletic department and build a reputation for your team as being responsible and helpful. You understand better than anybody what the sport of Ultimate and its players can offer. You don't need to convince everyone to think like you. You just have to make the strategic moves to win most of the battles, if not the war. Above all, never give up. See table 10.1 for suggested responses to some negative statements.

Recruiting Players

Although the core of most new Ultimate teams is usually a group of friends, you will usually need to recruit. Players get hurt, lose interest, or graduate, and you will always want to play seven-on-seven at practice and have plenty of people to travel to a tournament. Before you start papering the hallways with posters, consider this question: How new is the concept of Ultimate to your school community? Answering this will help you put together an effective recruitment plan.

"Ultimate? What's That?"

Although the popularity of Ultimate has certainly grown since its birth in 1968, thousands of poten-

tial players have never heard of it. If this is the case, you will be in an educational role, and as any good teacher knows, you need appropriate materials. We suggest that you contact the Ultimate Players Association (see appendix) and see what they have to offer. You will be able to find posters, videos, and instructional manuals and discs for a nominal charge. You can also look on the Internet and find many novice-friendly Web sites.

At your first meeting, show an action-packed Ultimate video and serve some food. Many people will show up anywhere for a free slice of pizza, and if you pop the video in while they are eating, you have a captive audience. Place some educational materials in the room, in case someone is instantly smitten. Take down everyone's name and phone number and, as prospects leave, hand each a slip of paper with the time, date, and location of the next meeting, at which you will actually play. Schedule it within a week of your first meeting and keep the event short. You want to leave them wanting more. Here are some other suggestions to attract novices to your sport:

▶ Decorate a bulletin board in school, one that is in a high-traffic area. Cover it with action shots of Ultimate players, and post your notices in the middle of them.

▶ Ask a group of experienced players to demonstrate Ultimate at halftime of a football or soccer game.

▶ Give out free discs at a school activity. You can give out free tickets beforehand and hold a raffle during an intermission or halftime.

Table 10.1 They Say, You Say, or How to Win a War of Words With an Administrator

School official	Ultimate enthusiast
"We don't have enough money in the budget to fund any new team."	"That is completely understandable. We would be more than happy to raise funds for this year. Can you tell us when next year's budget is due, so that we can get our request in well ahead of time?"
"Ultimate is not a sport. You are wasting your time."	"We sure have found that lots of people feel that way. I think if you came out and watched us, you would be surprised. When would be a good time for you to see us play? And if you don't have the time, here's a video that can show you what we are talking about."
"We don't have any fields available."	"We are more than willing to practice before or after the varsity teams."
"We don't want our serious athletes quitting their sports to play Frisbee!"	"If your other athletes are as as serious about their sports as we are about Ultimate, we can't imagine that they would quit. All we need is about 15 kids."
"Get out."	"Thanks for your time. We'll be back soon."

"Ultimate Looks Like Fun, but I Don't Really Know How to Play"

Before your initial practice, call everyone who signed up at your first meeting. Potential players often need that one last reminder to get them to show up. Offer to give them a ride if you can. You now have a willing audience in front of you. Make sure that they enjoy the practice enough to commit to your team. You must be ready to do some serious teaching or find someone who can do it for you. Enlist the help of some experienced players, who will either run these practices or be there to support you. These experts should come prepared to play and clearly understand that their job is to teach, not show off. We often institute a few rules for these teaching scrimmages:

- ▶ No hucks or even half-field passes. The goal is for everyone to have lots of touches on the disc.

- ▶ Everyone must touch the disc at least once before a score occurs.

- ▶ Experienced players are not allowed to throw or score a goal.

In general, you want practices to consist mainly of scrimmaging and few, if any, drills. Remember, you are just trying to get your prospects hooked. You want the activity to be loose and fun. You can play short games to 3 or 5 points, and perhaps a longer one for the last half hour. Everyone will get a taste of what Ultimate can be. To avoid intimidating anyone, keep the intensity in check.

Before everyone leaves, announce that you have set up a short series of practices, perhaps four within 2 weeks. You do not want to schedule too many right away, because the scrimmaging could suffer if the sessions are sparsely attended. You do not want to schedule too few, because you may lose momentum. The last thing to do is to ask the prospects if they plan to come again. When people make verbal commitments in front of a group, no matter how loosely organized, chances are that they will honor those commitments.

"I Love Ultimate and Want to Play All the Time"

With any luck, Ultimate has become part of your community by this point. Achieving this milestone usually takes a year or more, but when Ultimate gets a foothold, curtailing its growth is almost impossible. Most organizers will struggle to keep up with the demand for playing opportunities. You will probably be more focused on retaining players than recruiting them, because word-of-mouth will work better than any pizza parties or guest coaches.

You still want to make sure to offer challenges to experienced players and encourage new players. Depending on the season, your school may field competitive traveling teams or form an intramural league. Along with growth comes growing pains. You may have to hold tryouts to eliminate some players. Many communities have summer leagues, as well as summer camps and hat tournaments. (In a hat tournament, individual players show up on a weekend morning and are put on teams for a tournament to be held *that day*. This event is a great way to meet new people and develop team chemistry in a short amount of time.) Whatever the venue, you should be happy to have these growth problems. Ultimate has arrived in your community and is no longer a guest sitting on the doorstep, waiting to be let in.

Forming a Team

As you formalize your commitment to Ultimate, you will likely experience the dynamics of forming a team. Although no group of athletes is exactly the same, patterns that can help or hurt a team are likely to develop. You must be able to recognize potential problems that occur on and off the field before they do serious damage.

- ▶ **Don't do too much.** Ultimate teams have traditionally enjoyed little institutional support, and its organizers are always in danger of suffering from burnout. Although one or two people should make the on-field decisions, a committee works well for the more mundane tasks, such as scheduling, finances, fund-raising, housing, and transportation. Unless you have run a team or tournament, you will have no idea of the multitude of tasks that need to be done. And the best way to silence the team complainers is to give them something to do. People become invested in the team when they contribute to its smooth operation.

- ▶ **Set goals as a team.** Whether you are trying to win your first game in pool play or repeat as national champions, goal setting is important to your team's success. Your team can hardly be expected to work together if its members all have different ideas of what you are working toward. You can ask everyone to cite individual goals and team goals. You can have people write anonymously about their experiences in the past and their hopes for the future. You can have the entire team walk across red-hot coals to prove their devotion. But whatever you do, you must have a genuine discussion in which everyone participates.

▶ **Develop a policy on playing time.** Probably the most contentious and potentially disastrous problem involves playing time. No player wants to stand on a sideline, watching player after player go in ahead of him and feeling as if the team does not need or want his athletic contribution. (Chapter 7 discusses the importance of sideline players.) Similarly, those on the field playing their hearts out will become frustrated if they see moping teammates sitting down or half-heartedly cheering them on. Discussing playing time is difficult because it is personal and subjective, and many teams try to avoid it if they can. If you have a coach, chances are that you will have little input. Coaches will make decisions about playing time by considering team goals and their own assessments. But the coach should still make it clear how substitutions will be run. All players should know what criteria the coach uses to determine playing time and how they can move up in the rotation. The coach should also encourage private meetings to discuss playing time. These meetings should happen off the field when everyone is calm, not during a game.

If players run your team, the same rules apply. The team will select one person to run subs, based on a policy that is clear and fair. Do not choose someone who is likely to favor her friends on the team. Every player will not get the same number of points, and the policy may change because of injuries or level of competition, but dealing early and positively with this difficult issue will build trust in the team. We also suggest that after a few weeks you discuss and reevaluate the policy on playing time.

▶ **Be positive.** Things will go wrong on your team. We guarantee it. People will be late, cars will break down, tournament lodging will fall through, and teammates will become angry with one another. All this is part of being on a team. The only thing you can control is how you react to these situations. Building a team requires skill. Just as learning to throw a forehand can be a struggle, the process of building a team can be frustrating. You may get advice that you don't really want. You may feel as if no one is listening to you. Still, you need to maintain a positive attitude. After all, you are lucky to be playing the great sport of Ultimate, and you need a team to do so. Otherwise, you'll end up playing disc golf by yourself.

Summary

Starting or maintaining an Ultimate program is not easy. Many people will want you to fail and will do their best to put roadblocks in your way. But if you find the right people, you can be part of building an active, strong Ultimate program in your school or community. All of us understand the appeal of chasing a flying disc. Teaching that concept to others, and organizing teams around it, is one of the most exciting and rewarding challenges in the world of Ultimate.

Appendix

Recommended Resources

Books

Bompa, Tudor O. 2000. *Total training for young champions.* Champaign, IL: Human Kinetics.

Brown, Lee, and Vance Ferrigno, eds. 2005. *Training for speed, agility, and quickness.* Champaign, IL: Human Kinetics.

Dintiman, George B., and Robert D. Ward. 2003. *Sports speed.* Champaign, IL: Human Kinetics.

Foran, Bill, ed. 2001. *High-performance sports conditioning: Modern training for ultimate athletic development.* Champaign, IL: Human Kinetics.

Gallwey, W. Timothy. 1997. *Inner game of tennis.* New York: Random House.

Goldberg, Alan. 1998. *Playing out of your mind: A soccer player and coaches guide to developing mental toughness.* Spring City, PA: Reedswain.

Goldberg, Alan S. 1998. *Sports slump busting: 10 steps to mental toughness and peak performance.* Champaign, IL: Human Kinetics.

Jackson, Phil. 1995. *Sacred hoops: Spiritual lessons of a hardwood warrior.* New York: Hyperion.

Lynch, Jerry. 2001. *Creative coaching.* Champaign, IL: Human Kinetics.

Radcliffe, James C., and Robert C. Farentinos. 1999. *High-powered plyometrics.* Champaign, IL: Human Kinetics.

Wooden, John, and Steve Jamison. 1997. *Wooden: A lifetime of observations and reflections on and off the court.* Lincolnwood, IL: Contemporary Books.

Wooden, John, and Steve Jamison. 2005. *Wooden on leadership.* New York: McGraw-Hill.

Web Sites

Competitive Advantage. Dr. Alan Goldberg's Web site provides many helpful products and links to guide readers to other resources.

www.competitivedge.com

Positive Coaching Alliance (PCA). PCA is a national nonprofit based at Stanford University. PCA believes that winning is a goal in youth sports but that there is a second, more important goal of using sports to teach life lessons through positive coaching.

www.positivecoach.org

Equipment

Discraft, Inc.

29592 Beck Road
Wixom, MI 48393
Phone: 248-624-2250
Fax: 248-624-2310
www.discraft.com
Source for the official disc of the Ultimate Players Association

Ultimate Players Association

4730 Table Mesa Dr.
Suite J-200
Boulder, CO 80305
Toll Free: 800-872-4384
Phone: 303-447-3472
Fax: 303-447-3483
www.upa.org
Provides links to licensed merchandisers

US Games

P.O. Box 7726
Dallas, TX 75209
Toll Free: 800-327-0484
Fax: 800-899-0149
www.usgames.com
Source for soft discs such as the Fun Gripper Flyer

VC Ultimate, Inc.

1541 Dundas St. West
Toronto, ON
Canada
M6K 1T6
Toll Free: (866) 844-2511
Phone: +1 (416) 588-4154
Fax: (416) 588-7363
www.vcultimate.com
Source for uniforms that meet the unique requirements of the sport

Glossary

1-3-3 zone—Variation of a zone defense.

3-2-2 zone—The basic zone in Ultimate.

absolute speed—Refers to an athlete's greatest pace or top sprint speed.

acceleration—Refers to an athlete's ability to increase his or her speed in the least amount of time possible.

"Away!"—A defensive command that indicates the force is toward the sideline opposite the defensive team's home sideline. Opposite of *"Home!"*

backfield—The area behind the thrower, often where an offensive reset pass takes place.

backhand—One of the basic throws in Ultimate, similar to a backhand in tennis. Sometimes called *normal.*

backing—To position behind a cutter to take away the deep cut or to force a cutter in toward the thrower.

bailing—To break off a cut and clear out of the area.

biting—When a defender is fooled and moved out of position by an offensive player's fake of a throw or a cut.

body-weight exercises—Exercises that use the weight of the body as resistance, such as push-ups, pull-ups, and squats.

box-and-one—A type of junk defense in which the short-deep position plays one-on-one on an offense's top thrower while the remaining six defenders play zone.

break side—The area of the field being denied by the marker and where the defense is not forcing or overplaying. Opposite of *force side.*

breaking the mark—When a thrower moves the disc into the area being denied by the marker.

brick—The designated penalty for when a defense's pull lands out of bounds. The offense may bring the disc to the brick mark.

brick mark—A mark in the middle of a regulation-size field that is 20 yards upfield from the goal line. (See figure 1.1.)

clam—A hybrid defense that combines principles of zone and one-on-one coverage.

clap catch—Basic receiving technique in which one hand claps down on top of the disc while the other does so from underneath, sandwiching the disc between the hands. Most effective when the disc is arriving at a middle level.

clearing—Offensive movement that creates space on the field for one's teammates. The offensive player maneuvers away from and out of a desired passing lane.

clogging—Opposite of clearing. The offensive player prevents the disc from getting to teammates by moving and positioning poorly, which allows a defender to play off of the cutter and linger in the passing lane longer, causing an obstruction.

continuation—A cut and throw that follows the prior completion quickly and fluidly, keeping the disc moving in its current direction across or up the field, particularly on the break side.

core (trunk) musculature—The muscles of the upper legs, hips, gluteals, and all muscles up through the trunk and shoulders. These are the relay center for explosive extremity movement, regulating the rate and intensity of action and reaction.

counter-cut—A cut that quickly follows one offered by another cutter and provides the opposite option for the thrower, or a cut that fills the role in the offense that the prior cut has vacated (e.g., the offensive player at the front of the stack taking the role of reset after the former reset has chosen an upfield cut).

coverage sack—This occurs when no receivers are open and a thrower's only choices are to force a pass into tight coverage, throw the disc away downfield, or be stalled.

"Crash!"—A command to alert defenders in the front of a zone that a receiver is approaching their area.

crosswind—Wind blowing from the left or right side of the thrower.

cup—Traditional zone formation closest to the disc.

cutting lane—Same as *passing lane.*

dead space—Area where the offensive players are stacked and from where cuts are being set up.

deceleration—Refers to an athlete's ability reduce his or her speed in the least amount of time possible, such as prior to a change of direction. Opposite of *acceleration.*

deep—An offensive player who often cuts downfield for a long throw.

deep-deep—A position in zone defense farthest away from the disc.

deep fill—A backup cutter who fills in, shallow or deep downfield, if a primary cutter in a sequence is unable to get open.

defender—A player who positions himself to foil any offensive movement that the cutter(s) want to make.

dictate—To determine where a cutter, thrower, or team's offense is able to attack.

downfield—Toward the end zone where an offense is trying to score.

downwind—Wind that is heading in the same direction as a throw. Also, when a team is moving in a direction with the wind at its back.

"Drop!"—A defensive call used to maneuver a teammate away from the disc.

dump—Same as *reset.*

dynamic stretching—Part of an effective warm-up that involves moving the joints through an ever-increasing range in an active manner, preparing the muscles and tendons for explosive movement.

external weight exercises—Traditional weight training that uses resistance provided by barbells, dumbbells, and various machines.

faking—When a thrower or cutter simulates the start of a realistic maneuver to mislead a defender, tricking or moving that defender out of position.

fast break—An offensive opportunity to score quickly after a turnover.

fill—Any secondary cut or cutter that enables an offense to continue flowing. See *short fill* and *deep fill.*

flick—Same as *forehand.*

flow—When the disc and offensive players are kept moving smoothly and quickly throughout the course of a point.

foot block—Blocking a throw on the mark with a foot.

force backhand—Allowing throws to the backhand side of the field.

force forehand—Allowing throws to the forehand side of the field.

force middle (FM)—Allowing throws to the middle of the field and not toward the sidelines.

force side—The area of the field to which the marker is allowing the disc to go. Opposite of *break side.*

force straight up (force flat)—Allowing throws toward either of the sidelines.

forehand—A basic throw in Ultimate. Also called the *flick* or *two-finger.*

frontal plane—In relation to the athlete's body, the plane of the body in which lateral (side-to-side) movement takes place.

fronting—To position between the thrower and a cutter to deny the in cut.

functional strength training—Training that focuses on improving strength using movement patterns commonly demanded in a given sport. This type of training more effectively incorporates important aspects such as core stability, balance, and proprioception.

give-and-go—When a thrower tosses a pass and receives it quickly back from that player.

"Go to!"—A call used to encourage a teammate to accelerate quickly toward the disc.

hammer—A basic throw in Ultimate, similar to an overhead in tennis.

hand block—Blocking a throw on the mark with a hand.

handler—Player who distributes the disc to cutters, similar to a point guard in basketball.

"Home!"—A defensive command that indicates the force is toward the defensive team's home sideline. Opposite of *"Away!"*

horizontal stack (H-stack)—An offensive formation which sets up a line of cutters perpendicular to the sideline.

huck—A long throw.

in cut—When a downfield cutter runs back in toward the thrower in order to receive the disc. Also known as an *underneath* or *comeback cut.*

individual coverage—Defensive strategy in which defenders individually cover offensive players. Same as *one-on-one* or *man-to-man.*

inside-out—A release where the outside edge of the disc is angled down. Other terms are *IO* and *invert.*

iso cut—An offensive strategy involving the isolation of an individual cutter.

"It's up!"—A signal to alert players that a disc is airborne.

junk—When teams combine facets of individual coverage with zone principles, creating a hybrid style of defense. A clam and box-and-one are examples of junk.

last-back defense—A strategy in which the defender who is then farthest downfield helps cover any long cutter.

layout block—When a defender dives to block a pass.

layout catch—When a player dives to catch the disc.

L-stack—An offensive formation used to defeat a sideline trap.

manipulative skills—Skills that involve grasping and letting go of an object, such as catching and throwing a disc.

mark—Synonymous with *marker.*

marker—The defender covering the thrower. Also called *mark.*

middle—An offensive player who often initiates continuation cuts and fills or a defensive player in the center of the cup.

middle-middle—The third member of the cup in a 3-2-2 zone formation, positioned slightly farther downfield but between the other two players in the cup (on-point and off-point).

movement portfolio—A set of physical conditioning skills that will allow success in all sorts of activities.

multiskill development—Training in a variety of activities and sports to promote a broad range of physical development.

"No around!"—A defensive call used to cue the current marker that a cutter is open in the area behind his outside (opposite of force-side) shoulder. Opposite of *"No inside!"*

"No big!"—A defensive call to alert the marker to flatten and widen her marking position in order to stop a long throw.

"No inside!"—A defensive call used to cue the current marker that a cutter is open in the area behind her inside (force-side) shoulder. Opposite of *"No around!"*

off-point—The point in the cup who is not marking the current thrower and who must stop a field-reversing pass to the side handler or a pass to the offensive wing.

on-point—The point in the cup who is currently marking the thrower.

outside-in—A release where the outside edge of the disc is angled up.

passing lane—The primary area to which the thrower intends to deliver a pass. Same as *cutting lane.*

pick—Occurs when an offensive player moves in such a way as to cause a defensive player guarding a receiver to be obstructed by any other player.

pivot—An offensive skill that allows the thrower to throw from both sides of the body. Also refers to the center handler in the zone offense.

pivot foot—The foot that must remain stationary during a player's pivot. This foot is opposite the hand used to throw.

plyometrics—A type of exercise that trains the neuromuscular system to lessen the elapsed time between the stretching (lengthening of muscle, storing of energy, and force reduction) and shortening (shortening of muscle, use of stored energy, and force production) cycles of muscles. Quickness and explosive acceleration and deceleration result from training the body to reduce this stretching–shortening cycle.

poach—Occurs when defensive players momentarily leave their cutters in order to obstruct a passing lane or block the disc intended for another receiver.

point block—When a marker blocks a throw.

popper—Offensive player in a zone positioned downfield beyond the cup.

pre-act—A term that emphasizes an important concept of constantly seeing and thinking ahead (being in position and prepared physically before actually needing to be) in order to preempt an offensive player's head-start advantage.

pull—A long throw to initiate a point, similar to a kick-off in football.

pull play—A full-field plan that an offense runs when receiving the disc at the start of a point.

reaction cushion—A strategy in which the defender sets up a short distance (1-3 yards) away from a cutter in the force-side passing lane in order to absorb the quick movements the cutter is making in an attempt to get open. This space provides the defender a head start when covering a cutter on the force side.

red zone—The area that includes the end zone and approximately 20 yards upfield.

reset—When a handler receives a short pass that restarts the offense. Also refers to the player cutting for a such a pass. Same as *dump.*

reverse—To move the disc to the opposite side of the field, thus improving the offensive options. Typically follows a backfield reset completion. Also used to identify the cut provided to reverse the field following a reset. Synonymous with *swing.*

sagittal plane—In relation to an athlete's body, this is the plane in which forward and backward movements take place.

seventh person—A bailout (or fill) handler placed at the front of the offense when running a four-person play.

short-deep—A zone position behind the cup and in front of the deep-deep.

short fill—A backup cutter who provides help near the front of an offense if the primary flow is stifled.

side handler—One of the two handlers on either side of the pivot, or center handler, in a zone offense. Sometimes called a *spreader*.

slice cut—A cut that is prompted by a thrower's pump fake to a reverse cutter, inducing the reverse cutter to plant and cut perpendicular to the sideline, sweeping back across the field toward the force side.

snap—A forceful extension of the wrist that gives spin to the disc.

speed endurance—The ability to run fast and do it repeatedly.

spin—Rotation on a disc. Sometimes called *Zs.*

spread—An offensive formation that splits the downfield cutters into two groups, each placed near one of the sidelines in order to open up the middle of the field for cuts. Also called the *split stack.*

stack—A single line of cutters placed downfield from the thrower.

stall count—Counted out loud by the marker, this is the amount of time within which the thrower must release the disc. Exceeding this count results in a turnover.

static stretching—A stretching technique in which the athlete maintains a gentle stretch for 45 to 60 seconds. This technique allows the muscles and tendons to lengthen, which is vital to increasing dynamic mobility.

"Strike!"—A defensive command alerting the mark to briefly prevent a force-side throw.

strong side—The side of the field where the disc is currently located. Opposite of *weak side.*

swing—Synonymous with *reverse.*

switching—The strategy used by defenders in one-on-one coverage in which they trade defensive assignments (i.e., the offensive players each had been guarding).

touch—A flight characteristic in which the speed of the disc is purposely slowed by the thrower.

transitional defense—A change from one defensive strategy to another within a point.

transverse plane—In relation to an athlete's body, this is the plane in which diagonal and rotational movements take place.

trapping—Defensive strategy in which the thrower is forced toward the sideline and the closest cutters are aggressively covered.

triangulate—When a defender is positioned to see both the cutter and the disc simultaneously.

two-handed rim catch (TRC)—A technique that offers greater reach for a catch made out in front of the receiver's body.

upwind—A wind that is heading in the opposite direction of a throw. Also, when a team is operating against the wind.

weak side—The side of the field opposite the current location of the disc. Opposite of *strong side.*

wing—Offensive or defensive position in zone play, usually located near the sideline.

zone—A defensive strategy in which areas are covered instead of opposing players.

Index

Note: The italicized *f* and *t* following page numbers refer to figures and tables, respectively.

About the Authors

Michael Baccarini, BS, is director of physical education at the Paideia School in Atlanta, Georgia. He has been playing Ultimate since 1978 and has taught and coached it for the past 13 years. Coaching the U.S. boys' junior Ultimate team with Tiina Booth, he has won two world championship titles (1998 and 2004) and received a bronze medal in the 2000 World Championships. He also coached the U.S. boys' junior Ultimate team to gold at the 2006 World Championship, has won two high school national championships, and he finished second in a third championship (in a match against Tiina Booth's team).

Baccarini has led several coaching certification clinics for the Ultimate Players Association's Youth Outreach Program and served as national junior director for the UPA from 1999 to 2002. He is also a veteran Ultimate youth camp director; he founded the Paideia Ultimate Summer Camp and developed it into a large and successful sports camp.

Michael Baccarini

Tiina Booth, BA, is an English teacher at Amherst Regional High School in Amherst, Massachusetts. She won national high school championships in 1998, 2003, and 2004 as coach of the ARHS boys' team. An Ultimate player and coach for more than 25 years, she also won world c hampionships as coach of the U.S. boys' junior Ultimate team in 1998 and 2004 (coaching with Baccarini). She is the founder of the oldest high school Ultimate tournament in the United States—the Amherst Invitational, founded in 1992. She cofounded the high school national tournament in 1998. Booth is a trainer for coach certification for the UPA and is the founder and camp director of the National Ultimate Training Camp, the first overnight camp for high school Ultimate players. NUTC has attracted players from throughout the United States, Canada, and South Africa.

In 1997, Booth was featured in *Sports Illustrated's* "Faces in the Crowd" for her coaching achievements, and in 2005 her team had a record of 57-3—including more than 20 wins against colleges—and won a college tournament championship title.

Tiina Booth

VC ultimate

Team uniforms built to your specifications and satisfaction.

Front

MEPHISTO ULTIMATE

22

Devil logo place 1" down from base of collar.

Devil and text together should be approximately 3.5" high by 6" wide

Numbers should be 8" high

Number font is Eras Bold ITC

White of flames should be approximately 4mm in width

Red of flames should be approximately 3mm in width

Right Sleeve

The arm shield logo is 3" high and is centered on the sleeve when viewed from the side

Back

Gradient starts from 60% K at the bottom, and goes to full black by the third flame up

Red of flames is also a gradient going from dark red at the bottom to standard red at the top

Left Sleeve

Photos courtesy of Matt Lane and No Tsu Oh

1-866-844-2511
www.vcultimate.com

You'll find
other outstanding
physical education resources at

www.HumanKinetics.com

In the U.S. call

1-800-747-4457

Australia	08 8372 0999
Canada	1-800-465-7301
Europe	+44 (0) 113 255 5665
New Zealand	0064 9 448 1207

HUMAN KINETICS
The Information Leader in Physical Activity
P.O. Box 5076 • Champaign, IL 61825-5076 USA